T0334439

This book provides the most comprehensive synthesis of the different theoretical approaches to the topic of strategy. It is also a pleasure to read. I agree entirely with Manuel Becerra's view that the most useful way to think about any company is in terms of an entity whose twin goals are: first, to create value and, second, to appropriate a fair share of this value for its own shareholders. I recommend this book as the first thing that any Ph.D. student in strategy should read before tackling the details of the strategy literature in doctoral seminars.

Anil K. Gupta
Ralph J. Tyser Professor of Strategy & Organization, Robert H. Smith School of Business, University of Maryland

This is a fantastic book that will fill a major gap in the strategy literature. It provides a thorough review of prior theory and research concerned with the economic basis of strategic management. Management scholars and practitioners alike will find this to be a landmark publication that enhances our understanding of strategic decisions.

Luis Gómez-Mejía
Council of 100 Distinguished Scholar and Regents Professor at the W.P. Carey School of Business, Arizona State University

An excellent and very timely book. In times of strategic turbulence the importance of sound theoretical grounding is accentuated. A must read for any serious student of strategy.

Øystein D. Fjeldstad
Professor and Telenor Chair of International Strategy and Management, BI-Norwegian School of Management

Theory of the Firm for Strategic Management

Strategic decisions deal with the long-term direction of the firm and its main activities, usually the responsibility of the top managers in an organization. Because the firm is the critical unit of analysis in strategy, we need to define what firms are, how they create value, and what their organizational boundaries are, in order to understand their overall performance. However, this must be done in a manner that is most useful for strategic analysis and decision making. In other words, we need a theory of the firm for business strategy. *Theory of the Firm for Strategic Management* integrates and expands key existing theories, like transaction costs economics and the resource-based view, to develop a value-based theory of the firm. This provides a framework to show how firms can create value for customers and, at the same time, capture economic profits for their owners through business, corporate, international, and social strategies.

MANUEL BECERRA holds the Accenture Chair in Strategic Management at the Instituto de Empresa Business School (IE), Madrid. His research interests include topics in corporate strategy, the economic theory of the firm, and trust.

Theory of the Firm for Strategic Management

Economic value analysis

MANUEL BECERRA

Instituto de Empresa Business School, Madrid

CAMBRIDGE
UNIVERSITY PRESS

CAMBRIDGE
UNIVERSITY PRESS

University Printing House, Cambridge CB2 8BS, United Kingdom

One Liberty Plaza, 20th Floor, New York, NY 10006, USA

477 Williamstown Road, Port Melbourne, VIC 3207, Australia

314-321, 3rd Floor, Plot 3, Splendor Forum, Jasola District Centre, New Delhi - 110025, India

79 Anson Road, #06-04/06, Singapore 079906

Cambridge University Press is part of the University of Cambridge.

It furthers the University's mission by disseminating knowledge in the pursuit of
education, learning and research at the highest international levels of excellence.

www.cambridge.org
Information on this title: www.cambridge.org/9780521863346

First published 2009

A catalogue record for this publication is available from the British Library

Library of Congress Cataloging in Publication data
Becerra, Manuel, 1964–
Theory of the firm for strategic management : economic value analysis / by Manuel
Becerra.
    p.   cm.
Includes bibliographical references and index.
ISBN 978-0-521-86334-6 (hardback) – ISBN 978-0-521-68194-0 (pbk)
1. Strategic planning.   2. Management.   3. Business enterprises.   I. Title.
HD30.28.B43   2009
658.4′012 – dc22   2008037805

ISBN 978-0-521-86334-6 Hardback
ISBN 978-0-521-68194-0 Paperback

Contents

List of figures   *page* xi

List of tables   xii

Preface   xiii

Part I   Theories of the firm

1   Introduction   3
   The emergence of strategic management   3
   The scope of the field   7
     The multidisciplinary basis of business strategy   8
   The concept of firm   11
     The firm as a production unit   11
     The firm as a decision-making process   13
     The firm as a contracting solution   16
     The firm as a collection of resources   17
   The theory of the firm for strategic management   19
     A value approach to the analysis of firm strategy   21
   Structure of the book   22

2   The contracting view of the firm   27
   Coase and the nature of the firm   27
   Williamson and transaction costs economics   31
   Property rights and incomplete contracts   35
   Agency theory   39
   Limitations of the contracting view as a theory of the firm   41
     The role of opportunism, hold up, and trust in the
       emergence of firms   42
     Comprehensiveness of the contracting view   45
     Usefulness for strategic management and its practice   49
   Contributions of the contracting view to a theory of the firm
     for strategy   51
   Contractual analysis in a make-or-buy decision and its
     limitations   53
     Example of an in-house cafeteria   53

3 The nature of the firm in strategy   56
     The resource-based view of the firm   56
       Firm growth   57
       Competence building   59
       Firm heterogeneity and differences in performance   60
     Questions about the resource-based view   64
       Does it provide tautological explanations about
          performance?   64
       Is it a useful theory?   66
       Does it explain why firms exist?   68
     The firm in strategic management   70
     A value-based model of firm strategy   71
     The effect of firm boundaries on the value created by
       internal resources   76
       Internal effects   77
       External effects   79
     Why do different firm strategies exist?   80

4 Creating economic value   85
     What is economic value?   85
       Value in economics   86
       Value in marketing   88
       Value in finance   90
       Value in strategy   91
     Sources of customer value creation   92
     Value creation through enhancing customer benefits   95
       Greater utility in existing product or service features   96
       Different combinations of product or service features   97
       New products and services   98
     Value creation through reducing customers' costs   99
       Reducing monetary costs (price)   99
       Reducing nonmonetary costs   100
     Value creation through reducing firms' costs   103
     The influence of externalities   104
     Innovation, entrepreneurs, and new value creation   106
       The role of entrepreneurs in value creation   108
     Value analysis versus transaction costs economics (TCE) as
       drivers of firm boundaries   109
       Williamson's example of mines and houses   109

5 The appropriation of value by firms   114
     Where do profits come from?   114
       Profits as a residual income in neoclassical economics   115

Profits as implicit compensation to factors of production   117
Profits as retribution to the entrepreneur   118
Contextual conditions for profits   120
   Uncertainty   121
   Innovation   122
   Specificity   124
Profit generation through resource combinations   127
The sustainability of profits through barriers to competition   129
   Barriers with perfect replicability   131
   Barriers with asymmetric replicability   132
   Barriers with limited substitutability   132
Value analysis, profits, and competitive barriers   134
   Profit sustainability of a new restaurant   134

Part II   Firm strategies

6   Business strategy   141
   Elements of business-level strategy   141
   Managing resources to create value for customers   143
      Value created by products   145
      Value created by professional services   147
      Value created by networks   148
   Market positioning   152
      Segmentation   153
      Differentiation   156
   Competitive dynamics   160
   The interaction among the different elements of strategy   164
   The influence of the industry and the top managers on
      business strategy   165
   Value analysis at the business level   168
      Why do schools exist, but not firms for long-term
        secretarial services?   169

7   Corporate strategy   174
   Value creation at the corporate level   174
   Horizontal diversification into new businesses   177
      The benefits of diversification   177
      The costs of diversification   181
      The effect of diversification on performance   184
   Vertical integration   186
   Mergers and acquisitions   189
   Strategic alliances and cooperation   192

Value analysis at the corporate level   195
   The integration of channel and content in Vivendi   195

8 International strategy   198
  The theory of the multinational   198
  A value approach to the MNE   203
  International presence   207
  Global strategy   209
  Value analysis in internationalization   213
   The internationalization of retailers Wal-Mart and Ikea   213

9 Strategy and social value   216
  Markets and social value   216
  Market imperfections   217
   Monopoly   218
   Externalities   221
   Other market imperfections   223
  Wealth distribution   225
  Corporate social responsibility   226
  Value creation and CSR   231
   A dual standard for business and CSR activities   236
  Ethics and social strategy   237
  Value analysis in corporate social responsibility   242
   CSR in The Body Shop   242

10 Value analysis in strategy   246
  Economic value and the theory of the firm   246
   What is a firm?   246
   Why do firms exist?   248
   What determines firms' boundaries?   249
   What causes performance differences across firms?   250
  Implications for strategy research and practice   252
   The strategic definition of firm boundaries   252
   Focus on the customer's perspective   255
   Sources of differentiation   257
   Industry change and replacement   259
  Towards a value theory of the firm in strategic management   260
   Areas for future research   261
   Limitations of value analysis   264

Further reading   267
References   272
Index   293

Figures

3.1 A value-based model of firm strategy *page* 74
6.1 Elements of business-level strategy 143
9.1 Monopoly and deadweight loss 218
9.2 Cost–benefit analysis of CSR activities to the firm
and overall society 233

Tables

1.1 Alternative approaches to the theory of the firm   *page* 23
5.1 A categorization of profits, resource combinations,
    and barriers   134
6.1 Configurations for value creation   151

Preface

The theory of the firm addresses the fundamental questions that we could ask about business organizations, including those regarding their role, their organizational boundaries, and their performance. It is not surprising that economists have made substantial contributions to our understanding of these issues, from neoclassical economics to the new industrial organization economics. However, it is more puzzling that the field of strategic management has not been able to absorb selectively the abundant literature on the economic theory of the firm and to adapt it to its own goals regarding strategic decision making. Simply put, economic theories like transaction costs economics were not designed to facilitate strategic analysis.

At this moment, strategy does not yet have a core theory of what firms do and their performance in the market, although the entire field somehow deals with an applied and instrumental perspective about the actions of firms and their implications for business performance. A large variety of approaches to the nature of the firm coexists within strategic management, currently dominated by the resource-based view of the firm. Unfortunately, the lack of a core foundation makes progress for the field more difficult through unnecessary controversies, such as market positioning versus resource analysis of competitive advantage.

This book is one step towards the goal of developing a reasonably comprehensive theory of the firm for strategic management. Relevant ideas from transaction costs economics, the resource-based view, competitive dynamics, diversification, globalization, and even corporate social responsibility can be integrated within a framework that begins with the most basic questions and leads to critical strategic decisions of a firm regarding how it should deal with its customers, its resources, and its competitors. I will argue throughout the book that the systematic analysis of how firms create and capture economic value is an especially useful approach to address these questions as far as strategic analysis is concerned.

I wrote this book for academics and advanced students in business administration who may look for a structured map of state-of-the-art ideas in strategic management from an economic perspective. The analysis of value provides the glue that connects the wide range of topics covered by the book. Obviously, a few hundred pages cannot summarize the huge literature in strategic management, but a value-based theory of the firm can serve as a basis to get acquainted with the economic foundations of the strategy field. The first part of the book covers these theoretical foundations and the second part explores the implications of economic value analysis for the key strategic decisions of a firm, including business, corporate, international, and social strategy.

Three years were necessary to finish the book. It would have been impossible without the support of many people, including the great editorial team from Cambridge University Press. I would also like to thank all of my colleagues at IE Business School (Madrid) and very especially Juan Santaló, who helped me with lively discussions and detailed comments to each chapter.

More than anyone else, I have to thank my wife Yoana, who made writing this book much easier and life much happier.

Manuel Becerra
Madrid 2008

PART I

Theories of the firm

1 | Introduction

The emergence of strategic management

As an area of knowledge, business administration covers a wide variety of fields that contribute to our understanding of the management of firms, such as marketing, finance, accounting, human resources, operations, and strategic management. Since business education quickly spread in the mid-twentieth century, undergraduate and graduate programs have traditionally included some courses in strategic analysis and implementation, though their names, contents, and methods have evolved through time. Let us begin this investigation into the core questions about the theory of the firm in strategy with a brief review of its evolution as an academic field.[1]

The origins of strategic management can be traced back to the core course, usually called Business Policy, which used to be part of most programs until it was changed to Strategic Management in the late seventies. Following the lead of Harvard, this course provided an integration of the different functional areas from the perspective of the general manager.[2] One influential early textbook claimed that business policy was the study of the responsibilities of senior management, the crucial problems that affect the total enterprise, and the decisions that determine its direction.[3] This approach relied heavily on careful analysis of real business cases that was presumably valid only for the specific organization that was analyzed. Strategic management was

---

[1] Rumelt et al. (1994) provide a brief history of the research and the teaching in strategic management in the first chapter of their edited volume as well as some of the fundamental questions in the field, discussed later in the following chapters. Hoskisson et al. (1999) provide a more detailed description of the evolution of the field, focusing particularly on the internal versus external debate about sources of competitive advantage associated with the resource-based view and the Porterian industrial organization approach.

[2] Early contributors to the foundations of the strategy area include Barnard (1938), Selznick (1957), Chandler (1962), and Ansoff (1965).

[3] See Bower et al. (1991).

mostly considered an art that requires analytical skills rather than a science to be expanded through empirical testing.

According to this highly applied perspective with little theoretical core, strategic analysis is primarily based on the internal appraisal of a firm (its set of resources, strengths, and weaknesses that may generate its distinctive competence) and the external environment (trends, threats, and opportunities, from which key success factors can be identified). The main goal of strategy was considered to be the appropriate matching of key success factors at the industry level with the distinctive competences at the firm level in order to achieve high performance for the firm.[4] A firm's strategy can be regarded as an adaptive response to the external environment and to the critical changes occurring within it.

Environmental influences and how to deal with them have played a key role in strategy from the very beginnings of the field. For instance, the importance of understanding the industry in which the firm operates has been stressed by scholars such as Michael Porter in the eighties, who were inspired by industrial organization (IO) economics. From a very different perspective, the fit between the organizational structure and the environment, as well as a firm's dynamic capability to learn from and change its environment, have been studied by contingency theorists in the 1960s and also by scholars from the resource-based view of the firm in the 1990s.

This match between internal resources and external conditions underlies the foundations of strategic management and its crucial goal of understanding the reasons for the success or failure of businesses. Many of these ideas can be traced to the early framework suggested by Andrews (1971). In short, the appropriate matching between the external environment and the firm's resources may converge into an internally consistent strategy that potentially results in a sustainable competitive advantage leading to the superior performance of some firms.[5] Expanding from this basic model, most undergraduate

---

[4] For instance, Amit and Schoemaker (1993) refine the notion of external key success factors and internal resources as an essential part of strategy. Vasconcellos and Hambrick (1989) provide a supportive empirical test of its effect on firm performance for mature industrial products. A more critical view about "industry recipes" is developed by Spender (1989).

[5] See Rumelt (1997) for a summary of this approach applied to the evaluation of business strategies.

and graduate-level textbooks analyze the so-called strategic management process, frequently going through topics like vision, external and internal analysis, strategy formulation at different levels and industry contexts, and implementation issues like structure, planning, and control.

Despite its widespread use for teaching strategic management, the notion of matching internal resources and external environment is neither sufficiently powerful nor precise enough to be the cornerstone of strategy on which the field can be built and developed further.[6] Many important topics cannot be addressed within this framework, including critical questions like why firms exist in the first place, what determines their size, and how they should innovate. Furthermore, it is hard to explain precisely performance differentials from the concept of internal–external fit without falling into after-the-fact theorizing about firms that must somehow fit better with their environment if they have proved to be successful.

Fortunately, the strategy field has expanded well beyond this model of internal–external matching,[7] using the traditional scientific method of theory development and hypotheses testing. Despite the important debates among strategy researchers, a distinct academic field has emerged in the last three decades.[8] At the turn of the century, strategy is an established field within business administration alongside other areas like finance, marketing, and organizational behavior. Having absorbed and moved beyond its highly applied but unscientific initial stages, the field is still in search of a theoretical core that could provide greater coherence and consistency to the fundamental issues in the theory of the firm that this book explores.

---

[6] As an analogy of the limitations of this internal–external fit approach, we can observe the development and decline of contingency theory within organization theory. See Child (1972) for the role of strategic choice in the performance consequences of the structure–environment fit.

[7] See Mintzberg *et al.* (1998) for an interesting critical review of the major approaches to strategy, including the matching "design" approach.

[8] The Business Policy and Strategy (BPS) division of the Academy of Management was created in the US in 1971, and the first academic journal dedicated exclusively to strategy, the *Strategic Management Journal*, was launched in 1980. In the early eighties the first graduates from doctoral programs in strategy came out as academics specialized in this growing field. In 2007 the BPS division was the second largest within the Academy of Management, very close in size to the Organizational Behavior division.

A model of strategy as organization–environment match

Kenneth Andrews provided a highly influential view of strategy in his book published in 1971. In his own words, "Corporate strategy is the pattern of decisions in a company that determines and reveals its objectives, purposes, or goals, produces the principal policies and plans for achieving those goals, and defines the range of business the company is going to pursue, the kind of economic and human organization it is or intends to be, and the nature of the economic and noneconomic contribution it intends to make to its shareholders, employees, customers, and communities." (Andrews, 1987: 13)

This elaborate conceptualization of strategy combines aspects of formulation (goals), implementation (plans and organization), firm boundaries (pursued businesses), and value (personal, economic, and broader social contributions). Andrews identifies four main components of strategy: (1) identification of opportunity and risk, (2) determining the company's resources, (3) the personal values of the chief executive and his/her team, and (4) the noneconomic responsibility to society. Basically, these four components refer to what the firm might-can-want-should do, respectively. He first raises the critical questions that top managers should address when they go through the entire process of strategic analysis and implementation, and then makes some recommendations, e.g., is the strategy in some way unique?

In this early and highly applied approach to strategic management, the performance of an economic strategy is primarily determined by the match between the market opportunities that the firm pursues and its distinctive competence (a concept introduced by Selznick, 1957). On the one hand, the firm can identify the possible opportunities and risks from the analysis of environmental conditions and trends. On the other hand, the firm should analyze its distinctive competence and the corporate resources (i.e., strengths and capabilities) that can be applied to exploit market opportunities. The best match between opportunities and resource should drive the strategic choice of products and markets for the firm, which today we summarize in an analysis of SWOT (strengths, weaknesses, opportunities, and threats) and key success factors. Though not yet fully developed, the main elements of strategic management that we will discuss throughout this book were already present in Andrews's model.

The scope of the field

The field of strategic management is particularly broad in its scope, disciplinary background, and methodologies. Probably the common thread in the widely diverse topics covered by strategy is the concern with top managers and their problems within the organization as a whole.[9] It is therefore multifunctional in nature, since top managers need to consider the different aspects that a strategic decision may require. For instance, a decision to diversify through the acquisition of another firm includes aspects of finance, marketing, human resources, and organizational behavior, presumably within a long-term vision of what type of organization the firm should be in the future. The strategist, as well as the strategy student, should be reasonably knowledgeable in these different areas to be able to understand the overall problem, and not rely on just one specific functional perspective.

Strategic decisions deal with the long-term direction and survival of the firm, usually the responsibility of the top managers of the organization. In contrast to tactical or functional decisions, they typically require substantial resources, cannot be easily reversed, involve the entire organization, and have a significant impact on the firm's performance. More formally, Chandler (1962: 13) has defined strategy as, "the determination of the basic long-term goals and objectives of an enterprise, and the adoption of courses of action and the allocation of resources necessary for carrying out these goals." However, this definition requires an explicit planning effort by top managers that does not always exist. Following Mintzberg (1978), we may consider strategy as a pattern in a stream of actions or decisions. Strategy is just the collection of strategic decisions that the top managers of a firm make about how the firm should compete in the market. Strategic management is the field that studies how these decisions are made and implemented, giving rise to strategy content and process issues respectively.

But strategy is studied not only for descriptive and taxonomical purposes. Being an applied field within business administration, its ultimate goal is to provide recommendations to management,

---

[9] The *Strategic Management Journal* webpage indicates that they publish papers dealing with topics such as strategic resource allocation; organization structure; leadership; entrepreneurship and organizational purpose; methods and techniques for evaluating and understanding competitive, technological, social, and political environments; planning processes; and strategic decision processes.

especially regarding the improvement of firm performance. In fact, most of the existing empirical research in strategy has some measure of performance as the ultimate dependent variable and virtually the entire field can be directly or indirectly connected to the understanding of why some firms fail and others succeed to a different degree. Obviously firm performance varies substantially across and within industries, in different countries, and through time. Part of this performance is attributable to management, and managers can influence it through the strategies that they formulate and implement in their firms. Leaving aside the uncontrollable factors that are not the responsibility of management (e.g., luck about the outcome of innovation efforts), those firms that can generate a competitive advantage through their strategy should be able to enjoy superior performance when compared with competitors without such an advantage.[10]

The multidisciplinary basis of business strategy

In order to investigate strategic decisions and their consequences for performance, strategy scholars draw on different disciplines, including economics, sociology, and psychology. The combination of its multifunctional nature with this interdisciplinary focus gives strategy its uniquely broad perspective on management. Though not every strategy scholar has a similar disciplinary background, most models in strategy borrow from microeconomic theory, especially for issues dealing with the analysis of markets, resources, and organizational economics. In particular, the field of industrial organization (IO) has been the source of current models of industry analysis and barriers to competition, like the highly influential five forces model of Michael Porter (1980).

However, in contrast to the usual practice in the economics field, strategy scholars do not rely on the analysis of equilibrium and constrained maximization to understand firm behavior. Strategy scholars do not usually assume that the existing practices and institutions are necessarily the most efficient ones and do not try, as economists

---

[10] The idea that competitive advantage leads to superior performance is really a central premise of the field rather than a testable hypothesis, as Powell (2001) argued. It is, however, useful for investigating the basis of a firm's success or failure because it helps us to focus on the reasons behind its performance.

typically do, to discover through mathematical modeling the implications for an equilibrium situation. In fact, game theory and the formalization of the interdependence among firm strategies has had limited impact on strategic management, both in its theoretical development and its actual practice.[11] Nevertheless, economics remains the core discipline that impregnates most of the strategy field, though it requires contributions from other disciplines to more fully and realistically understand how firm strategies are formulated and implemented, and their consequences for performance.

Because the unit of analysis is usually the organization or its business units, sociology is another important discipline that contributes to strategic management. In particular, organization theory has been very useful in understanding process issues, like organizational structure, culture, environmental adaptation, and stakeholder management. Even if we are concerned largely with business organizations, the profit motive does not adequately describe the purpose and behavior of firms in all circumstances. For instance, institutional theory has been used to study the isomorphic pressures across firms to gain legitimacy (versus efficiency) and how certain practices become institutionalized. Similarly, resource dependence helps us recognize the emergence and the use of power within the organization as well as the formation of a dominant coalition among top managers that sets the direction for the organization. These sociological theories bring an important element of realism to the analysis of firm strategy, though they are not as focused on performance outcomes.

Finally, the field of psychology also has an important contribution to make. Strategies are designed and carried out by managers and all individuals obviously have biases, personalities, cognitive limitations, and personal motivations. Psychology is particularly useful for topics like strategic decision making, information processing, and managerial interpretation. For instance, top management team research has shown that the demographic and social-psychological characteristics of top managers have important effects on the strategies that their organizations follow, including diversification, strategic change, and innovation. Cognitive and social psychology can be especially helpful

---

[11] See Saloner (1991) and Camerer (1991) for a discussion of the relationship among economics, game theory, and strategy.

to address how top managers enact their environment and the mental maps that they form about their businesses.

The influence of economics in the strategy field, sometimes considered excessive, has been the subject of debate since the beginnings of the field.[12] In many top business schools courses about strategy content and analysis are dominated by scholars with training in economics, while strategy process and implementation courses are typically covered by professors with sociology and organization theory backgrounds. In the last two decades economists have started to look inside organizations and have used their traditional tools to study issues like organizational structure, coordination, compensation, and motivation, which were previously the exclusive domain of sociologists and psychologists working in organization theory and organizational behavior. There is occasional tension about the role of economics within the strategy field.

Economic, sociological, and psychological concepts intertwine within the strategy field to help us understand how firms compete, as a result of the strategic decisions that their managers make. Economics is certainly at the core of strategy, because it is directly concerned with concepts closely linked to organizational performance, such as profit theory, customer utility, and market structure. Thus, this book will draw primarily from the existing economic theories to search for the ideas that could be useful in our understanding of the fundamental questions about firm strategy and performance.

However, sociology and psychology also bring in important concepts and theories to better understand how top managers actually run their firms, with the individual limitations and the social pressures that they have to face in managing their businesses. Being an applied area of knowledge, strategic management is not defined by its disciplinary basis or methodological approaches to conducting research, but by the problems that top managers face when running their organization. Economics provides a particularly fertile ground for the questions that we investigate in this book dealing with the nature of the firm, but other disciplines also have some important ideas to contribute to the advancement of knowledge about the strategic management of business organizations. This is our ultimate goal and economic

---

[12] See the debate between Barney (1990) and Donaldson (1990).

theories are only discussed to the extent that they can be useful to develop a stronger theoretical core for the strategy field.

The concept of firm

Because the firm constitutes the fundamental unit of analysis in strategy, it is necessary to define what we mean by "firm" or business organization. The concept of firm that we use has important implications in how we study them and ultimately in the type of recommendations that we may provide to top managers about how to improve their performance. There are actually a wide variety of conceptualizations about the nature of the firm and each one focuses on a certain aspect of what firms do.[13] All of them have therefore something to contribute to the analysis of how firms compete and their performance, though no widely accepted or comprehensive conceptualization has yet developed in the strategy field. Let us now introduce some of the existing approaches, so that we can start exploring the theory of the firm from a strategy perspective.

The firm as a production unit

The most important role for business organizations in our society is probably the supply of products and services. The theory of production in economics builds directly on this notion of the firm as supplier of goods, typically formalized through a production function, which constitutes the neoclassical theory of the firm.

It is important to note that economics has traditionally focused on the understanding of markets and the determination of prices, rather than the analysis of business behavior. Until the mid-twentieth century, economists considered the firm as a mental construct that allows us to model the supply side of markets, but not the very real organizations that we encounter in our every day life.[14] Their impact in the economy

---

[13] Just in economics, Machlup (1967) identified twenty-one concepts of firms. He claims that no concept of the firm can be the most important or useful, because each one serves different purposes. The choice of the theory has to depend on the problem to be dealt with and the research approach to use.

[14] Fritz Machlup (1967: 9) claimed about the theory of the firm in traditional price theory that it is not "designed to serve to explain and predict the behaviour of real firms; instead, it is designed to explain and predict changes in

could be captured through their production functions, which transform inputs (traditionally labor, capital, and land) into the products exchanged in the markets. These firms were typically presumed to use the best technology available to them, located in the so-called production possibility frontier. What actually happens inside firms was not of interest to most economists until the 1970s, particularly after the emergence of theories based on contracting. Firms were regarded as "black-boxes" that attempt to maximize profits through their decisions regarding supplied quantities and choice of inputs, which contribute to set the market-clearing prices at the level where supply intersects with demand functions.

This view of the firm as a production function has been instrumental in developing the basis of both micro and macroeconomics.[15] Though very useful on which to build a theory of markets and their efficiency based on the notions of equilibrium and perfect competition, its potential as a theory of the firm is rather limited and it is truly a theory of plant size. From this perspective, firms basically have the choice to enter or exit specific markets through a plant of certain size. Most of their decisions directly depend on their production function and its underlying technology. For instance, firm size depends entirely on the shape of their production function and in the long-run equilibrium they will produce at the level where their production function is at the lowest average cost of production. At that level, marginal revenue, marginal cost, and price are equal. Firms are price-takers in this perfect competition model developed by neoclassical economists. New entry into the industry will take place until overall supply equals demand and, thus, no extra profits may exist in equilibrium, except for difficult-to-maintain differences in costs among firms. Deviations from the perfect competition model are associated with some degree of monopoly power that allows firms to limit output and increase prices. However, even if firms enjoy some level of influence over prices, monopolistic

observed prices (quoted, paid, received), as effects of particular changes in conditions (wage rates, interest rates, import duties, excise taxes, technology, etc)." He referred to the "fallacy of misplaced concreteness" to the confusion of this theoretical concept with a real organization like General Motors. Though this is probably so for economics, strategic management is concerned with real firms.

[15] This includes the traditional microeconomic neoclassical theory of supply and demand as well as the Walrasian general equilibrium and the modern theory of value as modeled by Arrow and Debreu (1954).

competition would drive extra profits to zero as long as new entry is possible.[16]

The core apparatus of microeconomics is based on this conceptualization of firms as constrained optimizers, which has produced an enormous amount of knowledge. However, this view has been criticized on many grounds as a theory of the firm in economics as well as other fields. First, the profit-maximizing goal of firms is not always a reasonable description of how businesses behave and the decisions that managers make, which is a particularly damaging criticism for those of us interested in strategic management of real organizations. Herbert Simon and the proponents of a behavioral theory of the firm have stressed the shortcomings of this view, particularly the bounded rationality of managerial decisions inside organizations. These authors have opened up the neoclassical black-box of the firm and basically found managers making decisions within an information processing structure. Second, this neoclassical view of the firm provides a technological answer for plant size to what is really an organizational question. Economies of scale and any other technological constraints may be dealt with in many cases by a group of independent firms instead of one larger firm. Information and incentives issues inside the firm are totally disregarded. In other words, regardless of technological issues, firms may collaborate through market transactions governed by a set of contracts. From this contracting perspective initially suggested by Ronald Coase, the firm becomes an alternative to the market as a means of governing transactions, instead of the organizational result of a purely technological issue. These two criticisms of the neoclassical theory of the firm have led to new conceptualizations of firms.

The firm as a decision-making process

In contrast to neoclassical economists, organization theorists have focused on what happens inside firms and their relationship with their environment.[17] This descriptive and more realistic view differs

---

[16] See the analysis of imperfect (monopolistic) competition of Robinson (1933) and Chamberlin (1933).

[17] Of course, organization theory is a well-established field that has a large variety of conceptualizations of organizations in general, and firms in particular. It is not the goal of this book to review the large number of approaches to the analysis of firms that exists in organization theory, like

substantially from the normative and highly stylized nature of the neo-classical firm. From this perspective, coordination of specialized units and individuals is the major role of the firm. However, effective coordination does not happen easily nor automatically, but only through the appropriate decisions of its executives, primarily regarding the structure, control, incentives, and goals of the organization and its members.[18] Studying how managers make decisions is therefore critical to the analysis of organizations and their actual behavior.

As the seminal author of the behavioral school, Simon (1997: 18) defines the term *organization* as "the pattern of communications and relations among a group of human beings, including the processes for making and implementing decisions." Also from the Carnegie school, Cyert and March (1992: 202) describe the organization as a "decision-making process," because it is a system the primary output of which is decisions such as pricing, production, inventory, advertising, and investing. These scholars have made clear that profit maximization is not the critical goal that drives managerial decisions, as considered by the neoclassical theory of the firm. Managers can only dedicate limited attention to a reduced set of problems and possible solutions, while dealing with conflicting goals. Thus, bounded rationality leads managers to satisficing, rather than maximizing, behavior.

The behavioral approach has helped us better understand strategic decision making.[19] Alternatives for actions are discovered through simple search processes, often biased, and continuously adapted through organizational learning. Goals are not consistent throughout the organization, as different departments try to carry out their own responsibilities, thus resulting in the formation of coalitions within the firm. This leads to sequential attention to goals and decision rules based on

classical management theory, contingency theory, population ecology, resource-dependence theory, and institutional theory. In this chapter we will briefly discuss one of the seminal theories that remains at the core of most subsequent approaches within organization theory. For an excellent scholarly review of the field, see Scott (1992).

[18] See Barnard (1938) for an early analysis of how coordination among people takes place inside organizations, including the role of the informal organization, incentives, opportunism, and authority.

[19] See March and Simon (1958) and Cyert and March (1963) as the basis for the analysis of how decision making takes places inside organizations. Later on, strategic decision making has become an important area in strategy (Eisenhardt and Zbaracki, 1992; Nutt, 1998).

merely acceptable levels, rather than the maximization of an overall goal for the entire firm. Feedback-react decision procedures are also set, as well as possible negotiations with the environment, in order to reduce the uncertainty that organizations need to face.

The behavioral theory of the firm may be regarded as one core conceptualization of firms on which much of organization theory has built. There are many other approaches within the field,[20] but most of them draw from, or at least are consistent with, the notion of firms as decision-making processes that coordinate a variety of units and individuals with different goals, somehow integrated within the broader environment. Information processing remains the mainstream approach to understand the internal structure and coordination mechanisms of a business.[21] Considering firms as decision-making processes, better performance can potentially be obtained by improving the management of information and knowledge inside the firm and in relation to its external environment. Some scholars have gone as far as claiming that the only real sustainable source of advantage lies in an organization's architecture, i.e., "the way in which it structures and coordinates its people and processes in order to maximize its unique capabilities over the long haul, regardless of continuous shifts in the competitive landscape." (Nadler *et al.*, 1997: viii). However, empirical research in contingency theory that studies the relationship of organizational structure and coordination mechanisms with the external environment has not yielded strong explanatory power about firm performance.[22]

The neoclassical theory of the firm has been a very useful tool for studying business organizations as the basic production units in an economy, but it does not allow for the many differences that may exist among them. In contrast, the behavioral theory of the firm brings greater realism about what happens inside organizations, but at a heavy price. We can study how managers actually make their decisions, including those about the size and scope of their firms, but

---

[20] Morgan (2006) provides an interesting review using different metaphors for the implied nature of organizations across the major perspectives in organization theory.

[21] See Galbraith (1977) for an analysis of the firm, its internal structure, and its coordination mechanisms from an information processing perspective.

[22] Classical studies within contingency theory include Burns and Stalker's (1961) analysis of mechanistic and organic structures, and Lawrence and Lorsch's (1967) analysis of the departmental differentiation and integration within the structure to deal with the complexity of the environment.

this perspective does not offer much help about the implications of these managerial decisions on firm performance. This is because firm performance, and particularly profits, occupy a central place in economics, but it is much more loosely defined in organization theory, which typically prefers to analyze multiple criteria of organizational effectiveness shaped by political factors and institutional processes. Nevertheless, it seems clear that firms are much more complex than production functions that transform inputs into outputs through some kind of constrained optimization. Their internal structure varies substantially and it can make some firms more efficient or react faster to environmental changes, which should be part of a theory of the firm in strategy.

The firm as a contracting solution

The two theories previously discussed have provided great insights in their respective domains, but they have not specifically focused on why firms exist in the first place. On the one hand, the benefits of team-production are not sufficient to explain why different individuals should be part of a firm, instead of independent agents coordinating through market exchanges and contracts. On the other hand, though the decision of individuals to join existing organizations has been studied in terms of inducements and contributions of participants in the employee–organization labor relationship,[23] the initial emergence of the organization itself and its scope of activities, such as make-or-buy decisions, can scarcely be understood only in terms of information processing. In fact, information processing is necessary within the boundaries of the firm and also across them (for instance, with suppliers providing just-in-time inventory) and cannot by itself define firm boundaries.

For the contracting view of the firm, the defining characteristic is neither technology nor information, but the hierarchical relationship that exists within an organization, in contrast to the independent contractual relationships that manage market transactions. From this perspective, it is the efficiency and effectiveness of using market contracts

---

[23] See Simon (1982) for an analysis of the formal employment relationship from this perspective.

versus organizational arrangements to deal with economic exchanges that determines the emergence of firms.

Different theories have followed the insightful path of Ronald Coase's conceptualization of the firm as a governance structure of transactions. For these theories the possibility, the effectiveness, and the costs of writing contracts are essential for understanding why firms displace the market. We will review some of them in greater detail in the following chapter, including transaction costs economics (TCE), property rights theory, and agency theory, the latter focusing only on the management of vertical principal–agent contractual relationships. For all of these theories, the nature and the contractibility of the exchange, buyer–supplier or boss–subordinate, determine whether an organization should emerge and the internal management of such an exchange within the organization or through the market.

The importance of the contracting view of the firm should not be understated. The traditional method of constrained maximization in economics can be used to deal with problems of internal management of organization (agency theory) and the boundaries of the firm (property rights). Efficiency still occupies the core of the theory, but, in addition to production costs, minimizing transaction costs and agency costs become the challenge for understanding firm boundaries. As a nexus of contracts, firms emerge to solve contracting problems, so that a better design of the contracts in which a firm is involved should be the main way to increase efficiency and, consequently, improve performance.

Though the comparative analysis of firms versus markets has been very useful to understand issues like make-or-buy decisions, the contracting theory of the firm offers very limited insight into the sources for differential performance of organizations beyond efficiency, neglecting important aspects of strategy like differentiation and innovation. In addition, its particular focus on exchanges and opportunism may obscure other potential rationales behind the nature of the firm that we will explore later on. Given its importance, we will review in greater depth in the next chapter some of the main contributions and limitations of contracting as the basis for a theory of the firm in strategy.

The firm as a collection of resources

While the contracting view of the firm is the mainstream approach in economics, strategic management is currently dominated by the resource-based view (RBV) as the main conceptualization of the firm.[24] In the RBV, the firm is considered a collection of resources under one administrative framework, as suggested first by Edith Penrose and later developed substantially in the 1990s. In her words: "the primary economic function of an industrial firm is to make use of productive resources for the purpose of supplying goods and services to the economy in accordance with plans developed and put into effect within the firm." (Penrose, 1959: 15). This perspective forms the basis of our investigation of the theory of the firm for strategy, as we will discuss in greater detail in chapter three. To complete the comparison with the previous three approaches, it is worthwhile summarizing some of its key elements.

The most important feature of the RBV is its reliance on internal resources as the unit of analysis for strategy, including in this concept any financial, human, physical, and intangible resources, i.e., any possible asset that firms may use to conceive of and implement their strategies (Barney and Arikan, 2001). The industry in which a firm is operating becomes secondary when defining its nature, while the bundle of resources available to the firm dictates the direction towards which the firm can grow and the industries in which it can compete. Thus, available resources determine the scope of activities inside and outside the discrete set of productive opportunities available to the firm.

This view is particularly useful in explaining the process of growth of the firm. As Penrose pointed out, the growth process allows us to understand the issues of size and scope, which are ultimately its byproducts. The evolution in the bundle of resources that constitutes a firm (thus its size and scope) evolves through time in a path-dependent

---

[24] Usually considered as the alternative to RBV within the strategy field, the model suggested by Porter (1980, 1991) is condensed primarily in the five forces of industry structure, the three generic strategies (cost leadership, differentiation, and focus), and the value chain. To a large extent, Porter's ideas are based on the structure-conduct-performance model in early industrial organization, which builds on the neoclassical theory of the firm. Thus, the highly influential Porterian model of strategy, which we will discuss later in chapters five and six, does not develop a new theory of the firm. However, it achieves substantial sophistication in the conceptualization of the firm as a production unit, primarily through the notion of value chain. This model may be used to understand the set of discrete activities that a firm does within a given industry, which determines its possible competitive advantage.

process, in which the steps taken early on determine the set of options that exist later. The emphasis on how actual growth takes place based on internal factors also characterizes other approaches that share a similar view of the nature of the firm, including evolutionary economics (Nelson and Winter, 1982), core competences (Prahalad and Hamel, 1990), knowledge-based theories (Grant, 1996), and dynamic capabilities (Teece *et al.*, 1997). From this perspective, it is the superiority of accumulated resources, especially unique knowledge that determines the performance of an organization. The characteristics of resources that give rise to sustainable competitive advantage have become the core of the RBV.[25]

Certainly, the RBV has brought great richness to the analysis of sustainable competitive advantage, but it still has some important limitations and lags in its conceptualization of firms that, to some extent, can be filled by drawing from other theories of the firm. For instance, the RBV does not currently explain which resources should be bundled under the same administrative framework in the first place. Other challenges for this perspective deal with a more precise analysis of the value that individual or bundled resources may generate and how the returns from these resources are appropriated and distributed among different resource owners. Thus, this perspective still needs further development to become a fully fledged theory of the firm for strategy.

The theory of the firm for strategic management

The four theoretical lenses briefly described above have been very successful with regard to the specific problems that they intended to investigate: the determination of prices and quantities in markets (neoclassical), the processes for decision making and the internal structure of organizations (behavioral), the choice of governance mechanism for exchanges (contracting), and the analysis of competitive advantage and the process of firm growth (resource). However, none of these theories was initially developed to probe into the nature of the firm from a pure strategy perspective, so that the main questions within the field could be investigated building from this conceptualization.[26] Let us briefly

[25] The main characteristics of strategic resources have been described by Barney (1991) and Peteraf (1993).

[26] Even the RBV, primarily developed by strategy scholars, was initially intended to understand the process of firm growth in the work of the economist Edith

identify the questions that a theory of the firm for strategy should deal with.

It is generally agreed that a theory of the firm should address the fundamental questions about what a firm is and its role in society. For instance, Holmstrom and Roberts (1998) argue that the central questions in the economics of organization are: why do firms exist, what is their function, and what determines their scope?[27] Besides these questions, given the applied nature of the field and its concern with top management, a theory of the firm for strategy should also address what drives their overall performance, in other words, why some firms have better performance than others, because strategic management is especially concerned with understanding firm performance and its sustainability through time versus competitors in order to provide recommendations for management. In fact, several authors have already suggested the need for a strategic theory of the firm to directly address the issue of heterogeneity across firms and their differences in performance, for example, Rumelt (1984), Grant (1996), and Foss (2005). Thus, a theory of the firm for strategy should basically address four major types of questions:

a) Definition: What is a firm? What are its defining features? How should they be conceptualized so that we can study them?
b) Role: Why do firms exist? What is their role in society? How do firms emerge?
c) Scope: What determines their size? How far can they grow? What drives their scope of activities with regard to products (vertical/horizontal integration) and geographical presence (internationalization)?
d) Performance: What determines their performance? Why do performance differences exist among firms? How are they sustained through time?

Penrose (1959). Later on, it focused on the analysis of competitive advantage, drawing heavily from the literature on economic rents (e.g., Peteraf, 1993).
The issue of why firms exist was not central to the theory, at least in its origins. Its concern with competitive advantage has placed this theory at the center of strategy, despite some of its limitations as a theory of the firm. Current work in the area tries to reconcile the RBV with the contracting theory of the firm to provide a more comprehensive theory of the firm, like Foss (2005).

[27] These same questions have been identified within the strategy field by authors reviewing the existing theories of the firm, like Conner (1991), and Seth and Thomas (1994).

The four theories briefly reviewed earlier offer their own answers to these questions in a more or less satisfactory manner as far as strategic management is concerned. Each of these theories has something to contribute to the theory of the firm for strategy, though all of them have some limitations because they put their emphasis on different questions and goals. The last two perspectives can be considered the main footholds for the foundations of the strategy field. Some authors have expressed their preference for some type of contracting theory to explain the nature of the firm for strategy, notably economists Oliver Williamson and David Teece; others argue in favor of a resource or knowledge approach (e.g., Robert Grant, C. K. Prahalad, and Bruce Kogut); while others are pushing towards a more integrative approach of these two perspectives in our field (like Jay Barney, Joseph Mahoney, and Nicolai Foss). For instance, Foss (2005) argues in favor of integrating the contracting and the resource perspectives, instead of considering either one as broad enough to provide the foundations for the field.

A value approach to the analysis of firm strategy

In this book, instead of the mere addition of TCE and the RBV to provide an eclectic approach, we will try to develop a comprehensive approach that captures the main ideas from both perspectives, while using the notion of *value* to integrate and expand further their explanatory power. Value analysis can be used to integrate and develop a more comprehensive approach to the theory of the firm in strategy.

I will claim that we need a broader theory that incorporates elements of both, glued by a conceptualization that better captures the competitive nature of firms. In other words, this theory should not be the mere combination of contracting and resource perspectives, using a transaction costs rationale to explain the boundaries of the firm and a resource perspective to study performance and competitive advantage. Instead, we need to develop a broader perspective with the potential to build a strategic theory of firms as independent competitive units, i.e., the basic subject in strategy. As we will see throughout the book, the concept of *economic value* allows us to do so and to study how firms create and capture value. In fact, much of strategy research has focused on how to appropriate value, usually through the ownership of unique resources and building barriers to entry. More recently, the emphasis has changed towards how firms create value.[28]

I will argue that the most useful conceptualization of the firm for strategy is that of value-creating units in direct competition with other firms for resources and customers. From this perspective, we will explore how firms create value for customers and appropriate part of it for its owners. One of our key challenges in strategic management is to understand the process of value creation and appropriation, which constitute the major role of firms in our economy. Very briefly, those firms that can create more value by combining cospecialized assets will enjoy higher performance and the replicability of these resource combinations by competitors will determine firm performance in the long run. It will be necessary to consider contracting issues and resource characteristics to analyze firm size and scope, but the critical underlying concept will still be *economic value* to which the analysis of contracting and resources will need to be connected. The analysis of value will allow us to define the firm as an independent entity and, later on, study its role in society, its boundaries, and its performance in the rest of the book.

Table 1.1 summarizes the four approaches to the theory of the firm that we have briefly introduced in this chapter and introduces the value perspective that we will explore throughout this book.

Structure of the book

We have begun our analysis of the theory of the firm in strategy by briefly reviewing the historical development of the field of strategic management, its scope, and its multidisciplinary background. Because the firm is the critical unit of analysis in strategy, we need to define what firms are, their function, their defining boundaries, and their overall performance. However, we should do so in a manner that is most useful for strategic analysis and decision making. In other words,

---

[28] See, for instance, Brandenburger and Stuart (1996), Ghoshal *et al.* (2000), Stabell and Fjeldstad (1998), Ramirez, (1999), and DeSarbo, Jedidi, and Sinha (2001). There is a growing interest in how firms create or destroy value, including the analysis of new business models for value creation triggered by the growth of the internet and the reconstruction of value chains. A recent special issue from the *Academy of Management Review* has been dedicated to value creation (Lepak *et al.* 2007).

Table 1.1 *Alternative approaches to the theory of the firm*

Theory of the firm	Definition	Role	Scope	Performance
Neoclassical	Production function	Supply of products and services	Technology	Production costs and market power
Behavioral	Decision-making process leading to action	Coordination of specialized units through information processing	Rationally bounded decisions of management coalitions	Effectiveness of internal structure to deal with the environment
Contracting	Nexus of contracts	Governance structure of transactions (vs. markets)	Transaction costs	Total costs, especially transaction and agency costs
Resource	Collection of resources under one administrative framework	Develop and exploit available resources	Relatedness among resources	Resource characteristics, especially uniqueness
Value	Independent competitive unit	Value creation for customers and its capture by firm owners	Value specificity across resource combinations	Replicability and substitutability of resource combinations

we need a theory of the firm for business strategy. I have argued that, despite the contributions of the existing conceptual approaches introduced in this first chapter, we still need a theory of the firm in our field. It is particularly critical for this theory to guide scholars in the understanding of performance differentials across firms and its implications for managerial practice. In the first five chapters of the book, we will review the existing literature that can help us develop such a theory of the firm for strategy based on the notion of value and its creation and appropriation by those independent value-creating units that we call *firms*.

Chapter two analyzes in greater detail the theory of the firm as a contracting solution for managing relationships, which is the currently accepted view in economics around the notions of transaction costs, property rights, and agency costs. This well-developed perspective provides clear answers to why firms exist, their scope and their internal management, but I will argue that it is not a comprehensive theory, sufficient to understand the emergence of firms in all cases, nor to understand performance differentials across firms. We will focus especially on TCE and review critically its strengths dealing with the analysis of vertical integration as well as its limitations as a theory of the firm for strategy. I will claim that a broader analysis of value that includes transaction costs is necessary to understand the emergence, the size, the scope, and the performance of firms.

The third chapter reviews some of the main contributions of the RBV to the theory of the firm. The view of the firm as a collection of resources has contributed significantly to the development of the strategy field, particularly as an alternative to the traditional perspective to strategy based on IO economics and TCE as the rationale for firm scope. However, it has run into some problems in becoming a fully fledged theory of the firm for strategy. We will review these key problems dealing primarily with vagueness and tautological threats, which could be solved by probing further into the notion of value. We need a better understanding of how firms create value for customers through the combination of resources; in other words, why resources under a common corporate umbrella create more value than separately. This chapter will develop a value-based model of firm strategy that builds directly from the RBV and the conceptualization of the firm as a collection of resources to create and appropriate value in competition with other players in the market.

Chapter four takes up the challenge of examining value creation. Firms combine resources to create value, but we have to explore further the different ways in which this may happen. We will analyze different sources of value creation through enhancing customer benefits, including innovation and differentiation. We will explore two other ways to create value, namely increasing firm efficiency and reducing customer costs. Though they have not yet received much attention, the nonmonetary costs to the customer of accessing and using the product (e.g., information and physical accessibility to the product) also affect how much value they receive, in addition to the intrinsic characteristics of the product and its price. This chapter discusses how firms can combine certain resources, and only those, to create value for customers, including different alternatives like product innovation, differentiation, efficiency, and nonmonetary customer costs.

Chapter five moves one step further, taking us from the analysis of value created by firms into the value that they actually appropriate, that is, their profits. Most of the value created by any single firm is usually appropriated by its customers, resource providers, and competitors, but part of it is kept by the firm's owners as normal and even superior profits. The understanding of where profits come from is probably the core of business strategy. This chapter builds on the economic literature on profit theory and rents, which can be absorbed and reinterpreted in the field of strategy. Our goal will be to understand the contextual conditions for profits to emerge as well as the barriers to competition that may sustain profits through time.

After reviewing and integrating the existing research inspired in economics, particularly TCE and the RBV, the first five chapters develop the basis for a value theory of the firm. However, being an applied area within business administration, the ultimate goal of the strategy field is to provide sound recommendations for managerial practice. Firms do not create value and later decide on how to appropriate it, but do both at once through the continuous management of their resources to achieve a profitable position in different product and geographical markets. The last five chapters investigate the strategic management of firms from this value perspective.

To generate and appropriate value, firms have a set of options about how to deal with customers, competitors, and internal and external resource providers. A firm's strategy essentially defines how the collection of resources that constitute the firm jointly create value for customers in competition with other players in the market. We will analyze in chapter six the main strategic decisions, including the resource management processes inside the firm, the alternatives for market positioning, and the dynamics of dealing and interacting with competitors in the markets for customers and resources. All these elements of business-level strategy are interconnected through the notions of value creation and appropriation.

The main corporate level issues are discussed in the next chapters. We will study how firms can create value combining resources across different industries (diversification in chapter seven) and across countries (internationalization in chapter eight). Because these are questions about the product and geographical scope of the firm, the analysis of value creation, transfer, and exploitation offers additional insight over the traditional approach to firm boundaries inspired in TCE.

Chapter nine discusses some of the social and ethical implications of this perspective of the firm as combiner of resources to create and appropriate value. We will analyze the circumstances under which the creation of value for the firm will not be consistent with greater social value as a result of market imperfections. We will also explore the corporate social responsibility (CSR) of firms that may exist beyond their economic purposes. We will address these questions from both perspectives, economics and ethics, and suggest a dual standard for business versus social activities that can be used for decisions regarding the boundaries of the firms.

The concluding chapter deals with the contribution of economic value analysis to the field of strategy. Most topics covered by strategy researchers in the last few decades deal to some extent with how firms and their managers create and appropriate value. In this chapter we will summarize the key features of a value-based theory of the firm in strategy and the answers that it would provide to the fundamental questions about the nature of the firm, its scope, and its performance. We will conclude with a discussion of the implications and limitations for both research in strategic management and managerial practice.

2 | *The contracting view of the firm*

Coase and the nature of the firm

The contracting theory of the firm has displaced the neoclassical conceptualization of the firm as a production function and constitutes the mainstream approach to the analysis of organizations in modern economics. The defining feature of organizations is not so much the production function that they carry out (for which other institutional arrangements would be possible), but the way in which firms organize economic activity in contrast to the market. From this perspective, firms are governance mechanisms for transactions and they allocate and control resources in a manner inherently different from markets. This theory of the firm is based primarily on contracting issues that firms contribute to solve. Ronald Coase planted the seed of this approach, which was then refined and expanded by Williamson, Jensen, Hart, and other economists inspired in the notion of transaction costs and contract design.

In his classic article on the nature of the firm, Coase (1937) addressed directly the question of why there are firms in our economy. His answer comes from the apparently simple realization that exchanges can take place either inside organizations or outside the firm contracting through the market. Using a traditional optimization principle, firms would internalize those exchanges to operate more efficiently as long as the cost of doing these exchanges inside the firm is smaller than transacting through the market. He referred to them as "transaction costs," including finding the exchange partner, bargaining over prices, writing a contract, monitoring and enforcing such an agreement, and any other possible costs of using the price mechanism, i.e., contracting through the market. The logic of this insightful argument is very strong and it has become the standard approach to the analysis of firm size and scope of activities in economics.

The tremendous influence of this Coasian perspective on the field of economics is very reasonable. Classical and neoclassical economics were particularly strong in the analysis of markets and prices, but weak in what happens inside the black-box of the neoclassical firm. With this new approach the decisions of firms to internalize any activity can be studied with the standard tools of economics (e.g., marginal analysis) applied to market transactions in contrast to intra-firm transactions. Thus, a large part of the existing apparatus to understand markets can be used to probe inside organizations, which Arrow (1974: 33) defined as "a means of achieving the benefits of collective action in situations in which the price system fails." Put in other words, any kind of collaboration between economic agents that cannot be efficiently achieved through the price system may trigger the emergence of an organization that integrates these otherwise separate actors. Thus, organizations are an alternative governance mechanism to market transactions, in which authority replaces the price mechanism as the method to allocate and coordinate resources.

These ideas triggered an interesting and productive departure from the earlier conceptualization of the firm as basically a production function. Coase (1937) stressed his disagreement with Knight's (1921) ideas about uncertainty driving the authority relationship inside organizations and the reason for firms to exist. For Knight, the distinguishing mark of the firm is the mode of payment of the employed people. Different individuals have different preferences about risk and uncertainty. Entrepreneurial people, willing to take up the uncertainty involved in the firm's activities, may provide the authority within the firm while taking on the fluctuating residual income. On the other hand, employees are willing to obey the directions of their bosses for a pecuniary remuneration within certain limits. Therefore, for Knight, differences in individual approaches to uncertainty determine the emergence of organizations. In contrast, the fact that hierarchical authority supersedes the market, and more efficiently in some circumstances, characterizes organizations for Coase.

The central contribution of Coase is the identification of transaction costs and its role on the emergence, size, and scope of firms.[1] He

---

[1] Coase (1960) also explains the relationship between transaction costs and market externalities, which we will discuss later on.

showed how costs other than production exist in our economy and they are extremely important, despite not being explicitly disclosed when exchanges take place. Though Knight is probably right that there are usually differences in the risk profiles of an entrepreneur and his or her employees, the value generated by organizations as institutions may be related to using authority, rather than being a risk or uncertainty broker between owners of the firm and employees. In Knight's theory, authority itself does not create value.[2] In fact, Coase argues convincingly that Knight's ideas about uncertainty do not require that authority should be used inside organizations at all, that is, there is no explanation of why the price mechanism should be superseded by authority to allocate resources, as it happens inside firms. Coase claims instead that authority is the main feature of organizations and the benefit of authority is arguably the reduction of transaction costs. Individuals' approach to risk may determine their willingness to become entrepreneurs or their compensation package inside firms, but it does not explain why organizations use authority internally. In contrast, Coase provides an explanation of why authority is better than the price system when market transaction costs are high, which lead to the emergence of organizations that supersede markets as a governance mechanism of transactions.

The same criticism can be made to the proponents of the organization as a necessary coordination mechanism that results from the specialization and the division of labor in our economy. Coase also argued that the price mechanism and authority are both means of coordination and integration of different activities. Transaction costs determine which of them is more efficient in different circumstances. Thus, merely the need for coordination is not sufficient to understand the nature of firms.

---

[2] Knight (1921) pointed out the distinction between risk and uncertainty; there is an element of uncertainty regarding the future performance of business that is inherently different from the traditional definition of risk that is insurable because the possible states of nature can be associated with some probability of occurrence. Thus, a firm is not just a consolidator of risk, which could otherwise be traded by individuals independently with specialized economic actors, but it deals with greater uninsurable uncertainty. For Knight, entrepreneurs (i.e., firms) shield their employees from this uncertainty, but require that they follow their authority. Ultimately, it is the bearing of uncertainty that constitutes the essence of firms from this Knightian perspective.

Firm size is also clearly explained by transaction costs. In Coase's (1937: 23) words: "a firm will tend to expand until the costs of organizing an extra transaction within the firm become equal to the costs of carrying out the same transaction by means of an exchange on the open market." The limits to firm growth are also included in this explanation. Given that there are diminishing returns to management, firm size eventually reaches a limit. Beyond such a limit, market transactions will take place between economic agents; otherwise only one firm would exist, which would actually become a planned economy.

The Coasian perspective regarding the nature of the firm is so compelling that it has become the cornerstone of the prevailing contracting theory of the firm in economics. Decades later, economists continue to build on Coase's ideas about transaction costs. For instance, Oliver Williamson has studied in detail when we can expect the market to be more or less efficient than the firm as alternative forms of governance. Other researchers have probed into the analysis of property rights and incomplete contracting caused by transaction costs. As we will discuss in greater detail later on in this chapter, the Coasian perspective and its further refinements have been very useful to address issues like vertical integration and modes of entry in international markets, for instance, when the analysis of alternative choices to operate through the market or internally through the organization arise naturally.

This influential theory was developed by Coase, a brilliant Nobel Prize winner working at the intersection between law and economics. His goal was never to provide recommendations to management when dealing with strategic decisions, but the understanding of the economic system and especially its implications for social welfare. It is the efficient allocation of resources that matters most for economists. The firm is in this regard an alternative authoritarian means for resource allocation to the price mechanism. For this reason, the applicability of transaction costs to strategy is naturally limited to a narrow set of important topics, but it can hardly become the central theory in strategic management that can be used to understand the emergence, the growth, and especially the competitive advantage and performance of firms. We will analyze the contributions and limitations of this transaction costs perspective as a theory of the firm for strategy later on, after we discuss its more recent evolution and further development by Williamson, property rights, and agency theorists.

Williamson and transaction costs economics

Oliver Williamson built on the insights of Coase about transaction costs and the firm as a governance mechanism to develop a fully blown theory that today we refer to as transaction costs economics (TCE). Though there are other approaches to the analysis of firms that deal with contracting issues like property rights and agency theory, TCE is certainly the one that has been used more often in strategy to explain the emergence of firms and their scope.[3] Let us review briefly some of its main characteristics and its implications for strategic management.

Williamson uses a truly multidisciplinary approach drawing concepts from economics, law, and organization theory to study the market versus firm dichotomy suggested by Coase. He frequently uses the term "hierarchy" to refer to the firm as a governance mechanism of transactions, thus stressing the authority element inside organizations. Indeed, organizations do not resort to the legal courts for dispute resolution among its parts, but to higher positions in the hierarchy. His major contribution is probably the analysis of why and under what circumstances we can expect transaction costs to be higher through market exchanges or inside the hierarchy.

First, it was necessary to clarify the concepts of transaction and governance costs. He distinguished between transaction costs taking place before or after an agreement. There are ex-ante transaction costs, e.g., drafting, negotiating, and safeguarding the agreement, while ex-post transaction costs, like haggling, monitoring, and bonding, occur after the initial agreement to carry out the exchange. On the other hand, governance costs (bureaucracy) include increasingly limited managerial attention to new activities, internal procurement biases, bureaucratic delays, politicization, and any other cost associated with using the hierarchy. The firm internalizes those transactions that can be

---

[3] For instance, two of the leading textbooks in strategy, Barney (1997) and Grant (2005) draw heavily on Williamson's ideas to explain the emergence of firms and their decisions about corporate strategy, particularly regarding vertical integration and diversification. Its influence on research in corporate strategy issues is enormous and it could be considered the most widely used "theory of the firm" in strategy, only challenged by the resource-based view and related learning perspectives. Williamson's views are covered in his two books (Williamson, 1975; 1985) and a long list of journal articles. Williamson (1999) directly compares TCE with the learning perspective as lenses for strategy research and Williamson (1991) with the traditional approach based on market power and competitive dynamics ("strategizing").

more efficiently managed inside the hierarchy than through market exchanges, that is, when market transaction costs are greater than the bureaucratic costs of managing those transactions inside the firm.

The implications of transaction costs on organizational structure are analyzed in detail in Williamson (1975). Hierarchies are the response to different types of market failures, which can be explained by high transaction costs. For instance, he considers that vertical integration results from market failures in intermediate goods and labor markets. In contrast, the multidivisional structure can be regarded as the organizational substitute for failures in the capital market, and it serves to facilitate unrelated diversification.

The feasibility of spot market transactions breaks down and a hierarchy replaces the market for certain frequently recurring exchanges as the joint result of the following factors:

a) Bounded rationality and environmental uncertainty. As Simon (1957: 88) claimed, "human behavior is *intendedly* rational, but only *boundedly* so." The information processing capability of humans is limited and the complexity of our uncertain environment is so large that it is impossible to optimize fully every decision. This places a limit in the possibility to write full contracts that could otherwise regulate all relations among independent actors. Complex transactions surrounded by greater uncertainty will tend to be internalized inside the firm.

b) Opportunism, defined by Williamson as self-seeking behavior with guile. Some people may behave opportunistically if they have a chance, specifically when a contract with them leaves some gaps. Firms essentially emerge to solve those situations in which the threat of opportunism is particularly large and damaging to at least one of the parties.

c) Small numbers bargaining. For exchanges that may only be carried out with a limited number of parties, these can impose their bargaining power and take advantage of the other party, due to the impossibility to write complete contracts and the likelihood of opportunism discussed above. The implications of bargaining, however, are better captured and ultimately caused by asset specificity.

d) Asset specificity. Investing in an asset that is very specific to an exchange with another party (i.e., "quasi-rents" in which the asset's next best alternative use with a third party is far less profitable) creates an acute problem of vulnerability for the weak party forced to maintain the exchange relationship that, in the joint presence of opportunism and bounded rationality, makes contract-based market transactions a highly inefficient alternative for the weaker party. Asset specificity thus generates a hold-up problem for at least one of the parties, which may be taken hostage by the other party after the former invests in the highly specific asset.

Williamson (1985) stressed the presence of asset specificity as the critical determinant of transaction costs. In this context, the party that invests in the highly specific assets (i.e., site, human, physical, or merely dedicated assets to a particular customer) would either limit the invested amount or suffer the high costs of managing the contractual relationship, in order to avoid the possible abuse from the other party. In both cases, managing the relationship through contractual market exchanges would incur higher costs than integrating both actors within a hierarchy, though some governance costs would obviously be suffered inside the hierarchy as well. The firm is, therefore, a means to economize on bounded rationality and attenuate opportunism in the cases when market transaction costs are particularly high, mainly in the presence of asset specificity.

An interesting question that needed to be addressed was the possibility for hierarchies to engage in selective intervention. Certainly, the hierarchy is not intrinsically superior to the market because it has to bear internal governance costs, which are often greater than the costs of transacting through the market. However, one could argue that hierarchies may take advantage of their greater efficiency to organize internally through authority only those transactions with particularly high market transaction costs, while at the same time replicate for other exchanges a type of coordination *as if* they were taking place in the open market, in a similar way that the M-form (multi-divisional form) may allow its different divisions to deal with each other as apparently independent corporations. Williamson argued, however, that this possibility of selective intervention is severely limited by the low-powered incentives that indeed take place inside the organization in contrast to fully independent firms competing in the market, whose survival depends exclusively on themselves.

Overall, it seems fair to say that Williamson, almost single handedly, has fully developed and exploited in a well structured and elegant manner the insightful views of Coase regarding the firm as a governance mechanism of transactions. TCE has been used to analyze issues of vertical integration, complex contracting (e.g., hybrid organizational forms like franchising and exclusive dealings), long-term commercial contracts, multinational corporations and foreign trade agreements, and even informal agreements, among many other topics. The empirical support for the theory is quite remarkable, particularly for vertical integration issues like "make-or-buy" decisions.[4] However, it has some important limitations as a theory of the firm for strategy that will be discussed later, after we analyze two other contracting perspectives on the firm.

Underlying assumptions of alternative contracting processes

Williamson (1985) analyzes in great detail the nature of the firm as a governance structure for managing transactions between economic agents. The alternative solutions that could be used depend on the underlying attributes of the contracting processes. Four contracting processes that may result from the combination of the two critical behavioral assumptions behind TCE, and the possible presence of asset specificity, are shown in this table.

Behavioral assumptions		Economic attribute	
Bounded rationality	Opportunism	Asset specificity	Contracting process
0	+	+	Planning
+	0	+	Promise
+	+	0	Competition
+	+	+	Governance

If rationality were not bounded, then the parties could fully anticipate all future scenarios and incorporate possible contingencies into a contract. Even if the transaction required an investment in

---

[4] For a detailed review of the TCE empirical literature, see Shelanski and Klein (1995). We will analyze vertical integration and horizontal diversification in greater detail in chapter seven.

highly specific assets and the parties could behave opportunistically when given the chance, appropriate *planning* would be sufficient to manage exchanges in the absence of bounded rationality (0 means absence and + means presence in the table above). Adequate mechanisms could be designed in ex-ante negotiations to deal with potential future problems, which would be efficacious and enforceable by a third party or the legal system.

Problems between the parties would not arise when opportunistic behavior can be ruled out of their relationship. Though gaps may appear in the contract, a *promise* to deal fairly with any unexpected events between the parties would suffice to manage the transaction in a joint profit maximizing manner, regardless of the level of asset specificity. Hierarchies would not be necessary either in this second case to manage relationships in the absence of opportunism.

When the parties do not need to make relationship-specific investments, traditional market mechanisms can be used to manage exchanges between the parties. "Parties to such contracts have no continuing interests in the identity of one another" (Williamson, 1985: 31). Arms-length contracts can be efficient because both parties cannot take advantage of the other and hold it hostage of a relation-specific investment. This is the traditional context of *competition.*

For Williamson, the hierarchy will emerge as the *governance* solution only when the two behavioral assumptions of bounded rationality and opportunism are present and the economic exchange requires investment in relation-specific assets. In this case, governance allows the firm to "organize transactions so as to economize on bounded rationality while simultaneously safeguarding against the hazards of opportunism" (Williamson, 1985; 32).

Property rights and incomplete contracts

Just like Williamson's TCE, property rights theory is also concerned with the institutions of capitalism, particularly firm ownership. It directly focuses on the assignment of property rights to resolve the problems of incomplete contracting and hold up. Though very similar to TCE in many regards, it has been more formally developed in recent years and, in contrast, it concentrates on distortions of ex-ante investments, rather than the ex-post transaction costs which are at the center of TCE.[5]

The early views on property rights deal with the problems of monitoring and incentives in joint production. Given the nonseparability of the productivity of different inputs in the joint production of different factors (e.g., a team of people lifting a heavy weight), some individuals may behave opportunistically and not pull their weight. One way to reduce this risk is for someone to specialize in monitoring the effort of the team members. Alchian and Demsetz (1972) argue in their seminal paper that this monitoring specialist should gather several rights that actually define ownership in the classical firm, being the residual claimant after all factors of production receive their compensation.

Property rights are social institutions that define and delimit the range of privileges granted to individuals over specific resources. They comprise the right to use an asset, to appropriate its returns, and to change or transfer the asset itself. At a given time, these rights reflect the conflicting interests and bargaining strength of the parties affected and, thus, they are formed and enforced by political entities.[6] The critical idea from this literature at the macro level is that well-defined property rights are a necessary condition for an efficient economy. As we will discuss when we talk about externalities in chapter nine, if property rights are poorly defined, then individuals will not account in their decisions for the influence of the actions of others (i.e., externalities), creating deviations between the social and private products. In other words, some exchanges that are not efficient socially, though profitable for just a few individuals, will be undertaken. Similarly, some exchanges that are good for society overall will not be carried out by individuals on their own, if nobody may be excluded from their benefits. Thus, without well-defined property rights, exchanges will not be optimized and resources will not flow to their most appropriate use.

---

[5] Property rights theory has become the cornerstone of the theory of the firm in mainstream economics and more widely accepted than TCE, which is more multidisciplinary in its background and goals. Some of the major contributions are Coase (1937; 1960), Alchian (1965), Demsetz (1967), Alchian and Demsetz (1972), Klein *et al.* (1978), Libecap (1989), North (1990), and the more modern approach of Grossman and Hart (1986), and Hart (1995). Mahoney (1992), for instance, has discussed its large influence on strategic management.

[6] See Libecap (1989) and North (1990) for the analysis of institutional change and the role of property rights.

For Hart (1995), ownership essentially means to hold the residual control rights of a firm's assets, that is, the right to decide all usages of the assets limited only by a prior contract, custom, or law. For anything outside these obligations, which could be interpreted and enforced by a third party or judge, the owners have the right to decide what to do with the assets. Ownership matters because complete contracts are impossible, given that it is very difficult for the parties to think ahead about all contingencies, to negotiate about them, and to write down in a way that they could be understood and enforced. This is particularly important for transactions in which the firms need to invest in relationship specific assets.[7] Assigning property rights to one or other party in a transaction will move the incentives to make relationship specific investments because the party that takes residual control rights also receives a greater fraction of the ex-post surplus created by such investment. Consequently, the most efficient solution would be to assign the ownership of the merged firm to the party that needs to make more relationship specific investments in order to reduce overall transaction costs, even though the acquired party would then have less incentive to make any additional relationship specific investments, as it no longer has residual control rights over such investments.

Property rights theorists claim that given the presence of transaction costs and incomplete contracting, organizations emerge as an institutional solution to exchanges in which there are appropriable specialized quasi-rents. The main argument essentially follows the same rationale that Williamson suggests in TCE. However, the process by which this happens is explained somewhat differently by this theory and it explains which party should be assigned the property rights. Basically, joint ownership of specialized assets would serve to economize on contracting costs to insure nonopportunistic behavior.[8] For highly specific assets, it is better to give all control rights to one party, the one that needs to invest most in relationship specific assets. Otherwise, the two parties may fear that the other party may hold up later

---

[7] Hart (1995) identifies two other implications of contractual incompleteness, though less important than relation specific investments: asymmetric information between parties may prevent an efficient agreement to be reached, and haggling over the terms of the contract, which is time consuming and wastes resources.

[8] See Klein *et al.* (1978) for an analysis of postcontractual opportunistic behavior in some examples of appropriable quasi-rents of specialized assets.

on and, thus, they may underinvest in highly specific assets. The quasi-rents that result from the investment in specialized assets would not be generated unless there is integration between the two parties. Only in this case the single owner, having residual control rights over the specialized assets, will then be willing to invest in them. The firm is a combination of physical assets, which make possible the authority over the human resources that use these assets. Firm boundaries are set to optimally allocate residual control rights over assets.

Evidently, transaction costs play a critical role in property rights theory. The Coase theorem claims that if property rights are well defined and transaction costs are nonexistent, then all socially efficient exchanges would take place through the market using the price mechanism, i.e., all transactions that create wealth for society will be carried out. Under these unrealistic circumstances the initial assignment of property rights would be irrelevant, because market transactions would drive the economy towards the best possible allocation of resources and renegotiated property rights. The invisible hand that Adam Smith (1776) talked about would take care of it.

However, transaction costs exist and externalities matter. In our actual environment, we cay say that property rights develop to internalize externalities; in other words, their main allocative function is the internalization of beneficial and harmful effects.[9] If transaction costs are high or property rights are not well allocated among its members, society will stagnate. Along this line, North (1990) claims that the main reason for underdevelopment is the inability of societies to develop effective, low-cost enforcement of contracts and property rights. Within an inappropriate institutional framework, the economic gains from specialization and trade will not take place, because many exchanges (which are basically the mutual ceding of rights between two or more parties) will not be carried out.

The new institutional economics based on the seminal work of Ronald Coase and later developed by TCE and property rights theorists has opened up the door to the analysis of incentives and institutions from a very different perspective than the neoclassical theory of the firm. Contracting issues become the key to understand why organizations are formed, driven by transaction costs economizing.

---

[9] Of course, this internalization would only occur as long as the gains from internalization are greater than its costs, as Demsetz (1967) noted.

This perspective has been further developed by agency theorists who look inside organizations to analyze how contracts can be designed efficiently.

Agency theory

Transaction costs economics and property rights theory, both inspired in the seminal ideas of Ronald Coase, form the basis of a modern economist's approach to the theory of the firm, which explains why organizations displace the market for certain types of exchanges. They have had a large influence in the strategy field, particularly for decisions about firm boundaries. However, they were not intended to look inside the firm and analyze in detail the characteristics of the contrats that actually take place inside the organizational boundaries. Once authority supersedes the market to a certain extent, these theories have basically completed their goal. The hierarchy is formed and property rights, especially residual control rights over the firm's assets, are allocated so that transaction costs are minimized. It is agency theory that addresses the issue of how vertical hierarchical relationships are managed among other contractual relationships inside the firm.[10]

The firm is a "nexus of contracts," including those with employees and even contracting relationships with other parties, such as suppliers, customers, and creditors. Each contract is subject to some agency costs to the extent that the agent does not always behave in the best interests of the principal, who delegates on the agent to perform certain business tasks. The design of the contract becomes the center of agency theory. The contract should minimize agency costs, including monitoring (direct efforts of the principal to control the agent's behavior, like observing the behavior and providing incentives), bonding (expenditures by the agent to guarantee that he or she will not act against the

[10] Early positivist agency theory focused primarily on the separation of ownership and control (i.e., the relationship between owners and the top management of organizations), inspired in Berle and Means's (1933) classic treatment, including Ross (1973), Jensen and Meckling (1976), and Fama (1980). The more mathematical principal–agent model, including Harris and Raviv (1979), Holmstrom (1979), and Pratt and Zeckhauser (1985), has been applied to many other contractual relationships. Good review articles include Baiman (1982), and Levinthal (1988). Eisenhardt (1989) provides a very good review and assessment from an organizational theory perspective.

interests of the principal), and the residual loss (a very general category of costs suffered by the principal due to the remaining divergence in interests between principal and agent, and the resulting actions of the agent). Mathematically, the principal optimizes a function subject to several constraints that include the incentives provided to the agent and the use of external information and monitoring.[11]

The model is based on several reasonable assumptions. The divergence in interests between principal and agent is the critical assumption in the model, because otherwise there would be no agency costs that need to be minimized, nor incentive and control decisions to make. Also, the agent has some disutility for work effort, because otherwise there is no need to induce the agent to work hard. Finally, the agent is considered more risk averse than the principal, who is usually regarded as risk neutral because he or she can diversify and invest in other firms or contracts. If this were not the case, an optimal general solution is for the principal to transfer the entire business to the agent and receive a fixed payment in exchange.

Given these assumptions, the optimal contract would shift some risk to the agent to motivate him/her to work hard, but not all, because he or she is more risk averse than the principal. The transfer of risk to the agent generates a negative effect in overall wealth to be distributed between the principal and the agent, but there is also a positive effect of wealth because such a transfer induces the agent to work harder and, thus, they have a larger pie to share between them. The optimal solution would include some level of incentives and monitoring, usually based on some information or signal about the level of effort and the risk in the environment.[12] If there were no uncertainty about the outcomes or the agent's effort could be fully observed, then an optimal solution could be easily designed because the agent's marginal product

[11] For instance, the principal may minimize the compensation to the agent (which depends on some level of outcome), subject to two constraints: participation (the agent agrees on taking the contract), and incentives (the agent is motivated to exert the desired level of effort). The solution provides the levels of compensation that the agent would receive depending on the observed outcome and includes how much monitoring by the principal there will be.

[12] Holmstrom (1979) showed how any information, even if it is imperfect, about the agent's effort or the uncertainty regarding the environment can be used in the contract to improve the pay-offs of both principal and agent, because it allows a more accurate judgment of the agent's effort without having to shift risk to the agent.

could be perfectly assessed and his/her compensation directly tied to it.

This approach has been used in a wide variety of contractual problems, including issues of adverse selection (hidden information about the agent, who may misrepresent his/her ability and other characteristics) and moral hazard (hidden action by the agent, such as the lack of effort by management to behave in the best interests of stockholders). There is clear empirical support for the theory (including the choice of incentives based on behavior versus outcome), though the solutions provided by principal–agent problems are usually much more complex than the ones that we usually observe in reality. An important criticism is that of Williamson (1985) and Hart (1995), who question its exclusive reliance in ex-ante incentive alignment between principal and agent and the assumption that the contract is efficacious, i.e., complete contracting that can be enforced by court ordering without additional transaction costs.

A critical question is the extent to which agency theory is a theory of the firm that tries to explain the emergence of firms, instead of a tool or lenses for the analysis of contractual relationships. Agency theory analyzes the contract between principal and agents based on a set of assumptions and it is very useful indeed for such a task. However, it cannot be used to explain whether certain activities should or should not be part of the set of contracts that constitute the firm, i.e., whether one additional activity should be done inside the organization. In fact, technically the firm does not truly exist as a separate entity and we cannot talk about the boundaries of the firm, which is just a fiction. More properly, we should talk about individuals linked through a "nexus of contracts." Thus, we cannot use agency theory to analyze the possibility of a firm to diversify into a totally new business, for instance, though it can help us design the appropriate contract once the decision to diversify has been taken. Despite being a central element of the contracting view of the firm in economics and finance, agency theory is not just intended to explain the emergence of firms or to help in decisions about strategic management.

Limitations of the contracting view as a theory of the firm

The contracting view of the firm has added significant richness to economics by looking inside the organization, which has benefited the strategy field. In the neoclassical theory of the firm, the tasks that constitute the essence of management are performed inside firms without error and costs because the focus is on market analysis and the determination of quantities and prices. Production techniques, prices, input availability, and any other information are fully known at zero costs to the firm. The contracting view of the firm changes all these assumptions by making explicit the role of transaction costs. Besides the costs of production specified by the production function, transaction costs contribute significantly to determine firm size, scope, and to some extent profitability through their effect in total costs.

However, despite the important contributions of the contracting view, we are concerned in this book only with its applicability as a theory of the firm for strategy and the questions that it should help address for the strategic management of businesses. With these concerns in mind, there are several limitations of this view of the firm that should be discussed.

The role of opportunism, hold up, and trust in the emergence of firms

Both TCE and property rights theory argue that markets will be supplanted by organizations when the costs of using the market are greater than the internal costs of governance. Using the terminology of property rights, when there are complementary assets that generate appropriable quasi-rents, it is more efficient that only one party should hold the residual control rights over the complementary assets, instead of two independent actors transacting through the market. Otherwise, the two separate parties would underinvest in complementary assets, because of the risk of being held up by the other party after the initial investment is done and it becomes a sunk cost. Similarly, Williamson argues that, when asset specificity is high, transaction costs would be especially high, given the joint presence of opportunism, bounded rationality, and environmental uncertainty; in such case, the hierarchy becomes the institutional alternative to market transactions that Coase talked about.

Contracting theories focus on the possibility of opportunistic behavior, ultimately causing the emergence of firms. When opportunism is a bigger threat, transaction costs in general may be expected to be higher and, more specifically, investment in complementary assets is likely to be smaller. In these circumstances, firms that internalize these transactions are more efficient than others that rely on market transactions. If the opportunistic behavior from the economic actors could not take place, it would not be necessary to combine asset ownership under one hierarchical structure. TCE argues that a promise would suffice in such an unrealistic world; firms would not be necessary, contracts would dominate our economy, and hold up and underinvestment problems would not exist.

These arguments place opportunism at the heart of the theory of the firm and also trust as the other side of the same rationale.[13] But the reliance in the organization as the solution to opportunism has been widely questioned by sociologists and organization theorists. For instance, Granovetter (1985) has claimed that TCE presents an undersocialized view of markets, which fails to consider the social structure in which economic action is embedded. Similarly, he argues that Williamson also develops an oversocialized account of organization, where the efficacy of hierarchical power is overestimated.[14] Malfeasance is not only averted by institutional arrangements, nor by a generalized morality of individuals in our society, but by the role of social relations in generating trust and the widespread preference for transacting with individuals of known reputation. Trust matters and it certainly affects and is affected by social relationships, including whether the integration of complementary activities is necessary to curb opportunistic behavior.

---

[13] The importance of trust in our economy has already been noted by some economists, particularly Kenneth Arrow. He regarded trust as an externality: "an important lubricant of social systems" (Arrow, 1974: 23). The lack of social consciousness can be considered a distinct economic and political loss, and "among the properties of many societies whose economic development is backward is the lack of mutual trust" (Arrow, 1974: 26).

[14] Granovetter (1985) explores the embeddedness of economic action inside a network of social relations as the main determinant of vertical integration decisions. In his words: "Certain implications follow for the conditions under which one may expect to see vertical integration rather than transactions between firms in a market. Other things being equal, for example, we should expect pressures toward vertical integration in a market where transacting firms lack a network of personal relations that connects them or where such a network eventuates in conflict, disorder, opportunism, or malfeasance. On the other hand, where a stable network of relations mediates complex transactions and generates standards of behavior between firms, such pressures should be absent" (Granovetter, 1985).

On the contrary, Williamson has argued strongly against the usefulness of the notion of trust for business research, which may lead
to muddy the clear waters of an analysis of calculativeness based on
transaction costs and the design of effective contractual safeguards.[15]
From his perspective, the analysis of trust is irrelevant for the analysis
of commercial exchange and it should be reserved for purely personal
relationships (e.g., loved ones). Other scholars working within a TCE
framework develop a compromise position, claiming that trust can
lead to the constraining of opportunistic behavior by way of reputation and, thus, reduce transactions costs in the presence of asset
specificity to some degree.[16]

The main question, however, is to what extent the essence of firms
is the solution of problems of opportunistic behavior and cooperation
between parties. It seems that the importance of opportunism and hold
up is probably overstated as the main drivers of the emergence of firms.
Coase himself thinks that the avoidance of fraud is not an important
factor in promoting integration and argues against the critical role that
asset specificity plays in TCE and property rights theory. He explicitly
claimed that a defrauding firm may make immediate gains but, if it can
be identified, future business would be lost and this would normally
make fraud unprofitable for the firm. He based his skepticism about the
asset-specificity argument in the belief that "opportunistic behavior is
usually effectively checked by the need to take account of the effect of
the firm's actions on future business" (Coase, 1988: 71), an argument
fully in line with game theory research on sustaining cooperation and
firm reputation.[17]

The opportunism reducing effect of the hierarchy is not a necessary
condition for firms to exist from a pure Coasian perspective to transaction costs. All that is needed is varying levels of transaction costs
inside the organization and through the market to observe both types
of governance. This does not mean that the arguments behind TCE and
property rights are invalid. Indeed, some organizations may emerge to
solve problems of opportunism and investment hold up, but they do
not emerge necessarily always to solve this type of problem, nor is the
organization the only institutional arrangement to deal with them in

[15] See Williamson (1993), though he earlier argued in favor of the positive effect
of trust in reducing transaction costs in Williamson (1975).
[16] See, for instance, Chiles and McMakin (1996) and Gulati (1995).
[17] See, for instance, Kreps and Wilson (1982).

all cases. We should recall that there are other transaction costs not related to opportunism and hold up that also exist, like the marketing costs identified by Coase dealing with learning about and haggling over the terms of the exchange. It is the existence of market transaction costs (some of them related to asset specificity and opportunism, but not necessarily all of them) that make organizations more efficient in some cases. Even if promises are always kept and safeguarding costs do not exist, other transaction costs unrelated to opportunism may lead organizations to emerge, such as information and bargaining costs. Thus, we could criticize an over-reliance on opportunism as an explanation of firm boundaries, though transaction costs economizing can be an important factor to consider.

Comprehensiveness of the contracting view

The compelling logic of Coase's argument about the two alternative governance mechanisms for transactions, markets and organizations constitutes the basis of the contracting view of the firm. The analysis of opportunism and asset specificity has probed deeper into some of the problems of contracting, though they may have been overstated as the only determinants of transaction costs. In any case, the contracting view argues that either the market or the hierarchy (or a hybrid of both) will be the most efficient way for exchanges that take place in different contexts. TCE scholars analyze these contexts to understand the type of governance structure that emerges. Any question about the emergence and scope of firms can be answered through this analysis of the relative efficiency of market contracts versus hierarchical authority for resource allocation. In other words, if an organization replaces the market, presumably there must be some reason why the market is less efficient than the hierarchy in governing these transactions. TCE claims to be a comprehensive theory of the firm to the extent that transaction costs (in addition to production costs) primarily determine the relative efficiency of firms versus markets to manage transactions.

This argument has been used to explain why technology is not a sufficient reason for firms to exist, as the neoclassical theory suggested, and that transaction costs economizing is always behind the emergence of firms. If there are any economies of scope in undertaking two activities simultaneously, two independent firms could sign a contract and collaborate through market exchanges in the absence of market transaction costs, so that all possible economies would be realized.[18] If they indeed integrate, there must be some transaction costs that make contracting through the market an inefficient alternative. We should look for high market transaction costs somewhere because otherwise the market would be the most efficient option, at least when the assumptions of neoclassical economics apply. The analysis of asset specificity in particular should help us understand the origin of transaction costs.

However, this rationale prevents refutation that transaction costs are the only reason for firms to exist. In other words, it claims incorrectly that TCE is a comprehensive theory of the firm. The key is in the assumption that two firms can always collaborate through the market in the absence of transaction costs, *this option being equally as efficient* as the integration of the two firms.[19] This assumption negates any other possible explanation for firm integration, except for transaction costs. If we remove the assumption that all economies can be equally achieved inside or outside the organization, transaction costs economizing is just one determinant for the existence of firms, but not necessarily the *only* one. If there is any other influence besides transaction costs in the relative efficiency of conducting an activity inside one organization as opposed to contracting it out, such a reason could justify the emergence of firms, and the contracting view would not be a comprehensive theory of the firm. We should not simply rule out by assumption that transaction costs are the only difference between doing an activity inside a given firm or outside, but take them into account before we undertake a final analysis of a firm's boundaries.

Two other factors besides transaction costs have been clearly identified as having an impact on firm boundaries: (1) absolute cost differences between firms and (2) information and knowledge management. I will analyze them now briefly.[20]

1) Absolute cost differences between firms

Markets are not entities separate from organizations, but one type of institutional arrangement that allows different firms to conduct

---

[18] See for instance Majumdar and Ramaswamy (1994) for this traditional TCE criticism to a technological explanation of vertical integration.

[19] See also Conner (1991) for a similar point.

[20] In chapter three we will analyze in greater detail the reasons why two resources may create more or less value being part of the same firm rather than competing independently in the market.

exchanges with each other. In other words, as far as make-or-buy decisions are concerned, markets are really other firms. Coase was well aware that firms differ in their capabilities to make the best use of the factors of production.[21] Because costs differ across firms, businesses internalize those activities in which they have cost advantages, even in the absence of transaction costs or when market transaction costs are the same as the governance costs of managing those transactions internally. Williamson has also acknowledged that it is the combination of production and transaction costs that organizations try to minimize. However, the focus on costs other than transactions costs has become so marginal in the contracting view of the firm that it seems, erroneously, that the scope of firms is determined exclusively by transaction costs. As long as the costs of doing different activities actually differs across firms (e.g., gains from specialization), firms should internalize those activities in which they are more efficient than other firms (i.e., the market). This should be so even if market transaction costs do not exist or, much more realistically, they are very similar to internal governance costs.

2) Information and knowledge management

In an interesting departure from the Coasian logic, Demsetz argued that transaction costs exist and that, although they are very important, they are not the primary determinant of why firms exist.[22] He claimed that organizations may be better than markets in transferring information and knowledge and, therefore, the vertical boundaries of firms are also determined by the economics of conservation of expenditures on knowledge. Similar arguments have also been

---

[21] Coase first made this point in his 1937 article. Madhok (2002) analyzes in detail how differences in costs between firms lead to internalization of activities in a way that makes the resource-based view fully compatible with Coase's ideas.

[22] See Demsetz (1988: 151), who used the insightful analogy between gravity and transaction costs in the determination of chemical reactions and governance structure respectively: "gravity influences chemical reactions, but seldom is it the key variable whose behavior importantly explains variations in the reactions observed." He later argues: "There is much more to the problem of economic organization than is plausibly subsumed under transaction and monitoring cost. Perhaps the transaction and monitoring approaches to the theory of the firm have confined our search too much. Firms would exist in a world in which transaction and monitoring costs are zero, although their organization might be considerably different" (Demsetz, 1988: 154).

made in the field of strategy regarding the superiority of organizations over markets in managing and transferring competences.[23] Thus, apart from transaction costs considerations, firms may internalize those activities that need more effective ways to manage knowledge than what their coordination through the market may allow.

It could be argued that these two and any other differences in the efficiency of markets versus organizations to organize activities ultimately result from issues of incomplete contracting and transaction costs. Some firms could have lower costs because they have a superior factor of production that is not tradable or because their superior capabilities cannot be contracted through the market. These limitations to trading and exchanging through the market could be considered transaction costs in an all-inclusive interpretation of TCE. Transaction costs, defined very broadly as any barriers to transfer anything including know-how, would be behind all differences among firms and, in turn, these differences would determine integration decisions.[24]

However, such a broad conceptualization of transaction costs cannot be solid ground on which to build a theory of the firm.[25] This approach would confuse transferability with contracting issues, which presumably explain all possible transactions. For instance, truly unique tacit expertise, like that of Picasso, cannot be perfectly transferred between individuals or firms, regardless of contracting considerations that formalize and regulate the eventual transfer. The genius of Picasso is his and it is not fully transferable to his pupils, even if the best possible contract is written to facilitate such a transfer of skills. Some advantages of firms may also be intrinsic to them and they may not be adequately transferable, which as a result may make them not effectively contractible with third parties. In such cases, firms should internalize those activities that benefit from such advantages. But we should

---

[23] See, for instance, Liebeskind (1996) and Grant (1996).

[24] See Teece (1980) who analyzes the multiproduct firm from a TCE perspective, including the use of common and recurrent use of proprietary know-how as a potential reason why organizations may be more efficient than markets.

[25] Cheung (1998) defined transaction costs as including all conceivable costs in society, except production and transportation, and claimed that transaction costs were at least eighty percent of the GDP of Hong Kong. From this perspective, economizing on transaction costs is virtually equivalent to efficiency.

not fall into a reverse causality trap: it is not necessarily the impossibility to write complete contracts that causes Picasso to paint his own work, but the uniqueness of his skills and their limited transferability to other people.[26] Transferability is a prerequisite for contractibility and its influence may be more important than the latter in understanding firm boundaries. More generally, other reasons, besides contracting issues, may determine the emergence of firms. As we will discuss in greater detail in chapter three, any factor that influences the value that resources may generate when combined with other resources may affect firm boundaries (e.g., cross-selling or market power). Transaction costs are just one of them, but not necessarily the only one.

Usefulness for strategic management and its practice

The use of TCE has been criticized by some organization theorists for its emphasis on efficiency and opportunism, and even for being bad for practice.[27] To some degree, this is part of the old debate that can be traced to the human relations school about models of human nature and organizations.[28] However, regardless of disciplinary basis

---

[26] Leaving Picasso's preferences for teaching and painting aside, which could be easily included in the analysis, the great master should evaluate the time and the compensation obtained from the two alternatives: teaching (using the market) or painting (internalizing the activity of painting), to exploit his unique skills. Incomplete contracting could make the alternative of teaching undesirable if effective contracts could not be designed and enforced for obtaining superior returns from teaching versus painting. However, if Picasso could train a sufficiently large number of pupils per year and obtain a large percentage of their future income – of course, the only part that is attributable to Picasso's training – through an enforceable contract, then it would have been possible for Picasso to prefer teaching over painting. On the contrary, even if such a contract could be written and enforced, the transferability of his great skill to his pupils is very limited. It would be preferable for Picasso to spend his time painting rather than teaching if his returns from such a decision – even if supported by a complete contract – are not sufficiently large. Both incomplete contracting and incomplete transferability may drive Picasso's decision. Similarly, a firm's decision to integrate may come from not having the opportunity to write the appropriate contract or from having only imperfect transferability of advantages to another organization. The decision of a firm to internalize certain activities should not be attributed exclusively to incomplete contracting, because it could be due to imperfect transferability, which is an entirely different issue.

[27] See Perrow (1986), and Ghoshal and Moran (1996).

[28] See the classical work of Mayo (1945), and McGregor (1960).

and beliefs about personal values, it is particularly important for an applied field like strategic management to be useful for practice.

Efficiency is the central driver of organizational forms behind TCE. Williamson (1991) goes as far as saying that economizing is more fundamental than strategizing and, thus, the best strategy is to organize and operate efficiently in the long run. But it is obvious to all strategy researchers that increasing efficiency is not the only way for firms to compete.[29] As I argued in the previous point, firms may emerge for reasons other than transaction costs economizing and they may create value for society in other ways besides their internal efficiency in organizing exchanges. The possibilities for creating value in different ways should be part of a theory of the firm for strategy, which should help managers in their strategic decisions.

Firms are much more than efficient mechanisms by which to govern transactions. Though contracting analysis has opened the door to a more rigorous analysis of firm boundaries, managers need to consider many other aspects besides internal efficiency when making strategic decisions about how their firms compete in the market. They have to decide whether or not it makes economic sense for their organizations to carry out certain activities, so that their overall competitiveness in the market may be increased. Rather than designing contracting or ownership arrangements that require the expertise of lawyers, top managers have to decide whether certain assets in combination create greater value and profits than competing as separate units. This analysis cannot be reduced to the notion of asset specificity and contractibility, though these may be important aspects for some types of decisions. We need to understand better why the competitiveness of the firm in the market is affected by the strategic decisions of the firm at the business and corporate levels. Many critical strategic issues cannot be well analyzed from a contracting perspective, like market positioning, barriers to entry, differentiation, innovation, and competitive dynamics.

Just to mention one example, TCE can hardly be used to understand the success of Coca-Cola during the twentieth century in its domestic market and worldwide, and the remarkable strategy of Pepsi-Cola in

---

[29] Cost leadership is just one strategic option for Porter (1980) and he later argued that greater operational efficiency cannot even be regarded as a strategy (Porter, 1996).

carving a solid position, particularly in the US. Certainly, the contracting relationship between the two marketing powerhouses and other economic agents (e.g., their bottlers) is very important, but we should look elsewhere to understand their success, their strategic challenges, and the way they create value for society. Something else besides managing internal and external transactions matters for understanding strategic decisions and their performance consequences. A focus on contracts would detract from concerns such as competitors and customers that constitute the day-to-day activities of managers and their strategic decisions. In the words of Coase:

" . . . the way in which I presented my ideas has, I believe, led to or encouraged an undue emphasis on the role of the firm as a purchaser of the services of factors of production and on the choice of the contractual arrangements which it makes with them. As a consequence of this concentration on the firm as a purchaser of the inputs it uses, economists have tended to neglect the main activity of a firm, running a business." (Coase, 1988: 65)

The contracting view of the firm is not a good theory for helping managers run their businesses probably because it was not intended to do so. Its usefulness for strategic decision making is limited to the areas where alternative contracting takes center stage and can be expected to be the primary driver of such decisions. However, as a theory of the firm for strategy it can only be part of a broader theory of how firms create value for society and their performance.

Contributions of the contracting view to a theory of the firm for strategy

It seems fair to say that, at the very least, TCE and the broader contracting view of the firm has succeeded in opening up the black-box of the neoclassical firm. Despite its success in economics, however, the contracting view has important limitations to provide the basis for a theory of the firm in strategic management. In the points above I argued that (i) the importance of opportunism and asset specificity has been overstated as the only source of transaction costs; (ii) firms do more for society than just economizing on transaction costs, and (iii) the contracting approach is not particularly useful for strategic management. These criticisms, though important, only pose a limit on the applicability of the contracting approach to strategy, but do not question its major contributions. It is very reasonable for economists to study opportunism and asset specificity as one of the main determinants of transaction costs, often the most important. In addition, the displacement of the market as an institutional mechanism to govern exchanges is such a critical feature of organizations that it deserves to be studied by economists, even if this analysis is not particularly useful for strategic decision making, and given that there are other ways for firms to generate value for society besides transaction cost economizing.

The main point in this chapter is that we need a broader approach to the analysis of the central questions that a theory of the firm should address, including why firms exist, their size and scope of activities, and their performance. TCE has a lot to contribute to this theory, particularly with regard to some corporate strategy issues. With regard to firm boundary decisions, markets are really other firms and all of them compete to create value combining resources to satisfy certain customer needs. Rather than a firm versus market comparison, it is often more useful for strategic management to think of a firm versus other firms.

The comparative analysis in TCE can be redirected towards what makes two firms more competitive (with respect to the other firms in the economy). If they are organized under the same administrative structure as two firms competing independently: how can they gather more or better resources? Do they have better access to their customers under the same corporate umbrella? Can they innovate more effectively? And, of course, when are they more efficient, including the transaction costs that they bear? All of them are really questions about value created by firms.

In an analysis of value, economizing on transaction costs will certainly play an important part. As TCE argues, when two firms engage in frequent transactions where management through market contracting is inefficient (compared to internal governance), they should probably merge. Value for society will be generated from this overall savings in transaction costs, part of it probably transferred to customers via lower prices. To push further in the development of such a theory, we will need a conceptualization of firms different from mere governance structures of transactions, that is, less focus on the exchange and more on the value-creating activity side of businesses. As we will explore in the next chapter, the resource-based view and related knowledge

perspectives on the nature of the firm are particularly useful conceptualizations for strategy to build a theory of the firm of this type.

Contractual analysis in a make-or-buy decision and its limitations

To illustrate the strengths and limitations of the TCE approach to firm
boundaries, let us analyze a fictional case of a firm that wants to decide
whether or not it should internalize a service for its employees, like an
in-house cafeteria. In our example, a firm with a large facility and
several hundred employees needs to decide whether and, if so how, it
should set up a cafeteria on its premises, so that employees would not
have to go out for a cup of coffee and a quick lunch.

Example of an in-house cafeteria

The firm has several options: (1) not to set up an internal cafeteria and
let people go outside for lunch to a nearby small restaurant with good
sandwiches, (2) to build the cafeteria and operate it as an internally
managed activity, (3) to build the cafeteria and outsource it to the best
bidder, or (4) to auction the rights to the cafeteria to the best bidder,
which would then build and manage it.

A contracting approach would recommend the option with the lowest cost to the firm, particularly focusing on transaction cost economizing. If many employees waste precious time going outside to
the nearby restaurant, option 1 can be rejected. Option 4 can also
be rejected, because the restaurant operator would need to invest in
highly specific assets (the investment in fixed assets is not likely to
be recoverable if the contract is not renewed) and it would probably
underinvest in the restaurant's layout. In addition, contract negotiations would be the most difficult in this case, probably including discussions of which products to provide, quality of services, prices, and
future changes to these, such that option 4 generates high transaction
costs.

Assessing relative transaction costs of options 2 and 3 is more difficult. TCE would argue in favor of option 2 if bureaucracy costs are
lower than market transaction costs driven by asset specificity. However, in option 3 asset specificity of the necessary investments by both
sides is very small. The firm owns the premises and the investment

in most fixed assets can probably be used by an alternative operator. Similarly, the restaurant operator does not need to invest in highly specific assets either, because kitchen tools have alternative uses if the contract is cancelled. Thus, internal bureaucracy costs are likely to be greater and option 3 is probably superior in general terms.

The contracting approach provides a clear and logical answer, which may be correctly applied to many firms facing this decision. But it also has some limitations. First, it may give an excessive role to opportunism. Depending on the reputation of the firm and the expectations about its future behavior, restaurant operators may be willing to accept option 4 and design, build, and manage the facilities, despite being hostage to the firm. Contracts, though incomplete, are not so bad in protecting highly specific assets and many firms are actually willing to accept some risks and trust their partners, particularly when their reputation is at stake and their collaboration results in gains to be divided between them. Many chains do set up restaurants within the premises of other firms (e.g., inside theme parks). Similarly, though regarded ambiguously as a hybrid type of organization, all franchised restaurant owners are very similar to option 4 and nevertheless make highly specific investments with respect to the franchising chain. Firms often accept making highly specific investments particularly if it allows them access to sales with a reasonable level of confidence, like being an exclusive specialized provider to Wal-Mart. Organizational integration is not the only way to deal with situations that require highly specific assets and create potential for opportunism.

Second, there are other important factors for make-or-buy decisions apart from transaction costs, such as production costs and firm knowledge. TCE often (though not always) assumes that production costs are constant and only transaction costs differ, such that the governance structure of transactions would basically determine vertical integration. Sometimes it is argued that the most efficient party should carry out the activity under analysis and, then, an appropriate governance structure should be placed on top of it. However, production costs on their own could be enough to explain the choice of vertical integration. If we were to assume that transactions costs are constant inside and outside of the hierarchy, then obviously production costs would be the only factor left in the firm's decision to either run the restaurant by itself or contract it out. But in these two arguments above, transaction or operation costs determine firm boundaries only by assumption.

Any difference between internalizing the restaurant's management and outsourcing it needs to be considered, including the costs of managing operations, transactions, and any possible additional costs or benefits of vertical integration. For instance, in addition to transaction costs and operation costs, the company will certainly take into consideration how good the quality of the food and service is likely to be for each alternative under study. If the firm considers that it does not have the appropriate skills to properly manage the restaurant it will probably choose some sort of outsourcing. Transaction costs are only one type of cost to be considered in the decision, but not necessarily the ultimate driver of the firm boundaries, unless we assume that it is the only possible difference between internal management and outsourcing.

Third, TCE remains silent about nonefficiency aspects of the make-or-buy decision that can be especially important for strategic management. Managers do not always choose the lowest cost alternative and they have to consider other aspects of the decision, particularly those that may affect their competitiveness in the market. This would be the case if the firm wanted to use the cafeteria to attract and retain talented and mobile employees. The company might want to create a unique environment that promotes creativity within the organization, including the cafeteria, making it necessary to manage it internally. In such cases the transaction costs of managing the cafeteria would take a secondary role to the ability to run the operations as desired. Furthermore, transaction costs analysis would not really be useful when deciding whether the firm should build the activity from scratch or buy an existing company, like the nearby restaurant, to carry it out, after it has decided to internalize the restaurant's operations. An analysis of transaction costs alone would not be enough to fully understand the strategic implications of a make-or-buy decision.

3 | *The nature of the firm in strategy*

The resource-based view of the firm

As we discussed in the previous chapter, economists have been traditionally concerned with the understanding of markets and, more recently, their displacement by firms. In contrast, strategy scholars have focused on how businesses are actually managed and what determines their performance. It is not surprising that the reason for firms to exist has not been an important issue in strategy and the notion of competitive advantage has taken instead the central place within the field. In search for better understanding of why some firms succeed while others fail, strategy scholars have frequently drawn from economic theories. Interestingly, they have found a somewhat marginal theory in economics that analyzes the process of firm growth developed by Edith Penrose in 1959. This approach focuses on the firm as a collection of resources and it has inspired what today is called the resource-based view of the firm (RBV). This chapter explores this theory and some related perspectives that share a very similar conceptualization of the firm, like the literature on evolutionary economics, knowledge-based theories, dynamic capabilities, and core competences. We will build on them to discuss the nature of the firm in strategy and, later, we will push it forward to include the notions of value creation and appropriation.

Penrose's (1959) insightful analysis has become the basis of the RBV, which focuses on the process of growth of the firm. In contrast to the neoclassical approach centered on the characteristics of an objective production function, the productive opportunity of the firm depends on how managers think that they can use their available resources, as a result of their experience and their own view of their competitive position and their environment. In other words, exactly the same resources may produce very different services in a creative process that could be described as Schumpeterian. Penrose investigated how this process takes place, especially the limits to growth and its direction (i.e., diversification). During the eighties and nineties, the RBV and parallel internally focused perspectives were developed substantially far beyond the seminal ideas of Penrose.[1] Rather than looking at firms as collections of products and markets, the RBV focuses on the characteristics of their resources, which helps us understand their growth and competitiveness.[2] Let us review some of its main contributions.

Firm growth

Certainly, this area is where the influence of Penrose's original ideas has been substantial both in economics and strategy. She basically argued that resources determine the direction of firm growth and its limits.[3] Today it is widely accepted that unused available resources determine the direction that firms take to a large extent. There is abundant empirical evidence that firms diversify to put to use their excess capacity, though it is usually coupled with the existence of market failure for their underutilized resources.[4] To the extent that their resources may be used somewhere else, the degree of "relatedness" between their initial set of activities and their new ones also influences the path that firms follow in their growth process. Given that resources usually exist in discrete quantities (i.e., indivisibilities), there are always some unused resources that the firm tries to exploit engaging in new sets of activities that are somewhat related to the previous activities. As new activities are added to the firm, new possibilities for growth arise in this dynamic process based on the development and exploitation of firm resources, always driven and constrained by the resources available to the firm at a given time.

---

[1] See Barney and Arikan (2001) for a review of the origins of the RBV, its main features, and some of its contributions to strategy as well as other business fields.

[2] See Wernerfelt (1984) for an early analysis of the contrast between market position versus resource analysis.

[3] Penrose argued that "as long as expansion can provide a way of using the services of its resources more profitably than they are being used, a firm has an incentive to expand" (Penrose, 1959: 67). In modern economic terms, we could say that firms do not automatically reach the production possibility frontier. More precisely, such a frontier is subjective in nature and it should not be considered constant throughout the industry, because it depends on each firm's set of available resources and its experience.

[4] See for instance Wernerfelt and Montgomery (1988) and Montgomery and Hariharan (1991) for supportive evidence.

The influence of available resources in the direction of firm growth also means that firms cannot decide freely in which industries they should compete, because some resources, such as expertise in combining the necessary inputs or a useful reputation, cannot be acquired in the market. Thus, available resources, especially managerial expertise, place a limit on the future growth of the firm, at least in the short run, which is known as the Penrose effect. Penrose actually goes as far as saying that the external demand that firms face is probably less important than the resources of the firm to understand the process of growth.[5]

There is, however, more controversy about the speed of growth that a firm can handle and its maximum size. Resource constraints, including managerial capability to cope with growth and even financial requirements, certainly limit how fast a firm can grow in the short term, but this limit probably varies depending on the set of available resources that constitute a firm. Different firms, each one a different bundle of resources, may grow at different rates and their growth rate may also depend on the direction they take. For instance, growth into unknown areas is associated with greater risk and uncertainty, which demands greater managerial attention, which in turn constrains the growth potential of the firm in those new areas.

There is also debate about how far firms can grow. From the RBV, it seems reasonable to believe that the growth of the firm is potentially endless. In fact, Penrose argued that very small and very large firms would have more problems managing their growth and, thus, they should be expected to have a smaller potential growth rate than medium size firms, but all of them can grow forever. The existence of enormous organizations like General Electric, which has had several decades of strong growth, seems to question that there is indeed a maximum size, and it is not clear that managerial diseconomies of scale actually exist.[6] This question remains open, with some authors

---

[5] In this sense, Penrose (1959: 84) claims that "the anticipation of consumer acceptance is a necessary condition of entrepreneurial interest in any product, but the original incentive to a great deal of innovation can be found in the firm's desire to use its existing resources more efficiently." In other parts of her book, she argues that entrepreneurial versatility, ambition, ingenuity, and competence are essential determinants of the growth of the firm, rather than technological or demand reasons.

[6] See Gander (1991) who tested empirically the Penrose effect and found that firms experience constant returns to managerial resources.

arguing against the possibility for firms to continuously grow as suggested by the RBV. For instance, Coase and Williamson have argued against the possibility of infinite firm growth because the internal costs of coordination should eventually become greater than the costs of managing those transactions through market means.

Competence building

In her work, Penrose barely touched upon how firms and their managers develop expertise through time in their dynamic interaction with their environment. It was not until the eighties that scholars probed into the process of competence development inside organizations. This process has been very well described by economists Nelson and Winter (1982), through their analysis of how firms search for, develop, use, and discontinue *routines*, which are the regular and predictable behavioral patterns that rule virtually everything that is done inside organizations. Very much like genes do in biology, routines can be used to understand the evolution of organizations. A large literature on organizational learning has accumulated in the last two decades exploring issues like environmental scanning, organizational memory, absorptive capacity, knowledge management, and forgetting.[7]

This literature on evolutionary economics and organizational learning has been absorbed and pushed further within the strategy field in the analysis of dynamic capabilities. Teece *et al.* (1997: 515) argued that the key role of strategic management deals with "appropriately adapting, integrating, and reconfiguring internal and external organizational skills, resources, and functional competences to match the requirements of a changing environment." This dynamic development and exploitation of capabilities is the critical capability that firms need to have in order to be successful, particularly in high-tech industries. Appropriate time paths must be chosen to build a required set of resources, because factor markets usually do not exist for strategic resources.[8] Thus, new capabilities are developed in a path-dependent process, in which certain steps can be taken only after previous steps have allowed the firm to develop a given stock of knowledge and

[7] For a review of the early literature on organizational learning, see Huber (1991). The topic has been the subject of considerable interest during the nineties (Senge, 1990).

[8] See Dierickx and Cool (1989) and Barney (1986).

assets. It seems that the more firms know about one area of expertise, the more they can develop new competencies related to such an area, i.e., they have more absorptive capacity.[9] Choosing the capabilities that the firm needs to start developing today to enjoy tomorrow is the main responsibility of management from this perspective.

Competence development can be better understood from the RBV, though many of these ideas have really been developed in parallel to this perspective. They are all, however, connected to how one type of intangible resource (i.e., knowledge) develops within the organization and its presumed crucial effect on performance. Besides this focus on resources, the competence development literature provides insights that are fully consistent with Penrose's initial ideas and further work on the RBV.

Firm heterogeneity and differences in performance

If all information was publicly available to firms and all resources were tradable in markets, firms would be able to easily combine the appropriate resources in their search for maximum profitability, assuming perfect rationality in the decision makers. In this unrealistic scenario, differences across firms within a given industry could exist only in the short term and firms across all industries would have similar performance in the long run. Firms would enter into and exit from industries with higher and lower performance than average respectively, thus equalizing performance across the board. However, it is evident that firms and their performance differ very much from each other within and across industries even in the long run. The RBV has been very useful to understand why these premises from neoclassical economics do not usually occur in the real world. The analysis of what happens inside organizations and the resources that constitute a firm has allowed us to understand why there are substantial differences across firms and their long-term performance.

Organizational theory provides solid arguments that question the perfect rationality of decision makers, which should presumably lead firms to imitate each other and eventually have a similar performance in the long run. Since the behavioral theory of the firm was developed,

[9] See Cohen and Levinthal (1990: 128) for the seminal analysis on the absorptive capacity as "the ability of a firm to recognize the value of new, external information, assimilate it, and apply it to commercial ends," which is largely a function of the firm's level of prior related knowledge.

it seems clear that bounded rationality alone is sufficient to observe differences across firms, though there are many additional sociological explanations of why firms differ.[10] In a similar line of thought, Penrose and later approaches to entrepreneurship based on the RBV argue that managers have different perceptions of what their firms can do (i.e., the productive opportunity of the firm is subjective), which would drive them into different paths and, thus, increased heterogeneity of firms. Once firm heterogeneity exists, it is reasonable to expect performance differences as well.

A key contribution of the RBV to the understanding of firm heterogeneity and performance comes from the analysis of why all resources, including information, are not equally available to market participants. Causal ambiguity, in particular, has been stressed as a major limitation with respect to available information and knowledge. It is often unclear which is the source of the competitive advantage of a successful firm, so that it becomes very difficult to imitate what it does. In other words, competitors may not have the knowledge of what resources need to be assembled to achieve the expertise of other firms. The firm with superior expertise may not even know why it actually enjoys its superiority and how it achieved it. This causal ambiguity, typically unidentified knowledge that is presumably tacit, highly complex, and firm specific, can be a substantial barrier to imitation that results in companies being heterogeneous and with different levels of performance.[11]

Causal ambiguity has been formally modeled by Lippman and Rumelt (1982). They develop a mathematical model that results in firms and industries having differences in performance in the long run, even though entry and exit is allowed. The key to the model is the introduction of initial uncertainty regarding the future costs that the firms will have if they decide to enter. If there is uncertain imitability driven by causal ambiguity and imperfect mobility of factors, there will be differences in efficiency and performance across firms.[12] This argument expands substantially the traditionally accepted economic explanations of long-term performance differences, like the experience

---

[10] For different explanations of why firms differ from an organization theory perspective, see Carroll (1993).

[11] See Reed and DeFillippi (1990) for the role of causal ambiguity in sustaining firm competitive advantage.

[12] As Lippman and Rumelt (1982: 420) put it: "in the absence of uncertainty, the creation of a unique resource could be repeated and its uniqueness destroyed." But they also note that: "Factors of production cannot become mobile unless they are known."

curve, economies of scale, market power, and first-mover advantages, which are not contemplated in the model.

Causal ambiguity is an informational limitation, but the underlying reason why it results in performance differences across firms is ultimately the immobility of factors. In fact, causal ambiguity is just one explanation of why firms may encounter differences in efficiency leading to performance differentials. But the necessary feature for these differences to be sustainable through time is their inimitability. Traditional economics has placed in barriers to competition, especially barriers to entry at the market level, the ultimate explanation of why some firms and industries are more profitable than others. However, the RBV has probed deeper inside the firm to understand differences in their composition of resources and the barriers at the resource level (i.e., the market for factors of production) that contribute to prevent imitation among firms and long-term performance convergence. Several authors have identified *isolating mechanisms*, such as specialized assets, switching and search costs, patents, reputation, legal restrictions to entry, and causal ambiguity.[13] Though some of them are well-known barriers to entry at the market level, other isolating mechanisms are built around the strategic resources that confer competitive advantage to somehow limit their acquisition or replication of those factors.

Probably more important than the analysis of isolating mechanisms that prevent the perfect mobility of resources, the RBV has stressed the characteristics of those resources that may confer a competitive advantage. Barney (1991) has identified four characteristics of those strategic resources with the potential to provide sustainable competitive advantage: valuable, rare among competitors, imperfectly imitable, and imperfectly substitutable by another resource. Other similar approaches to the analysis of strategic resources have been discussed in the literature, dealing primarily with the identification of the earning potential of one resource and its appropriability by the firm that owns it.[14]

Despite the important contributions of the RBV to the analysis of firm competitiveness, there is still debate about the potential of this

---

[13] See Rumelt (1984) for the concept of isolating mechanism.
[14] See Peteraf (1993), Amit and Schoemaker (1993), and Grant (2005).

perspective to develop into a full theory of the firm for strategy.[15] In the next section we will review some of the controversy around it.

Characteristics of strategic resources

In what could be regarded as the foremost paper in the RBV, Barney (1991) explained which type of resources should be associated with a sustained competitive advantage and, thus, superior performance. This framework is based on two key assumptions: resource heterogeneity and immobility. Firms are presumably comprised of heterogeneous resources that do not move freely among them. Otherwise all firms could be imitated and none would be able to enjoy a sustainable competitive advantage.

Under these circumstances, which resources can give a firm a sustainable competitive advantage? Barney argues that these resources should have four characteristics, which have been qualified and expanded later on:

a) Value. Valuable resources are those that allow the firm to exploit opportunities or neutralize threats in a competitive environment, as Andrews (1971) already noted. More precisely, a valuable resource should allow the firm to decrease its costs or to increase its revenues in contrast to what its sales and costs would be without them.

b) Rarity. In addition, a valuable resource should also be rare to generate competitive advantage. Not every firm should have it because otherwise its possession would result in competitive parity at best and provide only average performance.

c) Inimitability. The resource should also be difficult to imitate, because otherwise the advantage would only be temporary as competitors may replicate such a resource. Barney identifies three main reasons why a resource may be difficult to imitate: unique historical conditions (path dependence), causal ambiguity, and social complexity.

d) Substitutability. Finally, the resource should not be easy to substitute entirely with another strategically equivalent though different resource.

---

[15] See the analysis of Conner (1991) and the criticisms from Priem and Butler (2001).

Some years later, Barney (1997) introduced some changes to these four traits of strategic resources to be able to generate a sustainable competitive advantage. He included substitution into the feature of imitability and added a new requirement: the firm must be appropriately organized to fully exploit the potential of its resources. He referred to this analysis as the question of organization. However, this is not a necessary characteristic of the resource and, in fact, it does not take place at the level of resources. It is an organizational feature that could be associated with organizational design and the usual elements of successful strategy implementation.

Firms comprised by resources with these four characteristics should enjoy a sustainable competitive advantage. This model highlights the importance of resource uniqueness, but it has not expanded much our understanding of value creation beyond the organization–environment match suggested by Andrews (1971) or the issue of value appropriation by the firm versus resource owners.

Questions about the resource-based view

The RBV has provided a new conceptualization of firms that is internally focused. This perspective is in sharp contrast to the more externally based model of strategy developed by Michael Porter, inspired in the traditional concepts of market positioning, barriers to entry, and competitive moves.[16] Looking at its influence on the strategy literature in the last two decades, the RBV has become one of the cornerstones in the field. However, the RBV has been questioned, not always with fairness, for its limitations regarding (i) possible tautological explanations, (ii) limited usefulness and applicability for management, and (iii) weaknesses in addressing firm scope.

Does it provide tautological explanations about performance?

The central argument of the RBV deals with the origins of sustainable competitive advantage that lead some firms to enjoy superior

---

[16] Porter (1991) has questioned the usefulness and the depth of the RBV by directly comparing it with the detailed analysis of the value chain activities within his market positioning model. This debate and the relative strengths of both approaches will be discussed in detail in chapter six.

performance. For RBV scholars, the analysis of firm resources, rather than market positioning, is the key to understanding competitive advantage. This critical analysis relies on the possession of resources with certain characteristics, especially being rare and valuable. However, as Priem and Butler (2001) noted, a sustainable competitive advantage is also usually defined in terms of being rare and valuable.[17] Thus, the argument above may be regarded as tautological in the sense that its truth can be derived from the analysis of the terms. In other words, only the possession of resources that give competitive advantage indeed give competitive advantage. We may just be moving down the level of analysis from the firm to the resource, but not really making much progress in understanding competitive advantage and superior profitability. From this critical perspective, the RBV is not really testable in its current form and furthermore it leaves out of the theory the understanding of some core concepts like value.

The threat of tautology and its relevance in science has been the subject of debate for a long time. In his analysis of the tautological argument that competitive advantage leads to superior performance, Powell (2001) argues that the RBV and many other alternative theories in strategy, as well as established theories in the physical and biological sciences, are built on tautological arguments that shield them from empirical refutation. However, from a pragmatist point of view, these theories may facilitate human problem solving. On similar grounds, Barney (2001: 42) argues that "because a theory is tautological does not mean that it might not be insightful and even empirically fruitful" and he goes on to explain that, even if the RBV can be stated in tautological terms, its main ideas can indeed be empirically tested, if its core concepts are appropriately parameterized.

Taking this pragmatist perspective, the tautology criticism does not seem very damaging. Actually, many well known theories have survived this criticism, like the Darwinian idea that natural selection drives the origin and evolution of species. It is not possible to refute that natural selection determines the evolution of species, but this insight has made possible great progress in the analysis of how random small cumulative inheritable mutations may result in a large variety of evolving species. Using his traditional wit against the critics to his ideas

---

[17] See the interesting debate between Priem and Butler (2001) and Barney (2001).

about transaction costs, Coase claimed that the tautology criticism is the one people make of a proposition that is clearly right. Refutability and the search for truth in the core synthetic arguments of a theory are not necessary for knowledge to advance. The view that firms are collections of resources may lead us to formulate other sets of testable hypotheses.

However, if the question of refutability is replaced by usefulness, the test of the RBV should be based on the results that its use has provided. Do the ideas that arise from the RBV have predictive power? In particular for our applied field, how useful is it for management?

Is it a useful theory?

The RBV has received many criticisms about its limited usefulness. For instance, it builds on ambiguous concepts (i.e., anything can be a resource); all firms are inherently unique combinations of resources and, thus, it becomes too easy to find ex-post explanations for their performance; causal ambiguity and the reduced possibility to manipulate key resource attributes severely limit its managerial applicability; and its predictive power is significantly reduced as a result of all these limitations.

It seems fair to say that many of these criticisms have been rebutted, at least in part. Jay Barney (2001) argues that the RBV never intended to provide a list of critical resources that every firm must possess to gain competitive advantage. This list cannot exist, because there are no rules for riches. In fact, the RBV explains quite well why this is so. For instance, either pure luck or private information about a resource's potential returns may lead a firm to possess a superior resource, whose acquisition cost has not been pushed up in the factors market so as to erode its above normal returns.[18] This is an important insight regardless of the resource to which it could be applied. In addition, the potential for different resources to generate a competitive advantage will change across different contexts and the RBV may help

---

[18] See Barney (1986) and also Peteraf (1993) for a discussion of ex-ante limits to competition. Makadok and Barney (2001) have studied more formally under what circumstances firms decide to invest in research to develop more accurate expectations about the future value of resources.

us understand how and why. Thus, it is a precise theory, even if the concepts on which it builds may be very broad. Its explanatory power is very large, which leads sometimes to the inappropriate use of the theory to analyze ex-post performance. However, this is not necessarily a problem with the theory itself. From this analysis managers may develop some insights about the earning potential of the resources that they have.

Looking at its impact in the literature, it is evident that the RBV has been central to strategy research in the last two decades. It has opened up the door to finer analysis of issues like competence development, imitability, and diversification by moving down from the product market level of analysis to the internal resource and core competences. However, despite its important contributions, adjusting the level of analysis does not fully resolve the main issue of strategy: the understanding of differences in performance. Even if the reason for the greater profitability of some firms is found at the level of resources, we need a better understanding of why some resources are superior to others, so that the theory can be used to provide sound recommendations for management. Arguably, the answer deals with the question of *value*.

Unfortunately, the RBV has not yet probed much into what it takes for a resource to be valuable. Barney (2001: 42) argues that "the determination of the value of a firm's resources is exogenous to the resource-based theory" and suggests the use of industrial organization models of perfect and imperfect competition, including also the structure-conduct-performance model. These models may help identify those resources that are valuable in the sense of exploiting opportunities and neutralizing threats. Thus, the RBV has basically moved the analysis suggested by Andrews for the firm to the resource level and added the economic analysis of rent sustainability, but it has not really pushed forward in a significantly new way the scrutiny of sources of rents. If there were single resource firms, the RBV would not have much to contribute to the analysis of their performance beyond what we knew in the seventies, though it would be very useful to understand their evolution and the sustainability of their performance, wherever it may come from. Thus, what constitutes a valuable resource in the first place remains an underdeveloped, but critical, issue. Without a more developed analysis of value, the RBV can only provide limited guidance for managers about the resources that the firm should try to develop and protect.[19]

Does it explain why firms exist?

Though there is some partial validity to the criticism of the RBV with regard to its usefulness, probably the main criticism of the RBV as a theory of the firm is that it does not really explain the boundaries of firms. The perspective of the firm as a collection of resources is indeed very useful to understand the evolution of firms and the sources of performance differences, but not their scope. The theory does not explain which resources should be included within the administrative framework that constitutes a firm. Along this line, Foss (2005) argues that the RBV indeed suffers from similar limitations to the neoclassical production function view of the firm, because it does not really analyze under what circumstances input factors (resources for the RBV) are optimally used inside the firm, instead of being exchanged through the market.

Some scholars, however, disagree with this criticism and believe that the RBV, and specially the notion of organizational capabilities, can be used to determine the boundaries of the organization. For instance, Conner (1991) argues that the level of relatedness with the existing resource base of the firm would determine the extent to which an additional resource may be more productive inside the firm than outside. Grant (1996) has also stressed the nature of the firm as an institution for integrating the knowledge that already exists within its members. In the context of the multinational enterprise, Kogut and Zander (1993) claimed that firms specialize in the transfer of tacit knowledge,

---

[19] Collis (1994) has questioned the value of organizational capabilities as sources of sustainable competitive advantage. He argued that one can always find a higher order capability (like learning to learn) that can make any capability no longer appropriate. Thus, pursuing the logic of capabilities will never identify the ultimate source of sustainable competitive advantage because of the infinite regress problem. Capabilities are just another element in the explanation of competitive advantage with no precedence over other possible levels. He recommends researchers to "generate lists of the enormous variety of capabilities and develop normative prescriptions for actually building those capabilities that have apparent potential for a particular industry in the near future, while recognizing that these might always be blindsided by a substitute or higher order capability" (Collis, 1994: 151).

which they can do better than market-based mechanisms. Much earlier, Richardson (1972) had argued that the appropriate coordination among activities could be obtained through different means (direction inside the firm, close cooperation between firms, and spot market transactions), which were determined by the organizational capabilities of the firms and the level of similarity and complementarity among the activities to be coordinated. Thus, organizational knowledge may be regarded as the main determinant of the boundaries of the firm, as implicitly assumed in the popular managerial recommendation in the eighties to "stick to the knitting" (Peters and Waterman, 1982).

Organizational capabilities are useful to explain at least some make-or-buy and internalize-or-license decisions. However, they are not a sufficiently solid standard for setting the firm boundaries. Relatedness is very hard to measure, particularly when we apply it to resources that are already loosely defined, like capabilities. The analysis of relatedness alone cannot become the basis for decision making at the corporate level. For instance, miniaturization has been regarded as the core competence of Sony (Prahalad and Hamel, 1990); however, the analysis of opportunities for miniaturization, which are so broad and indeed diverse, ranging from precision instruments to chip design and manufacturing, can hardly be used to define the set of industries in which Sony has been or could be involved, like the convergence between entertainment electronics and content.

The RBV seems insufficiently developed yet to be regarded as a fully blown theory of the firm, particularly if we consider the criticisms to this approach inspired in transaction cost economics (TCE). Some scholars have argued in favor of an integrationist perspective that combines both TCE and RBV in the place where each of them is stronger (Foss, 2005). However, because it is preferable to have less complex but sufficiently comprehensive theories, we should look for a new approach that facilitates and somehow expands the integration of TCE and RBV, rather than just adding two different theories. I will discuss in the rest of the chapter that the analysis of how firms create and appropriate value facilitates the integration of contracting and knowledge issues into a more useful, broader, and simpler approach for decision making about firm boundaries. For strategic decision making, the analysis of value creation and capture may be a better description of what firms can and should do in our society. In this approach, organizational capabilities and transaction costs have some part to play along other contributors to the understanding of where value may come from.

The firm in strategic management

The two major current approaches to the theory of the firm used in the strategy field, namely TCE and the RBV, have generated important insights for our conceptualization of firms and what they do. However, as discussed earlier, they have several limitations to providing the basic foundations for the strategy field, even though they have much to say about specific topics. A theory of the firm for strategy needs to be broader in scope to help us understand in a coherent and comprehensive way the four main questions that we identified in chapter one: what is a firm? What is its role in our economy? What determines its size and scope? And what determines its performance? Let us begin to address these questions from a strategic management perspective, starting with the first one. We will study all of them throughout the rest of the book and summarize the answers in the last chapter.

The definition of a firm and its boundaries can be related to strategic decision making, because in strategy we are specifically concerned with providing sound recommendations for managers about what they can do with their businesses. From our perspective, the firm is the collective subject that holds the responsibility for strategy design and its actual implementation, the boundaries of which we are trying to analyze. The organizational boundaries delimit what Penrose called an *administrative framework*, which holds together the resources that constitute the firm through one overall strategy. Thus, in line with the RBV, we can define further the boundaries of the firm in terms of the strategy set by the highest level in the organization around a collection of resources. Being part of one strategy is what determines the limits of a firm for our purposes, rather than ownership, coordination, and contractual considerations, which can be more relevant in other fields.

Both the firm and its strategy are defined concurrently. Firms, more precisely their top managers, are continuously making decisions about their boundaries, how to deal with their environment, and to what extent they should internalize or outsource certain activities. Even though it may be useful for analytical purposes, firms do not first exist with certain boundaries and then decide how they want to compete. This is a chicken-and-egg question, in which the current boundaries of the firm (i.e., the resources that are joined through a common strategy) are the result of the strategy followed in the past, though they may be taken as given to develop a new strategy for the future, which may change its boundaries again. Both the firm's boundaries and its competitive strategy in the market evolve jointly through time. Our ultimate goal is to understand why some strategies with their associated definition of firm boundaries are better than others, especially with regard to their performance.

The main challenges for this conceptualization of the firm alongside its strategy to be workable are basically two. First, we need a working conceptualization of what one strategy is and its boundaries. Second, we need to understand what makes one independent unit with its own strategy somehow economically preferable to having two smaller units, each one with its own independent strategy.

A value-based model of firm strategy

The concept of strategy has been debated for several decades.[20] There are many approaches regarding what it means for a firm to have a strategy and the term itself has received many definitions.[21] The inherent complexity in the notion of strategy results from the large number of possibilities involved in analyzing and categorizing what firms do and how they decide to do it. These possible analyses include the extent to which the strategy is internally consistent towards some overall goal or following a certain pattern, its short-term versus long-term focus, intended vs. emergent process of formation, cost vs. differentiation basis, customer vs. product orientation, and many other angles to describe what a firm does in the market and even its nonmarket activities.

---

[20] See Andrews (1971) for an early discussion. Other influential views include Mintzberg's (1978) analysis of the strategy formation process and Porter's (1996) market positioning approach. MacCrimmon (1993) develops an interesting analysis of the extent to which we can say that firm strategies exist.

[21] See for instance Barney's (1997) textbook for alternative definitions of strategy and strategic management. Hambrick and Fredrickson (2005) provide a practical conceptualization of strategy based on a set of questions that a strategy should deal with: (a) the markets in which a company competes, (b) the entry strategy into each of them, (c) its differentiation from competition and, (d) its plans for future actions, all of them presumably based on an underlying competitive logic that should allow the firm to obtain its returns.

For the sake of conducting strategic analysis, all firms have what we may call a realized strategy, following Mintzberg (1978). Firms compete in the market through the actions that their managers take, and the different ways in which they compete constitute the domain of the field. To the extent that a firm's strategy basically defines how the firm competes in the market, we can probe into the different elements of the market behavior of firms and their performance relative to competitors.

For competition among firms to exist, there need to be three main economic agents with whom to interact in the market: customers, competitors, and resources. These are the main stakeholders that have a direct influence in and are affected by a firm, though there may be other groups whose interaction with the firm also needs to be managed, like specific interest groups and government agencies. However, the role of other stakeholders becomes relevant for the firm's competitiveness in the market to the extent that they can affect the interaction with the resources, the customers, and the competitors of the firm, so that we can focus now on these three elements to understand a firm's business strategy.

First, firms compete to obtain the patronage of *customers*. It is evident that businesses fight to get sales as their main source of revenue that makes possible their long-term survival. Profit maximization has been frequently considered the main goal of businesses since classical economics, but obviously profits can only be obtained through selling to customers in the first place. Sales maximization is not a sufficiently accurate description of the goal of firms, but it is nevertheless necessary to obtain the support of their targeted customers. Customers include the final consumers as well as possible intermediaries that facilitate access to the consumer, and industrial customers that may further transform the product or service. This interface with customers is a critical component of a firm's strategy: who does it want to sell to? What does it do to attract these customers? How does it manage the relationship with them?

Second, firms have to fight for customers *against competitors*. Even monopolists have to be concerned with substitute products and innovations that could affect and even displace their industries. As we will discuss later on, understanding competitive dynamics, including for instance signaling and first-mover advantages, is essential for firms to deal successfully with competitors. When analyzing competitors, it is often useful to identify direct competitors as well as potential new entrants and substitute products from other industries that may satisfy similar customer needs. The interface of the firm with customers on the one hand and all possible competitors on the other hand defines what we usually call market positioning, that is, how the firm is positioned to attract customers in the market in contrast to what other firms do with the same goal.

Third, firms compete against direct and potential competitors *by managing resources* to provide some product or service to their customers. Using its owned resources and capabilities, firms usually acquire some inputs that are transformed and somehow rearranged by the organization, frequently in cooperation with other firms and often relying on complementary products and services as well. Drawing from the RBV, these resources include labor, inputs, fixed assets, technology, and any tangible or intangible resource. Resource management comprises all that the firm does, which materializes in activities, to finally deliver to the customer its range of products and services. This management of resources is the main way in which firms create value for customers. In the case of product manufacturing, this process can be modeled as a value chain from inputs to finished goods, though other value configurations also exist, as we will see in chapter six.

A critical part of a firm's strategy is, therefore, which resources are combined within the organization and how the firm's activities are integrated into the broader set of connected inter-dependent firms to jointly satisfy customer needs. The strategy area has focused especially on the barriers to competition that a firm can build around its most precious resources, as a critical factor in competitive dynamics. Superior profitability is often the result of creating barriers for potential competitors to either enter an attractive industry (barriers to entry) or replicate a strong market position within the industry (mobility barriers).

Figure 3.1 shows graphically the three main elements of strategy. This simple model allows us to begin our investigation of how firms create and appropriate value. Firms combine a set of internal and external resources so that they can create value for their targeted customers. This value-creating process of resource management constitutes the essence of what firms do in our economy. The process takes place in the presence of direct and potential competitors for both resources and customers. Consequently, firms have to decide how to develop and protect their resources as well as position their product in the

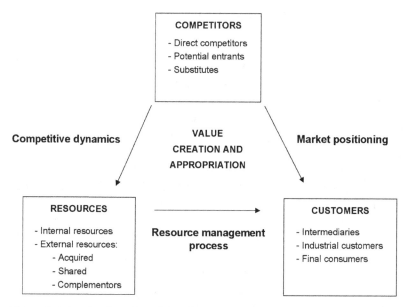

Figure 3.1 A value-based model of firm strategy

market in contrast to their competitors. The strategic boundaries of the firm can be drawn around the collection of internal resources that share a common integrated way to deal with customers, competitors, and other external resources, that is, a common strategy to create and appropriate value for the collection of internal resources as a whole. Value creation through the management of resources to attract customers provides the foundation for firm strategy, but not all the created value is actually appropriated by the firm. The bargaining power of resource owners and customers as well as the intensity of competition may lead to a significant part of the value to be finally appropriated by customers via lower prices, resource owners through higher costs, or competitors through imitation that takes customers away from the firm. The value ultimately appropriated by the firm is determined by the effectiveness of the strategy in dealing with its three main market stakeholders. Thus, the value appropriated by the firm is also at the center of the value-based model of strategy.

This simple model can guide us to continue our investigation of the theory of the firm in strategy. It allows us to describe the main role for firms in society (value creation) and it provides one way to measure their performance from the firm's perspective (value appropriation). We will explore how value analysis may help managers to make assessments about the effectiveness of one or more strategies against each other.

From a strategy perspective, firm boundaries are drawn around those resources that form part of one strategy so that more value may be created and appropriated by the firm and the resources that comprise it. Within a firm, internal resources no longer compete independently for customers and external resources against other competitors, but they compete as part of a larger strategic entity (i.e., the firm) to create and appropriate value. Based on this strategic definition of firm boundaries, internal resources do not compete as independent units with their own value-creating strategy, but they are part of a strategic direction set at a higher level and use the common interface that we call the *firm* in dealing with customers, competitors, and resources, including both external and lower-level internal resources. For instance, the acquisitions department of a firm does not compete as a player against competitors in the market, that is, it does not fight for its own customers and it does not have to obtain and manage its resources on its own (including financial resources, hiring, and setting alliances, for instance). Though it is true that many firms, especially large and diversified conglomerates, do not have only a single interface with customers, competitors, and resources, at least part of how they deal with them is usually decided at the highest level for the entire corporation. Having at least some elements of its strategy to deal with customers, resources, and competitors jointly managed is what provides the firm with strategic boundaries.

The analysis of strategic boundaries focuses on the conditions under which different resources within one higher-level strategy may create or destroy value as a whole versus separately or in a different combination. The boundaries of the firm set strategically in this manner may or may not fully coincide with the formal structure of the organization and its legal definition. For instance, fashion clothing companies like Zara (Inditex's brand) and Benetton usually outsource part of their labor-intensive production to individuals who work only for them. I will argue that the strategy of these firms actually includes these people, though they are not formally defined as employees, because they do not have to compete as independent units against other individuals to get their revenues, and often rely on Zara and Benetton to get their own inputs and resources. For an external observer they are part of the strategy of these businesses. Similarly, firms using franchises incorporate within their strategy its franchisees, even if legally they are defined as separate entities. In strategy we are mainly interested in understanding why certain resources give up a substantial part of their responsibility for decision making and compete as part of the collections of resources that we call firms. Contractual features are secondary to the market implications of moving strategic decision-making responsibilities.

This conceptualization of firm boundaries built on the reach of its strategy shares with other approaches similar problems with respect to precision. For instance, TCE has to acknowledge the existence of hybrid organizations between the market and the hierarchy. Even from a purely legal perspective, it is hard to define which organizations are part of a conglomerate, though fixed guidelines are set somewhat arbitrarily to facilitate formal consolidated accounting, for instance. Similarly, it is also hard to see in some cases the extent to which two potentially independent competitive units share a common interface in dealing with customers, competitors, and other resources and, thus, truly form part of a single strategy. However, as far as strategic management is concerned, it is preferable to define the firm boundaries in terms of strategy, even if the degree of strategy commonality among the firm's subunits is a continuous variable that cannot be easily dichotomized into inside–outside the strategy.

The effect of firm boundaries on the value created by internal resources

Having defined the strategic boundaries of the firm as a collective competitive unit, now we need to study why different resources that could compete independently may be more competitive as part of a firm with some elements of its strategy determined by its top management. Let us briefly identify some of the key reasons why some resources may create more or less value as part of a collection of resources within a firm than the value that they can create and appropriate as an independent firm, dealing on its own with customers and other resources versus competitors in the market.

The analysis of firm boundaries has typically relied on the relative costs and benefits of joining two sets of activities under the same corporate umbrella, primarily from a transaction costs perspective. TCE basically looks at the relative costs of managing transactions inside and outside the firm, which are driven essentially by asset specificity. In a nutshell, placing the transaction inside a hierarchy would create bureaucratic costs that need to be compared to the costs of using the market as an alternative. Comparative analysis of governance alternatives determines which transactions should be placed inside or outside the firm, as we discussed in chapter two. We can expand this type of comparative analysis to all potential costs and benefits of changing firm boundaries in addition to transaction costs. Combining two resources into one firm may have internal effects on how they are integrated as well as external effects in their relationship with customers, competitors, and external resources.

Internal effects

Placing two resources under the same strategic direction has important consequences on the relationship between them and how they can be managed. The integration between the two resources and the costs associated with its management will be substantially changed by putting them under the same corporate umbrella. This is a critical insight of TCE that has been widely accepted. However, beyond the costs of managing the transactions between two resources, moving boundaries allows a reorganization of the activities that includes, for instance, new options for the division of labor among the combined resources. *Synergies* can be realized driven by economies of scale or just reassigning activities based on the relative productivity of the two resources (i.e., their comparative advantage). To the extent that these synergies may exist, we should observe firm boundaries adapting to include these resources within the same firm, so that they may create greater value. Changing boundaries may facilitate the redistribution of these activities and the specialization of labor in new ways.

As we discussed earlier, it is misleading to assume that all synergies can be achieved independently of the governance of relationships, so that only transaction costs presumably determine the best possible contracting solution for managing transactions. This way we are assuming away the problem and forcing transaction costs as the ultimate reason for firm boundaries. Exactly the opposite conclusion could be reached, also mistakenly, if we assume that transaction costs are always constant and only costs and synergies between activities are allowed to vary across firms. Rather than looking for one single reason behind organizational boundaries, it seems more productive to identify how the efficiency and productivity of resources may change when we merge them with other ones under the same strategic direction. *Transaction costs* can be reduced on some occasions when merging two resources, but any possible rearrangement of the activities carried out by these resources may also lead to a change in their operational efficiency and their capability to generate more, better, or new output. Both lower transaction costs and lower production costs can sometimes be obtained by combining the management of two or more resources.

In addition to operational efficiency driven by technological and transactional reasons, the management literature has explored the *cognitive effects* of firm boundaries on its internal resources, particularly its employees. Kogut and Zander (1996) argue that firm boundaries provide a shared identity to all its resources that facilitates communication, coordination, and learning. Putting certain resources together makes easier the development of new related knowledge and competencies, thus facilitating innovation. As learning and innovation are critical for new value creation, any change in the composition of firm resources that facilitate them should be regarded as a relevant determinant of the boundaries of the firm. Human cognition, particularly regarding tacit procedural knowledge inside organizations, makes possible and puts limits on what firms can do effectively. From this perspective, not all technically feasible combinations of resources may actually take place because they have to be consistent with the firm's shared identity, which facilitates the effective transfer of tacit knowledge and its capability for learning inside the organization. Thus, the potential for learning and innovation is also affected by firm's boundaries.

Finally, *motivational factors* may also influence the value that resources may generate inside or outside specific firm boundaries. These have been identified by scholars from the knowledge perspective of the firm as well as TCE. For the former group, identity influences the attribution of self-interested behavior, so that people are more likely to infer an opportunistic behavior in those individuals outside their own group. Similarly, TCE stresses how the possibility of opportunistic behavior may displace the market in favor of the hierarchy, driven primarily by asset specificity. Certainly moving organizational boundaries has an impact on the motivation of the involved individuals, including any possible negative effects as well. In addition to positive motivational effects associated with lower opportunism inside the organization, in larger organizations there may be additional costs of people at lower level units trying to influence decisions of higher level managers in their favor. Furthermore, the greater protection that larger organizations may provide to specific business units may prevent them from feeling the heat of market rivalry, which results in less aggressive units than otherwise could be (i.e., low-powered incentives, as Williamson calls it).

By changing firm boundaries around different resources, we should expect a change also in the organizational efficiency of these resources, their cognitive framework, and their motivation. These effects on the resources' internal nature and productivity may lead the combined bundle to be more or less competitive than they would be independently.

External effects

Organizational boundaries not only have an internal impact on the bundle of resources that comprise the organization, but also on their relationship with external economic agents, i.e., customers, competitors, and external resources. Bundled resources within an organization share a common interface in their possible interactions with these stakeholders and, by changing the overall composition of the collection, their relative strength and effectiveness change with respect to what they could do independently.

Porter has stressed a firm's bargaining power versus suppliers (i.e., external resource providers) and customers as important structural forces that need to be managed. Organizational boundaries may have an impact on the *market power* that aggregated resources may have. By putting them under the same corporate umbrella, resources may reduce the acquisition costs of their possible external inputs. They may also increase prices by limiting the level of competition that resources could face if they were to compete independently, particularly against each other. In general, greater bargaining power has an important effect on the value that resources may appropriate when they are combined within the same organization.[22]

[22] Williamson (1991) develops an interesting criticism of the importance of power issues ("strategizing") vs. economizing on transaction costs. Contrary to

However, the external effects of combining resources go beyond market power and value appropriation from other market stakeholders. They may also affect how much value is actually created for customers. Combined resources may facilitate the consumption process by sharing a *common interface* with customers. For instance, cross-selling of related products through a common salesforce reduces the customers' costs of having to obtain access to different products separately, in addition to any possible synergies in distribution costs. In other words, better service can be provided to customers if some resources are bundled together to produce a broader set of related products.

Bundling resources may also provide greater value to customers for its *risk implications*. In many circumstances it is preferable for a customer to deal with a larger organization that is responsible for the entire product or service that he or she buys rather than just one smaller organization (or just one individual) at the end of a chain that assembles different components. Even if the costs of providing a product or service as a collection of independent resources or combined within one organization were the same, a customer may prefer a larger organization, which is more likely to have a solid reputation and be liable for potential problems later on.

In summary, bundling resources may create value either through the internal reorganization of resources that it may allow or by changing how these resources interact with their environment. Internal and external factors, like transaction costs, operational synergies, cognitive and motivational factors, bargaining power, customer service, and risk, may all have an impact on how much value can be created by combining resources within one organization.

Why do different firm strategies exist?

As discussed earlier, firms do not exist independently of their strategies *a priori*. Top managers determine the boundaries of the firm along

the view defended in this book, he claims that economizing, i.e., efficiency primarily driven by individual incentives and appropriate organizational governance, is the best strategy. In contrast, I argue, probably in agreement with many strategy scholars, that firms compete in other dimensions besides increasing efficiency, though technological and organizational efficiency (driven by transaction costs, agency costs, and other variations of contractual features) are certainly important.

other strategic decisions about how the firm creates and appropriates value in the market. The question of why firms exist is, therefore, analogous to the question of why firm strategies exist. There are many possibilities to manage the interaction with customers, resources, and competitors, thus giving rise to many firms, each one with its own strategy for value creation and appropriation.

To understand why different firm strategies exist, we should first analyze why the entire economy is not run as one single organization. This is an old question in political economy that has been debated for at least a century and its answer looks much more simple in the early twenty-first century after the collapse of the Soviet Union and other communist economic systems. In 1954 Arrow and Debreu proved formally the existence of a general equilibrium solution and its efficiency properties in a competitive economy that determines prices and quantities for factors and final goods. However, it could be argued that a planned economy may achieve the same result with some additional positive effects in egalitarian distribution.[23] Against this argument, Hayek (1945) provided the widely accepted explanation as to why free market economies are far superior to planned systems. He argued in favor of the decentralization role of prices in reaching the optimal allocation of resources, in contrast to one central board that integrates all knowledge and issues its orders about quantities and prices. Markets allow much faster action to sudden changes in any surrounding circumstances than central authority. Knowledge of relative prices is sufficient for economic agents to make their own independent decisions that result in the benefit of the overall economic system.

The enormous complexity that requires a centralized comprehensive plan and its lower decision-making speed make it less efficient than a free market economy based on decentralized knowledge and decisions. We could also stress the lower motivation for innovation and improvement that results from not having competition to attract customers. As far as economic value creation is concerned, and as the failure of communism has shown, many strategies (i.e., independent firms collaborating and competing against each other) are better than a single one for the world as an organization. In terms of customers, resources, and competitors, consumers in communist countries had lower wealth, their human resources often wanted to leave the

---

[23] Some economists, like Oskar Lange and Maurice Dobb, have argued in favor of the superiority of planned economies.

countries, and their overall competitiveness was clearly lower than for free market economies. As a collection of resources that aim at creating value for customers in competition with other countries, they have clearly failed. The human resources that constitute the basis of the economic system eventually dismantled it despite strong political pressure against their will.

Clearly, it is much better for economic progress to have independent firms competing through the market. However, following Coase, we could question why our economic system is not based on independent specialized individuals using the market to conduct their transactions without the need for organizations. In other words, why does not every individual compete in the market independently using market exchanges? The current answer to this question relies on the notion of transaction costs, which has also been used to place limits on the maximum size of organizations as well. Following Williamson, some transactions among individuals will be internalized inside organizations (and not others) because they differ with regard to their frequency, uncertainty, and, most importantly, asset specificity. Measurement problems also contribute to the problem of managing transactions efficiently through contracts. Thus, the larger the presence of these factors for exchanges, the more efficient it will be to internalize transactions to increase efficiency, so that the hierarchy replaces the market as a way to organize transactions. As Coase (1937) noted, firms emerge as islands of authority in the middle of an ocean of exchanges through the market.

The argument above based mainly on transaction costs constitutes the current explanation in economics of why firms exist. But we have also identified other possible benefits for resources to compete within one firm strategy besides reducing transaction costs. Under some circumstances it will be in the best interest of the potentially separable resources to compete jointly as part of one strategy against other competitors. Firms exist because there is competition for customers and external resources. Those firm strategies that create and appropriate more value against other players in the economy will prevail and grow. There would be no need for firms to exist if no matter how we recombine resources into different firm strategies, we could create the same value for society. Evidently, this is not the case and we should investigate how value creation and capture determines the emergence and the boundaries of the firm.

Strategy scholars have started to investigate why firms are so different from one another, particularly from the RBV. Even within the same industry, the degree of heterogeneity across firms is noticeable, for instance, in terms of size, performance, product variety, firm boundaries, and overall strategy.[24] Firms are not mere transformers of inputs into output through somewhat similar production functions, but they differ substantially in what they do, how they do it, and their performance even across direct competitors. To a large extent, these differences are actually created by their managers through the different decisions and actions that they take as a result of their different beliefs and expectations about their surrounding environment and future customer needs. These choices taken in the face of market uncertainty actually reinforce the potential differences across firms through time, because new routines, resources, and capabilities develop in a path-dependent manner as evolutionary economists and RBV scholars have shown. On the contrary, there are institutional pressures for organizations to conform to their environments and to gain legitimacy, which limits how distinct and differentiated firms can become.[25]

In conclusion, the analysis of value creation through resource combinations under one firm strategy is fully compatible with traditional explanations in economics about the emergence of firms, and it further expands our understanding of why they are so different from each other. Combining all resources into one centrally planned strategy or competing as independent units without organizations do not create as much value as selectively putting under one strategy a reduced set of resources. Firm strategies differ first because there is a large diversity of resources, including differences across technologies, locations, reputations, and human resources, which can be used to create value for customers. Every firm is, thus, a unique combination of resources and, just like there are no two individuals exactly the same, we cannot find

---

[24] See the three articles about this issue in the volume edited by Rumelt *et al.* (1994), including an orthodox strategic perspective based on managerial decision making, an evolutionary economics approach, and a sociological perspective.

[25] The isomorphic pressure on organizations has been analyzed by DiMaggio and Powell (1983). Deephouse (1999) provides an interesting analysis of the trade-off between achieving market differentiation and responding to institutional pressure.

two firms that are comprised of the same set of resources. The value that resources can create depends on the set of resources with which they may be combined, which allow further specialization and innovation that leads to new ways to create value. In the next two chapters we will analyze this process of how firms create value for customers and appropriate part of it for themselves.

4 | *Creating economic value*

What is economic value?

The question of what is value for individuals and overall society has been debated for centuries. It even has its own branch of philosophical inquiry, known as axiology.[1] Unfortunately, the notion of value is hard to operationalize for empirical analysis because of the difficulties in defining a concept that is personal (varying across people), situational (context-specific), and comparative (involving preferences among objects and concepts).[2] Given its subjectivity, difficult measurability, and noncomparability, the study of value itself could be regarded as unscientific.[3]

However, the analysis of value creation and appropriation cannot be discarded so easily because it is the core of what firms do in our economy. Giving up is not an acceptable way to deal with the challenges presented by the analysis of value creation and appropriation by firms through their strategies. On the contrary, this book argues that the notion of value should rightly occupy a central place in the theory of the firm in strategy. Fortunately, we are only concerned with the *economic value* that emerges from market exchanges of products and services, which limits the analysis to only one type of value assessment of products or services that may be potentially exchanged for a given price in the market. Anything that cannot be exchanged in the market for a certain price is not considered in our analysis of economics. Furthermore, we will not provide normative recommendations to customers about how they should value products or services, but only to

---

[1] See, for instance, Frondizi (1971).

[2] See Holbrook (1999) for a comprehensive conceptualization and framework to study consumer value from a marketing perspective.

[3] Using the difference between value in exchange (prices) and value in use identified by Adam Smith, David Ricardo in his *Principles* argued strongly in favor of studying prices, because "Value in use cannot be measured by any known standard; it is differently estimated by different persons."

firms regarding how they can carry out a value-creating strategy and appropriate part of it.

There are many rich ideas about economic value in the literature from different fields. First, we will briefly review those that can be useful to our analysis of the theory of the firm. Building from these ideas, we will analyze later in this chapter how firms may create value. Chapter five discusses value appropriation.

Value in economics

Since Adam Smith, it has been very clear for economists that price and value are two different things. Most economic theory deals with the determination of prices and output, and customer value only enters into the analysis to the extent that it can be used to understand prices. Classical economists like Smith believed that the relative prices of different products are determined exclusively by their total cost of production, though Ricardo thought that the relative quantity of labor was the most important determinant by far, disregarding the effect of changes in wage levels and profits (in addition to excluding capital and land rent).[4] This perspective was criticized by the proponents of marginal analysis in economics, like Jevons and Menger, who claimed that marginal utility fully determines relative prices. These economists argued that consumers maximize their total utility (i.e., the value that they receive) for the set of products and quantities so that their marginal utility from each of them divided by their market price is equal across all products.[5] Thus, if at given prices the marginal utility that consumers receive from getting one more unit of a particular product were greater than the marginal utility to price ratio that they obtain from all other products, they would switch to consume more of such a product and less of all others, which would result in an overall increase in the total utility they receive.

This equi-marginal utility principle is probably the core idea in demand theory in economics. However, it is not only demand, driven

---

[4] See Stigler (1958) for a discussion of Ricardo's labor theory of value and the differences with Smith and neoclassical economists.

[5] Neoclassical economics considers price as the only cost of customers. However, if consumers had to bear other costs besides price, their monetary value would have to be included in the appropriate denominator to compute this equi-marginal principle.

by consumers' utility decisions, that determines prices, just like production costs cannot fully account for prices either. Marshall reconciled these two effects and showed that both demand and supply jointly determine market prices, just like the two blades of a pair of scissors cut one sheet of paper. Neither one, utility nor costs of production, can be used exclusively to determine prices. Walras's general equilibrium formally modeled how prices of factors and final goods are mutually determined at market-clearing levels all at once.

Demand theory is one of the cornerstones of economics. It has produced important insights about the factors that affect demand and its influence on prices through the analysis of elasticities, indifference curves, wealth and substitution effects, hedonic prices, network effects, and many other concepts used to develop and understand demand functions in a variety of contexts. Utility theory has played a central part in the development of the theory of demand. However, the analysis of utility has some important problems, including its lack of a standard to measure it and the impossibility to make interpersonal comparisons. In fact, Stigler (1950) has argued that the negative-sloping demand function and the conclusions from its analysis can be fully developed without recourse to the unobservable and difficult-to-measure notion of utility, bringing back the discussion to prices as Ricardo recommended.

Overall, economists have made important contributions to the understanding of value, though they have also exposed its limitations. From the demand and cost functions, we can identify the total value created in a given market or economic surplus, which can be divided into consumers' and producers' surpluses. Graphically, the area below the demand function and above the market-clearing price is the consumer's surplus, which measures the maximum amount that the set of consumers would have been willing to pay for the total quantity of the product actually exchanged through the market. Because the demand function is just an aggregate of individual choices, there are no interpersonal comparisons and the surplus is clearly measured in monetary units based on the customers' willingness to pay. The area between the cost function and the market price measures the producers' surplus or the firm's profits.[6]

---

[6] Brandenburger and Stuart (1996) claim that we should also include the suppliers to the producers in the model to achieve a symmetric treatment in

Unfortunately, the mathematical tractability of the analysis of value becomes very quickly extremely complicated when we start changing the assumptions of the basic model. Though new models are continuously being developed, mathematical modeling is very difficult, for instance, for industries with firms that have different levels of product differentiation and asymmetric switching costs of buyers among them, which play a significant role in strategy. Nevertheless, the core models in demand theory have certainly made important contributions to our understanding of the critical variables that affect customer's purchasing decisions, such as heterogeneity in customers' tastes.

Value in marketing

Whereas demand theory in economics has provided the basis for the analysis of economic value as a key element in the determination of prices, the field of marketing has made its main goal to understand customers and how they form their preferences among products. Often drawing from utility theory in microeconomics, it has developed much further the analysis of customer value.[7]

The notion of customer value spreads throughout the entire field of marketing, which has probed into the nature and consequences of market orientation.[8] Zeithaml (1988) identified four possible definitions of value, always from the customer's point of view: (a) low price, (b) getting what the customer wants (i.e., the subjective measure of usefulness or want satisfaction that results from consumption or utility), (c) quality received for the price paid, and (d) overall assessment of received utility in contrast to the entire sacrifice of the customer for

customers' willingness to pay and producers' willingness to buy inputs from other suppliers. Thus, we could use the suppliers' opportunity costs in the definition of the lower end in total value creation, which would be distributed in three surpluses: consumer, producer, and supplier. Though the model is certainly more comprehensive and maybe more symmetric, the same ideas and consequences for strategy can be reached using a model with only customers and producers.

[7] For a recent review of this literature see Payne and Holt (2001). More detailed analysis of how to manage customer value can be found in Gale and Wood's (1994) book.

[8] For instance, Slater and Narver (1994) argued that market orientation (comprised by customer orientation, competitor focus, and cross-functional coordination) is necessary for creating superior customer value, which presumably leads to superior business performance.

getting it, including other elements besides price.[9] Though the use of the word *value* may differ across people and contexts, it seems reasonable to adopt the broadest definition in our analysis of value. We should take explicitly into consideration the three possible elements that may go into the computation of customer value: utility, price, and non-price costs to the customer. On occasions, however, customers may regard as fixed one or more of these elements when making their assessments of value.

The marketing field has developed a variety of techniques for estimating customer preferences and product positioning in the market and the consumers' mind.[10] Customer value, satisfaction, and behavior are critical concepts in the marketing literature, though they are typically applied to specific products.[11] Marketers have shown that products and services are much more than the intrinsic attributes of what is exchanged between the firm and its customer. From a marketing point of view, the brand includes elements beyond the physical product itself, like brand associations and symbolic benefits.[12] Thus, the analysis of value should not be restricted to tangible and intangible features of the product and the organization, but also to nonprice costs of customers, like learning, transportation, installation, and any other possible customer-born costs.

We will draw from this broad conceptualization of customer value in an augmented definition of products and services. However, because strategy is concerned with the entire firm and its leadership rather than

---

[9] See Oliver's chapter in Holbrook's (1999) book for a precise analysis of the concept of value in relation to quality and satisfaction.

[10] See for instance Kotler and Amstrong (1993).

[11] An important contribution to the analysis of customer value from a marketing perspective is provided in Holbrook (1999). His author identifies eight types of customer value (efficiency, play, excellence, aesthetics, status, ethics, esteem, and spirituality) based on a structured categorization of interaction of the customer, the product, and their social surrounding ($2 \times 2 \times 2$ category). However, there are questions of its comprehensiveness and parsimony. Because it is based on a deductive process, any type of value can be included within this framework, but some types may not fit clearly in any category and the differences between some of the categories are sometimes blurred. In addition, this categorization is basically a descriptive taxonomy, but it remains silent on how customers may evaluate among the different types. Despite these limitations, this categorization provides interesting insights and it is an important step towards the difficult analysis of customer value from a marketing perspective.

[12] See Keller (2007) for an analysis of customer-based brand equity.

the product-level management that constitutes the basis of marketing, we will adjust the notion of value to all the activities performed by the overall organization, both inside the firm and in coordination with external resources that coproduce value for the customer. In addition, we will have to include in our theory the noncustomer-based sources of value associated with organizational efficiency, which have been stressed in economics and operations management, but not explicit in the marketing notion of customer value.

Value in finance

The analysis of value takes a unique perspective in the field of finance, where it is associated exclusively with shareholder value.[13] Value-based management systems typically use some discounted cash-flow technique to estimate quantitatively how much a new strategy or given decision may affect shareholder value. This set of financial tools for strategic decision making, including option pricing theory, is widely used by managers, and the most basic of them is usually included in strategic management textbooks.

Despite their usefulness as quantitative instruments, these tools have one important limitation that needs to be identified about their ability to fully capture value analysis. They are primarily concerned with what we call in this book value appropriation, but leave outside of the analysis any guidelines about how and why overall value is created in the first place. In other words, once the numbers have been computed, these techniques allow the manager to compare, rank, accept, reject, and make sound decisions about possible alternatives for action. However, the critical analysis of value comes before these numbers are plugged into the financial formulas. Financial measures of shareholder value can certainly be decomposed into more basic elements, like the traditional Du Pont formula or a more strategic balanced-score card, but financial analysis is not really intended to understand where value ultimately comes from and, for instance, why sales or costs may change as a result of a strategic decision. There are important aspects of strategic management that are not facilitated by the use of these techniques, like the analysis of customers, competitors, and resources. How the firm

---

[13] See Rappaport (1986) for a financial analysis of creating value for shareholders.

deals with them will ultimately determine their financial implications on shareholder value.

Thus, the analysis of value creation, even limited only to shareholder value appropriation, is not captured by finance theory and its instruments, which are really measurement tools. We need to probe into the underlying reasons for value creation and appropriation, that is, how the numbers that go into financial computations are developed in the first place. Once managers have a better understanding of how their firm creates value, especially for customers, financial analysis may be used for managerial evaluation and decision making.

Value in strategy

The concept of value has always been at the heart of strategic management. For instance, Porter (1996: 68) claims that: "Strategy is the creation of a unique and valuable position, involving a different set of activities." The important place of the value chain in his influential model shows how relevant the notion of customer value is for strategic analysis and, more specifically, for understanding the behavior of costs and the existing and potential sources of differentiation. Barney (1991: 106) also argues that: "Firm resources can only be a source of competitive advantage when they are valuable," which he considers a critical characteristic of strategic resources in addition to rarity, inimitability, and nonsubstitutability. He believes that resources are valuable when they enable a firm to conceive of or implement strategies that improve its efficiency and effectiveness. For resources to be valuable, they should allow the firm to exploit opportunities or neutralize threats in a firm's environment, thus going back to the resource–environment match suggested by Andrews (1971).

Though the intimate connection between business strategy and the search for customer value is well established in the strategy field,[14] it is somewhat surprising to find only scarce research on how firms create value in contrast to the abundant ideas on value

---

[14] For instance, in his widely used strategy textbook, Grant (2005) regards business in general and, more particularly, strategy as a "quest for value." See also the special Academy of Management Review issue edited by Lepak *et al.* in 2007 on value creation at the individual, organizational, and society levels of analysis.

appropriation.[15] The notions of barriers to entry, isolating mechanisms, and first-mover advantages, which generally deal with appropriation, are widely used in strategy, but strategy scholars have not
yet explored what may create value for customers and how firms
should approach decisions about value creation. Some authors have
already argued in favor of greater emphasis in value creation, particularly building from the ideas of Schumpeter and Penrose about
entrepreneurial discovery and resource combinations (Ghoshal *et al.*,
2000). Recent work in strategy has started to focus explicitly on issues
of value creation and appropriation (Brandenburger and Stuart, 1996;
Stabell and Fjeldstad, 1998; Bowman and Ambrosini, 2000; Lepak
et al., 2007), which this book attempts to develop further.

Sources of customer value creation

Based on the ideas discussed above, we can define the total value created by one firm as the utility that customers receive from consuming
the products and services provided by the firm. In economic terms,
utility (gross) is reflected in the customers' willingness to pay for the
products and services that they actually buy from the firm. One customer's *net* value can be defined as his or her willingness to pay *minus*
the total costs in making consumption possible, including both monetary costs and other nonmonetary costs that the customer also has to
bear as well as the firm's costs. Though these concepts are often very
difficult to measure with sufficient accuracy, they are conceptually very
important and essentially reflect a cost-benefit analysis.

We should note that the total value actually created by one firm
depends entirely on the perspective of its customers. It is determined by
the number of exchanges with customers that the firm is able to attract
and the value created in each exchange from the customers' perspective.
Thus, strategic decisions should have some direct or indirect impact
on the interaction of the firm with the customer and the associated
costs to be relevant for value analysis. The total created value will
be distributed among the customers (net customer value surplus) and
the firm's profits and costs. The selling price of the product and the
prices paid by the firm for its inputs determine who appropriates the

---

[15] See Barney (2001) for a discussion of value creation and appropriation in the
resource-based view.

total value that the firm has generated for the customer: the customer, the firm itself (i.e., its owners), or the resources that it assembles and acquires.[16] This distribution of value created results in the customers' surplus, producers' surplus, and resources' compensation.

Economists and marketers have studied the factors that drive customer demand for any particular product and, more generally, for the composition of the basket of products and services that customers buy. The main variables are: (a) the price of the product itself, (b) the prices of all other available products and services (with different levels of substitutability or cross-demand elasticities among them), (c) the wealth of the individual, and (d) the tastes and preferences among existing alternatives, including the option for postponed consumption through saving. In addition to prices as the critical (monetary) cost of customers, we should also include in this list the non-monetary costs that the customer needs to absorb to acquire and use the product. An important part of a firm's strategy aims at changing some of these variables so that the customers may decide to buy more from the firm's offerings and, as a result, less from other firms that provide similar or alternative products and services. As long as customers are able to choose freely, any voluntary change in the composition of an individual's basket should result in an increase in total value to be divided between the customer and the firm.

It is critical for strategic management to understand what motivates a customer to choose a particular firm's products and not others. Many of the factors that determine the general composition of the type of products that go into customers' baskets are outside the control of the firm, because it cannot influence customers' wealth and the prices of other substitute products. In fact, customers' expenditure in different types of products changes very slowly through time, driven primarily by macroeconomic influences and technological development. However, firms have relatively greater influence on the choice of brand that customers buy within a given industry, which is associated with the cross-demand elasticities among directly competing products. Customers presumably decide to allocate a certain part of their budget to a specific type of product or service, but firms compete to persuade them

---

[16] See Brandenburger and Stuart (1996) for how total value may be distributed between the firm and its resource providers based on the opportunity costs of the resources.

to buy their own brand rather than a competitor's product. From a value perspective, they have two options. On the one hand, they can try to increase the total value that the product provides, i.e., the benefits associated with consuming the product. Alternatively, they may consider these benefits as given and focus instead on reducing their total costs, including those suffered by the customers and the firm. The following sections will explore these options as alternatives for value creation.

Generic strategies for competitive advantage

In his highly influential book, Porter (1980) proposed three possible generic strategies to outperform competitors in a given industry: cost-leadership, differentiation, and focus. He believes that only in rare circumstances could a firm pursue more than one of these generic strategies. In general, only one should be pursued in order to implement it effectively with total commitment. Otherwise, the firm may easily end up being "stuck in the middle" without any source of competitive advantage and consequently obtain below average returns.

The focus strategy is built around serving a particular target market, such as a particular type of customer, a certain segment of the product line, or a reduced geographic market. It is really a decision regarding segmentation and the breadth of the target market for the firm, but not truly an alternative to the other two generic strategies. In fact, once a narrow segment is identified and targeted, the firm needs to choose either cost leadership or differentiation as the basis of its focus strategy. Thus, there are essentially two alternatives for firms to create a defendable position in an industry independently of the segmentation decision.

First, cost leadership provides the firm with clear superiority over all competitors to the extent that its lower costs create a buffer against competitive pressures on prices. The cost leader can thus enjoy above-average profitability. However, cost leadership does not seem to be as sustainable through time as differentiation and it requires continuous efforts to keep cutting costs down to prevent imitation.

Second, a differentiation strategy also allows the firm to insulate itself from competitive rivalry. By differentiating from competition along certain dimensions, firms can reduce their customers' sensitivity to price and build some brand loyalty. Above-average margins are also possible through this strategic alternative to cost leadership.

Porter stressed the potential of these generic strategies to build a defendable position within a given industry, so that firms with either advantage should be able to obtain superior performance. These two generic strategies essentially correspond to the two sources of value creation discussed in this chapter, though they are not entirely equivalent. From a value perspective, firms can compete through either enhancing the benefits received by customers (including differentiation, but also innovation) or reducing overall costs (cost leadership, but also lower nonmonetary customer costs) relative to other competitors in the industry. In contrast to the exclusive focus of Porter's model on positioning, we will analyze separately issues dealing with value creation based on cost-benefit analysis in this chapter and business-strategy decisions dealing with resource management, competitive dynamics, and market positioning later in chapter six.

Value creation through enhancing customer benefits

Customers' benefits ultimately come from using the products and services supplied by firms in their life activities for final consumers or in their own value chains for industrial customers. Products and services constitute the interface between the firm and its customers and only through them may firms create value for customers. Broadly defined, a product or service may be regarded as a collection of tangible and intangible features, each of which is evaluated by the customers with regard to their own needs and expectations.[17] However, the utility that

---

[17] For the different conceptualizations of the product, starting from the core benefits and physical attributes to its augmented definition that includes surrounding elements and its potential evolution through time, see Levitt (1986) or Kotler and Amstrong (1993). Levitt introduced the importance of the surrounding features of a product in addition to its core characteristics, which jointly comprise this augmented conceptualization of a brand used traditionally in marketing. This broad conceptualization of products and services is widely accepted in the marketing literature; for instance, Kotler and Zaltman (1971) argued that price includes money costs, opportunity costs, energy costs, and psychic costs.

a product creates varies among customers and a person may even evaluate a product differently on different occasions. This heterogeneity in customer evaluations is the basis of the segmentation and differentiation strategies that we will discuss in greater depth later on.

Products and services create value for customers through the combination of different features and the utility that they may provide to customers from their own point of view.[18] By changing the combination of the features of their offering, firms may manipulate the utility that they create for customers.[19] With regard to the features of products, there are basically three ways to create value that we can describe briefly.

Greater utility in existing product or service features

Firms may create value by manipulating existing product features along a continuum, so that the product may provide more or less utility along a given set of product characteristics. In some industries a reduced number of specific product features are the fundamental drivers of customers' evaluations and, consequently, firms often engage in strategic races to improve that specific set of features as the key dimension of competition. In these cases new value creation is essentially limited to provide a better product along a reduced number of observable attributes. For instance, we can observe this type of competition in the microprocessors industry, where AMD and Intel compete primarily in the design of microprocessors with ever-greater speed.

This is what economists call vertical differentiation strategies, where the competitive focus is placed on finding an adequate level along a dominant competitive dimension. In the case of vertical differentiation

---

[18] Marketing experts have studied in depth how this combination of features takes place to create customer value. For instance, Holbrook indicates "the *dimensions* of the market space represent those characteristics, attributes or features of brands in the product class that provide *consumer value*." Furthermore, "an *ideal point* indicates a position of *maximum consumer value* for the customer segment of interest." Holbrook (1999: 3, emphasis in the original text).

[19] Hedonic prices have been used to study customers' monetary evaluation of different product features based on market prices (Rosen, 1974). This technique basically involves breaking down a product into a set of attributes and estimating through regression analysis of a variety of products the extent to which customers value their features in monetary terms.

all customers would agree in a preference ranking of available products, though they would choose to buy products at a given level along the ranking depending primarily on their wealth and the relative preference that they give to such a product type among all products available in the market. New value for customers is created when firms find new ways to increase the effectiveness of the product along its main dimension while keeping costs constant or increasing costs less than the perceived increase in the product's utility. However, vertical differentiation is not always based on strategic races to achieve a greater level with respect to a given feature. For instance, providing a more basic product with just the essential characteristics may give it access to a larger number of customers with lower income. Thus, firms may create value through vertical differentiation, that is, managing along one dimension the level of utility provided to customers.

Different combinations of product or service features

It seems unlikely that competition along one dimension can create more additional value after a certain period of time, because further improvements in an already highly satisfied dimension may not bring much additional utility to customers. Then, customer preferences may shift towards other dimensions of competition, such as design, performance, durability, reliability, reputation, warranty, status, price, and any other possible characteristics of the firm's product or service. For instance, AMD and Intel have started to introduce other features in their microprocessors, thus focusing less on clock speed and more on the integration of their microprocessors with specific tasks, like multimedia or wireless connection. Because there is wide variation in how customers value different features, firms may also segment the market and focus only on one subset of customers. Segmentation strategies are developed over a combination of features tailored to a specific market segment. These selected features provide greater utility only to those targeted customers, so that the firm may discard less relevant features that add more cost than the utility they provide to the specific targeted customer.

Strategies for horizontal differentiation basically involve creating value by combining different features in new sets. New value can be created by finding a customer segment with somewhat unique needs and then matching the specific combination of product features to demand characteristics. Both physical and emotional features may provide a differentiation advantage to firms, which increases their customers' utility by adapting to unique needs.

New products and services

In addition to better and differentiated products, that is, vertical and horizontal differentiation respectively, firms can create new value for customers through the development of entirely new products. The main challenge for product innovation deals with its chances of commercial and financial success, apart from solving its technical difficulties. From a value perspective, innovators believe that the recombination of resources in a new manner may result in new products that create more value for customers than the existing ones. In this sense, the critical analysis for innovators is why and to what extent will customers switch their current preferences towards the new products and services.

There is an intrinsic element of uncertainty in assessing the extent to which customers may value a change in the set of available products and features. Firms typically use prior information, market research, and experts' opinions to evaluate the possible market acceptance of innovations, though it is impossible to accurately estimate how much customers would be willing to spend on a product that does not yet exist.[20] It seems that the techniques for market research for relatively minor innovations like the product improvements discussed earlier, are well developed, but more radical innovations constitute basically a bet about the market acceptance of new products, i.e., the value that they may indeed create for customers.

---

[20] The introduction of the third generation of mobile phones provides a good example of the limited use of market research in practice. Though most market research showed that consumers would not be willing to pay extra for having a 3G phone and using its greater technological possibilities associated with Broadband, phone operators still pushed this technology and paid enormous license fees in Europe. They believed that customers could not estimate how much they would value the new services until they were in place and, thus, they could not anticipate which services would be truly valuable to customers later on. To support their claim, they frequently cited the huge and fully unexpected success of SMS text messages, which was not even identified as a potential service when the second generation was introduced in the early nineties.

Value creation through reducing customers' costs

Regarding value creation, the flip side of benefits is costs. Firms can also create value by reducing customer costs as well as firm costs. With respect to the former and taking the characteristics of the product as given, it is possible to reduce the cost to customers of having access to and using the products and services that the firm offers. There are two types of customer costs that we should discuss: monetary and nonmonetary costs.

Reducing monetary costs (price)

A basic principle of neoclassical economics is that price is determined by the market's total supply and demand and, thus, firms have limited influence over it in the absence of market power. Despite the clear role of price as the main market-clearing mechanism in economics, prices are actually set by firms and they are considered one more product feature by customers.[21] Consequently, they need to be managed by firms as one additional attribute of the product. In fact, the price can actually be regarded as the most important cost that they have to bear, particularly for the less wealthy customers who give greater preference to this feature of the product. Prices can be used to attract a certain type of customer and, thus, they are manageable within the constraints imposed by market conditions and firm costs.

Price reflects how the total value is split between the firm and the customer in an exchange, but it does not strictly affect the created value, i.e., the customer's willingness to pay. This is what makes the price unique versus other product features that indeed can alter the customer's willingness to pay. Changes in prices basically shift value capture between the firm and the customer for those exchanges that actually take place in the market, but they do not change customer's utility, nor do they affect firm costs. Prices, however, affect the number of transactions and, most importantly, value appropriation. For

---

[21] See Stigler (1968) for a comparison between price and nonprice competition and the greater efficacy of the former in eliminating monopoly profits. Essentially, price competition increases output very rapidly, while nonprice competition ends up increasing output very little, alongside an increase in costs for all firms.

instance, by increasing the price independently from firm costs, the firm is essentially reducing its target market to wealthier customers and capturing a greater part of the value created for them. Aside from this effect of market segmentation, price changes do not alter customer utility and under certain circumstances the total value created for society, which is split between consumers' and producers' surpluses.[22]

Despite their limited effect on the overall customer value (gross utility), pricing strategy is not irrelevant. Firms have some discretion about the prices that they can charge particularly in the short run. They can follow different pricing strategies, for instance, in the introduction of new products. Pricing strategies like penetration or skimming pricing will result in attracting a different number of customers. The impact of these strategies on value creation can be assessed in a longitudinal analysis of the number of attracted customers and the margins from these transactions versus those that are lost as the firm increases the prices of its products.

It is important to note that the prices that firms can charge heavily depend on their costs. Economists believe that prices should be equal to production costs in the long-run equilibrium, given free entry and exit into an industry. This close link between prices and costs has been stressed by Porter, who argues that cost leadership may provide a firm with a competitive advantage, but not low prices. As a result, we will focus primarily on firm costs rather than pricing strategy, because the key way to reduce prices is through cost reductions.

Reducing nonmonetary costs

Consuming a product also requires certain nonmonetary costs on the part of the customer that have been frequently overlooked because they are not clearly part of the product itself. Beyond the tangible and intangible characteristics of a product or service, its actual consumption may be easier or harder, which can be a substantial cost

---

[22] We will discuss in chapter nine the loss in overall value for society (the deadweight loss) that occurs when firms with monopoly power raise their price and, as a result, some customers prefer not to buy the product. For the customers that actually buy the product, raising prices only shifts value to the firm, so that price changes do not change total value. For this set of customers, more value can be created only by providing greater benefits to the customers (as reflected in their willingness to pay for the product or service), by reducing customers' nonmonetary costs, or reducing firm's costs.

for customers. These nonmonetary costs result from the interaction between the customer and the product and they are often behind the switching costs of customers from one firm to another.

Nonmonetary customer costs are inherently different from any attribute embodied in the product, both tangible and intangible, though they may be indirectly manageable by the firm through product attributes. Reducing customers' costs (i.e., consumption efficiency) has recently become a major challenge for firms as an important source to create value, which has expanded the traditional focus on firm efficiency to include the customer as well.[23] As society and individuals become wealthier, these nonmonetary costs are likely to obtain greater relevance. Let us briefly discuss the main nonmonetary costs of customers that broadly deal with the stages in the entire consumption process, from having information about the product or service to its actual consumption.

Information costs

For the customer to acquire a product, he or she needs to know that it actually exists and its key features, including its price.[24] Given that customer attention is limited and the number of potentially available products is enormous, the costs of gathering information about the products available and the firms that provide them are considerable. Actually, firms engage in advertising and promotion activities to develop well-known brands, which allow economizing on customers' costs of information gathering.

In the last few decades, information has been one of the hot topics in economics, including problems of information asymmetry and search costs, for instance. Despite the advancement in the formal analysis of information issues, we still need to investigate in the strategy field how customer value can be created through the management of information about the firm and its products. This includes the analysis of advertising and firm reputation, but also the risks that customers take

---

[23] See Prahalad and Ramaswamy's (2004) discussion of value cocreation with customers.

[24] Stigler (1961) first modeled in economics the search costs of customers with regard to product prices, which vary substantially across competitors. Caves and Williamson (1985) found empirically that information costs to customers is one of the two fundamental ways to differentiate a product, in addition to product features.

about the potential performance of the products and services that they acquire and how they can be mitigated, including warranties and other informational signals.[25] A clear example of a firm trying to reduce customers' information costs is Amazon, which informs its online store customers what like-minded customers are also buying.

Accessibility

There are also costs involved for the customer actually receiving the product, including any transaction costs absorbed by the customer and other costs of accessibility. Time, in particular, has been regarded as a critical nonprice cost that represents the customer's effort in getting the product, including traveling to the location, shopping, and waiting.[26] As well as time, the act of acquiring a product may be more or less pleasant in terms of physical and emotional effort, which also affects customer value beyond the intrinsic characteristics of the product itself. For instance, companies with mass distribution channels that facilitate product accessibility to customers reduce the costs of actually getting the product, while those with specialized channels often try to generate a favorable shopping experience.

Customer access is likely to become a more important matter for firms in the future as a source of differentiation and the potential to create value for customers. Having direct and privileged access to customers increases a firm's competitiveness versus other players, which seems much more difficult to replicate than specific tangible features of a product or service.

Usability

Using a product may also impose nonprice costs to consumers, such as learning how to use it, maintaining the product in working condition, or requiring other complementary products. In particular, the level of product "user-friendliness" has become more relevant in recent decades with the emergence of more sophisticated products like computer software, and its importance in the future is likely to increase. Firms can intentionally reduce the learning costs of buyers, who otherwise may have to sacrifice too much time and effort to use and

---

[25] For instance, firm reputation has been studied by Rindova *et al.* (2005) from a more sociological perspective.

[26] See Murphy and Enis (1986) for a discussion of the different characteristics of products, including monetary and nonmonetary effort and risks as well.

master the product. As recycling becomes more widespread, the disposal of the product may also become more relevant for customers as an additional nonmonetary cost that they have to bear.

For obvious reasons, the analysis of nonmonetary costs is particularly advanced in the marketing field. For instance, Anderson and Narus (1998) stress the importance of focusing on the total costs for customers, which is critical to understanding what customers value. The management of these nonmonetary costs has been regarded as a key feature of customer orientation versus product orientation. Narver and Slater (1990) claim that customer orientation includes all the firm's activities involved in acquiring information about buyers in the target market and disseminating it throughout the business. Customer orientation is a broad marketing concept that includes understanding customer needs as well as measuring and achieving customer satisfaction. The analysis of nonmonetary customer costs is indispensable to achieve this understanding and, ultimately, create customer value.

Value creation through reducing firms' costs

Firms create value for customers by enhancing customer benefits and reducing total monetary and nonmonetary costs. Customer benefits minus the costs that they absorb result in the customers' surplus. But the total value created by the firm also includes the firm's profits or losses.[27] By reducing their production costs, firms can create value, part of which may be transferred to customers via lower prices as discussed above, while the rest would be kept by stockholders. Porter's generic strategy of cost leadership is based on trying to reduce these costs, so that the firm may use prices to attract the most price sensitive customers. Firms can create value by reducing two major types of costs:

Technology costs
The costs associated with the technology of production are reasonably transparent. They are determined by the extent of economies of

---

[27] There are different ways to compute total value created, which is ultimately equal to total benefits as valued by customers minus customers' nonmonetary costs minus firm's costs. To avoid double accounting, if we also subtract customers' monetary costs (prices), only a firm's profits or losses should be added to compute total costs based on the two main components: customer's and producer's surpluses.

scale, capacity utilization, input costs, accumulated learning, automation, product design, and many other factors directly related to the engineering aspects of actually making the product or delivering the service to customers.[28] Because of their transparency and availability of markets for technology procurement, these costs are likely to be relatively easy to replicate in most industries, though some firms may enjoy a technology headstart advantage over their competitors. Process innovation and the rapid pace of technological progress have an evident impact in continuously reducing these costs.

Administration costs

It has become clear in the last few decades that a substantial part of firms' total costs are not driven by purely technological factors, but that they result from the way that these activities are organized and carried out inside the firm. We may refer to them broadly as administration costs. The two most widely studied are agency costs and transaction costs, which were introduced in chapter two.[29] In contrast to the continuous and evident advancement of technology, these costs are much more difficult to observe and measure and, consequently, to actively manage. Therefore, there may be greater differences among firms in administration costs associated with the management of the organization than in purely technology driven costs.

The influence of externalities

Customer benefits and total costs determine how much value the firm creates through its products and services, which is distributed between the customers and the firm's resources and owners. However, they do not necessarily reflect the entire value created for society. The total value created sometimes goes beyond market exchanges. A person or firm may inflict costs or benefits to third parties, though they may not be explicitly included in the market transaction and be fully compensated. Economists broadly refer to this possibility as *externalities*. For instance, the market price of a house may be negatively affected by the construction of a polluting factory near it. But the firm that builds the

---

[28] See for instance Porter (1980) for a discussion of cost drivers.
[29] See Milgrom and Roberts (1992) for an economics approach to the internal analysis of organizations.

factory does not fully consider all the costs of its decision, in this case the decrease in value of the surrounding houses and more generally the environmental damage, so that there are some negative externalities that are not accounted for. The presence of externalities leads to a divergence between social costs and benefits (i.e., for the entire society) and private social costs and benefits (i.e., for the firm that builds the factory and its customers).

The existence of externalities is an important problem for the efficiency of markets as the basis of economic activity, which has been a critical issue in economics in the twentieth century.[30] Externalities do not always imply negative costs that take place outside market exchanges that need to be somehow controlled and eliminated. They may also have a positive effect on third parties, like the spillovers from research that may benefit many other firms beyond the one conducting it. The firm doing research suffers the entire costs of research and development, but only keeps part of the benefits that are distributed to the rest of society. To account for the positive externalities of research, patents are granted to the innovator, so that firms have an incentive to innovate if they may keep part of the benefits that they created.

A particularly important type of positive externalities on the demand side are networks effects.[31] The value of certain products may be heavily driven by who else uses a similar product, so that they may interact in some way or rely on complementary products and services. This is the case, for instance, of computer operating systems, like Microsoft Windows. Operating systems have substantial network effects because (1) the transfer of files and data is much easier between computers using the same operating system (i.e., direct externalities associated with network size and direct exchanges among network members), and (2) software is developed specifically for a given operating system (i.e., indirect externalities that make a larger network more attractive to complementary products). In industries with strong network externalities and limited interconnections among networks, there is great pressure towards consolidation and winner-takes-all competition, like the computer operating system. To a large extent this is so because the

---

[30] For an early and highly influential discussion of externalities as a result of transaction costs see Coase (1960).

[31] Katz and Shapiro (1985) analyze in detail the nature of network externalities. Shapiro and Varian (1999) provide a great analysis of this type of industry and the unique strategic challenges that they face.

value that customers obtain from an operating system actually depends on the size of the installed base of similar systems, that is, the size of the network.[32]

As we will discuss in chapter six, managing network externalities becomes essential for firms whose business is basically setting up and running a network, including firms in telecommunications, banking, and other types of mediation services. The internet has facilitated the emergence of this type of firm (such as eBay and Google), whose logic for creating customer value relies primarily on managing connections, and is subject to strong network externalities. For strategic management in network based firms, it is very important to account for the possible externalities that may affect customer value, though they are not immediately incorporated into the costs and benefits directly associated with the product or service of the firm and, by definition, remain external to the transaction with the customer. Externalities also affect the overall effect of business in society and, thus, their corporate social responsibility, which we will discuss in chapter nine.

Innovation, entrepreneurs, and new value creation

The creation of economic value constitutes the essential feature of firms, which can be obtained through different means. Cost-benefit analysis may be used to make decisions about the specific features to include in a product and to allocate the monetary and nonmonetary costs of the customer, i.e., shifting costs between the firm and the customer.[33] By managing these different sources of benefits and costs,

---

[32] This is formally referred to as *Metcalfe's Law*, which basically says that the value of a network that connects people is proportional to the square number of people in the network. The idea behind it is that the value of being part of the network depends on how many people can be accessed through it. Thus, adding one person to a network of 100 people increases the number of possible new connections by 100, as opposed to just an increase in one more possible connection. Similarly, in a network of 100 people there are 100 × 100 possible connections, or 100 × 99 if we discard the connections of people to themselves.

[33] Ikea is a good example of switching some of the traditional production costs to the customer. By shifting product assembly to the customers, the firm's costs are substantially reduced in terms of their own assembly and, particularly, transportation and storage. The final decrease in production costs and prices more than make up for the extra assembly costs suffered by the customer. This business model also saves time for the customer, who does not need to wait for products to be manufactured and delivered, as traditional furniture firms do.

firms can create new value. But for new value to be created, some improvement over the existing situation needs to take place, that is, some successful innovation must occur.

As we will analyze in greater detail in the next chapter, innovation is at the heart of new value creation; otherwise the economic activity would remain stagnant at previous levels. Both product and process innovation may result in new value creation through new features and products or lower costs. Firms have relatively greater control over process innovation and costs. In contrast, product innovation faces much greater uncertainty about the market's response to the innovation. Radical innovation in value may produce high growth by disrupting existing markets and shaping the industry beyond its traditional boundaries and recipes for success.[34]

There is abundant research on which type of organizations and practices are more successful in producing and exploiting these different ways to innovate, such as the widely accepted idea of closing possible gaps between research and development, and marketing.[35] Nevertheless, developing better ways to analyze the value that innovations may generate for customers can be considered one of the key challenges for researchers in strategy that has not yet been studied. The technology bubble of the late nineties destroyed much wealth in our society and part of it could have been avoided if firms had been more rigorous in their analysis of value creation for customers, particularly the utility that new technology based products could deliver to customers.

Despite the importance of innovation for creating new value, there are some industries in which the amount of innovation is very small and the total value created for society remains stagnant or decreases, pushed by new substitute products. For commodities, product features are fairly standardized across competitors and they change very slowly through time. Increasing efficiency becomes then the critical

---

[34] See Kim and Mauborgne (1997) for an interesting analysis of radical innovation in the way that firms create value, which underlies high growth.

[35] See the classical work of Ed Mansfield on research and development, and innovation. From a management perspective, Brown and Eisenhardt (1995) discuss the characteristics of successful product development teams, such as team composition and communication. Also, Damanpour (1991) identified the characteristics of organizations that engage in more innovation (e.g., greater specialization and less centralization) from a meta-analysis of the literature.

source of new value. Firms will suffer the traditional margin squeeze in these stagnant industries.[36] Once similar production costs also spread throughout these perfectly competitive industries, prices should basically reflect average costs and only minimal profitability exists to keep the productive resources in place. In other words, no economic profits are likely to exist in stagnant industries.

However, even in commodity industries with virtually identical product benefits and production costs among competitors, there may be differences in profitability and some innovation. Nonmonetary customer costs may determine the relative profitability and market share of commodity producers. Without the possibility to change customer benefits and production costs, reducing nonmonetary customers' costs may be the only way to achieve some limited growth in the industry by grabbing market share from competitors. For instance, commodity firms may achieve lower accessibility costs to certain types of customers by focusing on a unique distribution channel, though the product features and price may be similar to competitors.

The role of entrepreneurs in value creation

Innovation and value creation has often been linked to entrepreneurial activity, though it may also take place inside organizations. The emerging field of entrepreneurship deals primarily with the specific challenges that entrepreneurs face in setting up their businesses and their role in the economy.[37] The process of entrepreneurial discovery takes center stage in this field, particularly the alertness of the entrepreneurs to opportunity recognition and their skills to exploit these opportunities, often against the odds.[38]

It seems that entrepreneurs have some unique characteristics in contrast to managers in large organizations, and probably process information differently.[39] However, regardless of how innovation is

---

[36] For a discussion of strategies for industries in the later stages of their cycle, see Harrigan (1980).

[37] Starting with Schumpeter (1934), the study of the entrepreneur and his or her role in the economy has become an important business field (Kirzner, 1979; Shane and Venkataraman, 2000).

[38] See Alvarez and Busenitz (2001).

[39] See Busenitz and Barney (1997) and Baron and Shane (2008) for how entrepreneurs think differently to some extent.

produced and who makes it happen, the success of any innovation ultimately depends on how much value they can create for customers.[40] Though entrepreneurs have specific problems and challenges that deserve to be studied, we do not need a different theory of the firm to explain the emergence of organizations by entrepreneurs and value analysis should also be applicable in this area.

The management literature since Barnard (1938) looks at personal contributions and inducements to understand the decision of individuals to join and leave organizations. A value perspective would focus on the final effect that either option would have on the ability of an individual, including a potential entrepreneur, to create and appropriate value, either inside an existing organization or as a separate competitive unit in the market. For instance, professional managers often leave their firms and set up on their own when they are convinced of an innovation's potential that its current organization is not willing to undertake, and when they believe that they can gather the necessary resources to carry out the innovation. An example of this is Ross Perot, who left IBM to form EDS and create value in a new way. Entrepreneurs drive the engine of economic development, as Schumpeter described, but they do so in a continuous search for new ways to create value for customers.

Value analysis versus transaction costs economics (TCE) as drivers of firm boundaries

Oliver Williamson (1985: 35–7) uses the example of a mine in an isolated location to analyze the firm–employee relationship and, more specifically, whether the firm (mine owners) or the employees (miners) should own the houses and the only store in the company town. Let us analyze this hypothetical case of firm boundaries from a contracting perspective and also from a broader value approach.

Williamson's example of mines and houses

This example assumes that miners cannot travel to other geographical areas to live and to shop. It is a clear illustration of the importance

---

[40] See Amabile (1983) for an analysis of creativity from a more psychological perspective.

of asset specificity in driving transaction costs and, consequently, the most efficient contract between the firm and its employees. The highly specific investment arises from the employees moving to a remote area, getting a house, and being basically forced to buy from the only store in town. As a result of this highly specific investment by the miners and the potential opportunism by the firm, it would be reasonable for them to require a wage premium, which would be an additional cost to the firm.

Williamson argues that the most efficient contract should reduce transaction costs caused by potential opportunism. He suggests house ownership by the firm, which writes long-term leases to the employees, though it allows easy termination by the employees. The store could be efficiently owned and operated as a cooperative, though there may be other options. The boundaries of the firm are presumably determined by contracting issues.

This is a clear example of TCE's impeccable logic of the important role of transaction costs. Different possible arrangements would have different overall ex-ante and ex-post transaction costs. As suggested by Williamson, the firm's strategy to own and rent the houses probably reduces a significant part of these costs that could exist in other contractual alternatives associated with other strategies.

These arguments can be directly incorporated into a value perspective without any significant change. We would need to study the extent to which different possible firm strategies create more or less value. In this case, efficiency issues determine the optimal solution and the critical question is which organizational boundaries generate lower firm costs. Certainly transaction costs would need to be considered, including all contracting costs of writing and enforcing contracts and the possible effects of opportunism in these costs. For instance, changing house ownership will affect the motivation of the miners and the potential for opportunism for both the firm and the miners. The firm could take advantage of the miners' large specific investment in the house, the traditional hold-up problem analyzed by TCE. Once the miners own the house, the firm may be less prone to provide salary increases in future wage negotiations. Also, renting a house rather than owning it creates a problem of moral hazard in the miners' behavior, because they may not take care of the house as much as possible, which increases maintenance costs.

However, in addition to any problems associated with opportunism, production costs also need to be considered as well as the knowledge and skills of the firms that could manage the activities. Who manages the store and who retains ownership of the houses may have an impact on the actual productivity of the store operations and the maintenance of the houses, not only for transaction costs of governance alternatives, but also for differences in skills, motivation, and overall costs associated with these strategic alternatives. We would need to analyze all factors that influence the costs of operations and not just transaction costs. Regarding the store, it is important who manages it because not all organizations can achieve the same cost efficiency. It is not so much the ownership of the store (employees or the firm) that drives overall efficiency, but the skills of the managers in charge of the store and the set of available firm resources. For instance, an outsourced firm could draw on its knowledge in managing this type of store in other similar locations, thus reducing its operational costs. In other words, the value that one resource (i.e., the store) may generate depends on the other resources that comprise the firm (i.e., its knowledge gathered through the management of other stores). Similarly, a single cooperative for just one mine or a small mining firm would not have as much bargaining power with the store suppliers as a larger specialized firm (outsourcing) or a large mining firm with other stores, which also affects the costs of operations.

Quite likely, the firm will just estimate the possible costs of running the store operations through a cooperative, through a license (outsource), and through internal management, and it will choose the lowest possible total costs, because any possible cost inefficiency of these operations would eventually be suffered by the firm via higher salaries for the miners. In addition to any possible transaction costs, the costs of operations do matter and the relative efficiency of each strategic alternative, including the costs associated with different governance structures, will have some impact on the final solution.

To the contrary, it could be claimed that once all the possible differences in productivity in managing the store are taken into account, the best possible solution should take place (i.e., the activities should be carried out such that the production costs are minimized) and the final solution of who owns the store is just a contracting issue. However, this argument does not prove that the boundaries of the firm are driven necessarily by contracting issues. Using the same type of logic, we could claim that once all different transaction costs are considered (or equivalently transaction costs are equal across different governance structures), it is just firm's costs that determine who should manage the store (i.e., the miners, an outsourced licensee, or the firm) and actual ownership would become irrelevant for strategy purposes, because the strategic direction of the store is set by the group of managers that can achieve the lowest cost of operations. As discussed in chapter two, in both cases the firm boundaries are established by assumption. We should keep in mind that in our field we are interested in who actually manages and dictates the store's strategy, rather than stock ownership (the employees, the firm, or another outsourced firm). The final solution depends on the relative efficiency of different specific firms as responsible for store management, in addition to any transaction costs created by governance structure. Furthermore, even the transaction costs of different governance structures are likely to depend on the specific mining firm that decides to choose between doing an activity internally or outsourcing it externally, as some firms may become better at managing transactions.

It would even be a mistake to conclude from this example that operations and transaction costs fully explain the boundaries of the firm in all cases. In this example, the strategic alternatives are all related to reducing firm costs as the only source of value creation, because the utility of firm customers (i.e., the buyers of the extracted mineral) is not likely to be affected by the ownership of the houses or the store. The final product is a commodity that allows no possibility of differentiation, innovation, or managing nonmonetary costs of customers. Customer value in this case is determined by the quality of the mineral and its price. Strategic decisions for this firm, including the ownership of the houses and the store, are thus limited to reducing firm costs, both administrative and operational. We only need to study the firm's costs as the single potential source of value creation in this example, but in other situations there will usually be more strategic options to compete for the firm than increasing efficiency.

We should keep in mind that, though this example may be good to focus on transaction costs and this is probably why Williamson chose it, this hypothetical case does not allow us to study the effect of firm boundaries on dynamically facilitating innovation and differentiation and reducing nonmonetary customer costs. If the decision about house ownership could somehow affect the quality of the extracted mineral, say, through its effect on employee motivation, we would need to consider its effect on market positioning in the analysis of comparative strategies. Similarly, these decisions would be much more complex and move beyond cost efficiency if the firm also tried to create value through the land development of the entire geographical area. Transaction costs are just one subset of firm costs, which in turn are also one alternative for firms to create value.

5 | *The appropriation of value by firms*

Where do profits come from?

We have stressed value creation as the main reason for firms to exist in the previous chapter. However, firms do not engage in business for the sake of value creation for their customers, but generally as the necessary condition to grow and obtain larger profits that they appropriate for their resources and owners. While value creation is, therefore, a precondition to value capture, it is the latter that firms ultimately pursue. We will now analyze how firms appropriate value.

It has been widely accepted since Adam Smith that the self-interest of two parties drives any voluntary economic exchange between them. The total value created in an exchange with a firm is divided between the customer and the producer's internal and external resources. Presumably, it is the search for producer's surplus (i.e., profits) that motivates the firm's managers in their business decisions. Profit maximization has become one of the cornerstones of economics, though it has received numerous criticisms regarding the extent to which it realistically describes firm behavior.[1] Despite its centrality in economics, there is no agreement about the origin of profits, which have frequently been considered a nuisance for economic theory in the models of general equilibrium. In this section, let us briefly discuss the three most prominent approaches to profit theory in economics.[2] In the rest of the chapter we will build on these ideas to understand the emergence and sustainability of profits from a strategy perspective.

---

[1] Herbert Simon (1957, 1982) has probably become the most influential critic of the central assumption of profit maximization in economics with his notion of bounded rationality and satisficing rather than optimizing decisions. His initial views were further developed into the behavioral theory of the firm.

[2] Mark Obrinsky (1983) provides an excellent review of the historical development of profit theory in economics.

Profits as a residual income in neoclassical economics

Profits occupy a central role in our market economy and in the fields of economics and business management. The presence of profits and losses signals possible improvements in the allocation of resources. Entrepreneurs and firms are attracted towards high profits, which expand supply in the more profitable industries until market prices are driven down presumably to marginal costs, the point at which no further new entry should occur. Under the assumptions of perfect competition, firm entry and exit eventually results in an equilibrium situation where no profits or losses remain. In this situation of general equilibrium, the different factors of production (traditionally land, capital, and labor) get compensated at the marginal product (rent, interest, and wages, respectively).[3] These inputs into the production process basically get what they contribute and there should be no residual left, that is, no extra profits should exist for firm owners but only "normal" profits (compensation for internal capital analogous to interest on external capital). This model from orthodox neoclassical theory in economics does not get us too far in the understanding of profits. The Walrasian general equilibrium models that are currently dominant in economics disregard the issue of profits entirely. Assuming the possibility for firms to enter profitable industries and leave unprofitable ones, profits are considered an elusive goal that cannot be maintained in the long run. Only a minimum level of profits to attract entrepreneurs to set up the productive activities of the firm seems possible and necessary and it should be added to the cost of goods, so that economic profits (net of this compensation to the owners of the firm) can be entirely disregarded. If we still observe profits in the real world, many economists believe that they are possibly due to the dynamic nature of the economy, which produces profits as a temporary phenomenon that results from changing from one static equilibrium situation to another.[4]

Despite the clear logic in these profitless models, firm profits or losses are ubiquitous in our economy and we need a better understanding of what causes them and why they continue to exist even in the long run.

[3] This is one of the key features of the Walrasian models of general equilibrium and the cornerstone of neoclassical distribution theory.
[4] This is basically the orthodox neoclassical explanation of Clark in the early twentieth century.

The field of strategy is entirely built on the belief that firms' strategic decisions in the market to a large extent determine their profits, which thus can be manipulated to some extent. The existence of profits has remained a puzzle for economists, who have been forced to develop a theory of profits somewhat reluctantly. The only well-analyzed situation for profits to exist is due to the presence of some level of monopoly power, i.e., the possibility for the firm to influence prices and raise them above the competitive level of zero profits. When single firms face a downward sloping demand curve, they may reduce output to increase prices above marginal costs and generate profits. Besides a transfer of value from customers to producers, this situation results in an absolute decrease in the total value created (i.e., the deadweight loss) in comparison to the no profit situation.[5] In a monopoly situation firms could produce more and sell it at a market price greater than their marginal costs, but they choose not to do so to increase prices and maximize total profits. Thus, profits can occur as a consequence of monopoly power, which signals a deviation from perfect competition and the optimal allocation of resources.[6] From this perspective, profits are residual income over the appropriate compensation to production factors that should quickly evaporate in the absence of monopoly power.

Though monopoly power will play a key role in the understanding of profits, there are some limitations with this approach that need to be acknowledged. First, it does not seem fully accurate to attribute the *emergence* of profits to restrictions to competition, i.e., monopoly power, which intuitively seem to be an issue of profit *sustainability*. Since the work of Cournot in the nineteenth century, it has been widely accepted that greater competition would put pressure on prices (via increasing total industry output) so that profits should decrease as the number of players grows and eventually disappear for a competitive market with an infinite number of players. As we will discuss later on, limited competition is the essential requirement for profits to be maintained, but it does not explain how and why profits are created in the

---

[5] In chapter nine, Figure 3, we will analyze the deadweight loss that results from monopoly power.

[6] However, in the models of monopolistic competition free entry and exit are allowed, even though firms still have some monopoly power. In these models, firms sell a differentiated product and face a downward sloping demand that allows them to set the market price, but there is no economic profit left. See the seminal work of Chamberlin (1933) or Robinson (1933).

first place. We should explain the emergence of a firm whose revenues are substantially greater than its costs, rather than take for granted its existence and study only its capability to raise prices, presumably driven by lack of competition. We will have to analyze the conditions for new firms to create value and capture some profits, at least until new competitors drive prices and profits down.

Second, profits certainly exist and they should not just be assumed away or consented as merely temporary disturbance. Abundant empirical research has shown that substantial profits (including some "rent" or economic profits) are maintained over long periods of time. For instance, Jacobsen (1988) has shown that profits tend to converge through time, but they do so very slowly. This process is moderated by the strategy followed by the firm (e.g., increasing vertical integration, market share, and marketing expenditures to reduce profit convergence), though surprisingly industry concentration does not seem to affect the persistence of return on investment (ROI) over time in this study. Thus, we have to look outside neoclassical economics and monopoly power for a more complete understanding of profits.

Profits as implicit compensation to factors of production

Other alternative explanations do not consider profits as the residual income that remains after all the factors of production have received their compensation, which should quickly disappear. Instead, they search for reasons why some factors of production may be compensated at a different rate than their marginal product, so that some factors may get more and others less of what they contribute. For instance, Marxist authors argue that profits result basically from the exploitation of labor, which receives lower wages than it should and, in turn, capital providers get the surplus from the alienation of workers from the production process in capitalist societies.[7] A more current approach that shares some similarities with the Marxist class struggle considers profits as the result of bargaining among different firm

---

[7] Marx reformulates Ricardo's labor theory of value, which basically claims that the price of any commodity results from the labor that goes into its production. If labor gets fully compensated, rather than getting subsistence wages, the possibility for profits entirely disappears. For a discussion of value and profits from this perspective, see Maurice Dobb (1973).

stakeholders.[8] From this perspective, the final distribution among the different stakeholders that participate somehow in the market process depends on the bargaining power of each one of the groups, including suppliers, labor, owners, managers, complementors, and customers.

It should be noted that profits are exclusively an issue of distribution for these perspectives based on exploitation or bargaining power. The main question is how to share the value created by the firm in the market. However, if profits are only a distribution issue, the search for profits should not create wealth and it should merely alter how it is allocated among stakeholders. Relative bargaining power probably plays some role on resources' compensation, but it is unlikely that profits and losses would only result from the relative power of different stakeholders without any underlying connection to the overall value created by the firm's strategy. Bargaining among resource providers can only take place after these resources come together to create value jointly. We will have to analyze what may trigger this process of integration.

Taking into consideration the possibility for factors to move, it seems unreasonable to believe that undercompensated factors will remain for a long time as part of a firm and market forces should drive their compensation towards their marginal product. The existence of profits (or losses) signals something that cannot be fully explained by the relative strength of the different firm stakeholders, particularly in a dynamic analysis of the emergence and sustainability of profits.

Profits as retribution to the entrepreneur

Finally, to close our brief review of profit theory in economics, we should discuss profits as the retribution to the entrepreneur, who may be regarded as an additional factor of production or just as a special contributor of labor and capital.[9] Profits may be the compensation

---

[8] See Coff (1999) for modern sophisticated analysis of competitive advantage, compensation, and bargaining power.

[9] For instance, Marshall regards profits as an additional productive factor that earns profit, just like labor earns wages. In contrast, Walras believes that "in a state of equilibrium in production, entrepreneurs make neither profit, nor loss. They make their living not as entrepreneurs, but as land-owners, laborers, or capitalists in their own or other businesses" (Walras, 1954, quoted in Obrinsky, 1983).

for the activities of coordination and supervision that the entrepreneur carries out as well as the capital that he or she may provide to the firm. These activities would need to be properly compensated to motivate the entrepreneur to gather the necessary factors of production and to ultimately assume the risk of the business. Thus, profits become the implicit wage and interest that the entrepreneur receives from his or her contribution to the firm. In contrast to the contractual relationship with the traditional factors of production, entrepreneurs receive whatever is left after all other factors of production have been compensated.

This entrepreneurial approach to profits, both as an additional factor of production and as implicit labor and capital, also has several limitations that, at the very least, require further elaboration. First, it is worthwhile to note that it is often very difficult to identify who is the entrepreneur in modern firms. Certainly, we could divide this hypothetical figure into managers and stockholders for large corporations, the former typically receiving a salary plus some share of the profits, while the latter is entitled to the remaining profits. However, the main problem is that it is not clear what exactly they are contributing that presumably generates profits. For instance, why are stockholders entitled to firm profits when they only contributed capital, but their compensation is so different and substantially greater than external capital providers that obtain interest? Entrepreneurial risk bearing may be regarded as part of the answer, but it does not seem to be a sufficient explanation because firms with the highest performance do not show significantly higher risk.[10] Empirical research has shown very wide dispersion in firm performance within industries and their convergence through time, despite facing a similar level of environmental risk.[11] More in-depth analysis of risk and uncertainty seems necessary to understand the origin of profits, though it is not likely that it will provide a fully convincing explanation of profit as compensation for entrepreneurial activities.

---

[10] See Mueller (1986). Jacobsen (1988) has also shown that unsystematic returns (i.e., after removing market returns) converge very slowly through time, in fact more slowly than total returns.

[11] See Cubbin and Geroski (1987: 440), who show that "the systematic persistence of profitability that we observe arises primarily from persistence in the firm specific component of above average profits rather than from the industry specific component."

An alternative explanation to entrepreneurial risk bearing has been proposed by Schumpeter (1934), who stressed the role of the entrepreneur in the economic development of society through innovation. For Schumpeter, entrepreneurs continuously look for new combinations of available resources at a given time, which disrupts any possible market equilibrium. Similar to the traditional neoclassical models, imitation by competitors would make any profits quickly disappear. In an iterative process, the introduction of new innovations by entrepreneurs would trigger further development that is compensated by profits, which remain temporary in nature until other innovations again change market conditions. Economic development and profits go hand-in-hand, both driven by entrepreneurial discovery. It is the active involvement of entrepreneurs in disrupting the market that generates profits, rather than external shocks that move the equilibrium from one situation to another. Thus, profits are a temporary phenomenon driven by entrepreneurial innovation.

Profit theory in economics has identified the main variables that could be useful for understanding value appropriation in strategic management, including limited competition, uncertainty, and innovation through new resource combinations. These ideas form the building blocks for a strategic theory of profits that we will develop in the remainder of this chapter.

Contextual conditions for profits

Strategy scholars and particularly the resource-based view (RBV) have analyzed how superior profitability may emerge and be sustained. For instance, Peteraf (1993) has provided a clear analysis of the conditions that allow a firm to obtain a competitive advantage and greater profitability. According to her model, some degree of resource heterogeneity needs to exist across firms so that they may obtain different types of rents. For these rents to be sustainable within the firm, the resources on which they rely need to be imperfectly mobile across firms. Furthermore, there needs to exist ex-post limits to competition (i.e., isolating mechanisms like traditional barriers to entry), so that these rents do not disappear through imitation; in addition, ex-ante limits to competition should also exist for these rents not to be competed away in the market for acquiring superior resources or a better position.

However, the conditions for the existence of profits should not be confused with the limits to competition (i.e., monopoly power) that make possible their sustainability through time. One issue is why profits emerge and another is how they can be sustained. In this section we will first discuss the contextual conditions for profits to emerge drawing from the literature discussed above. There are three critical conditions that may result in economic profits for firms: uncertainty, innovation, and specificity. These three conditions have to be present to some extent for profits to emerge; otherwise, the resources that comprise the firm would fully capture and divide among themselves the value that they create for customers, so that there would not be a residual left for the owners of the firm. Later on, we will study what firms can do to generate profits, given the presence of some environmental uncertainty and the potential to innovate through the combination of specific resources. Finally, we will discuss how different types of competitive barriers may prevent profits from eventually disappearing through time.

Uncertainty

Uncertainty is an important contextual requirement for profits to emerge. In a world of certainty there is perfect knowledge for every person, who could foresee without error the future and all the direct and indirect consequences of his or her actions. In this situation it is easy to measure precisely the contribution of all factors of production and no residual income or losses may exist, as long as they can freely move.

To investigate the effect of uncertainty on profits, we should note the distinction made by Knight (1921) between risk, which is measurable in advance and potentially insurable, and uncertainty, which is associated with insufficient knowledge of a decision's outcome to make any probability estimate at all. While the former can be included in the total costs of the firm and poses no real problem for the economist's notion of equilibrium, uncertainty limits mathematical tractability and it ultimately makes possible the emergence of profits and losses. Given the existence of uncertainty, compensation to productive factors would only very rarely be exactly equal to the actually generated revenues and, thus, profits and losses emerge at least in the short run while the limited information persists.

For Knight, there are basically two sources of uncertainty: production and demand. On the one hand, the production process involves some uncertainty because production is not an instantaneous decision and it is subject to some unpredictable factors that change through time. On the other hand, future demand cannot be estimated with certainty. This second source of uncertainty is particularly important, because the firm has very limited possibility to manage it. The managers' responsibility to forecast customers' wants cannot be insured, which leads to a natural specialization in managerial work: those individuals with greater ability to deal with uncertainty will assume managerial positions responsible for entrepreneurial decisions. The ability of these managers to deal with uncertainty should determine the size of firm profits from this Knightian perspective.

Profits may arise because people possess different beliefs driven by intuition or private information about the prices at which resources can be obtained and final products can be demanded.[12] Also stressing uncertainty, Kirzner (1997) studied how entrepreneurial discovery pushes back the boundaries of sheer ignorance (i.e., not knowing what you do not know) primarily by trial and error, which involves an element of surprise. Uncertainty makes possible that some firms may obtain higher unexpected returns just due to pure luck[13] and it is the ultimate reason behind causal ambiguity and uncertain imitability.[14] Some amount of uncertainty needs to exist for profits to be possible.

Innovation

Profits have also been attributed to innovation as the main driver for profits that moves firms away from a stagnant and profitless situation. Economists give the label "perfect competition" in a somewhat misleading way to those situations where there are no differences in product characteristics and costs among firms, and there is free entry into the market. If all products and costs are the same, then the situation becomes stagnant with every firm getting a similar market share

---

[12] See Shane and Venkataraman (2000) for the analysis of entrepreneurial opportunities.

[13] See Barney (1986) about the role of luck and expectations in obtaining superior performance.

[14] See Lippman and Rumelt (1982).

and zero profit, so that new firms are not attracted to enter the market. As Austrian economists have argued, this unattractive world in equilibrium provides a dead end to competitive improvements and entrepreneurial discovery that results in a large but stagnant consumers' surplus.[15] Everything that firms do is aimed at moving them away from this profitless scenario. To avoid this situation, innovation is the oil of our economic system that keeps it continuously running in search of greater value for customers.

The analysis of innovation was triggered by Schumpeter and Austrian economists, who focused on the critical role of the entrepreneur in introducing innovations to the market. For them, innovation is essentially the recombination of existing resources in novel ways through a process of creative destruction that renders obsolete previous ways to manage resources. The innovation process is driven by the natural alertness of the entrepreneur to possible opportunities, midway between deliberate search and pure luck. For instance, Kirzner (1997: 70) argued that "These opportunities are created by earlier entrepreneurial errors which have resulted in shortages, surplus, misallocated resources," stressing the active hand of the entrepreneur in economic dynamics.

The possible avenues towards innovation are very diverse. Schumpeter (1934) identified five types of change that lead to economic development, including new goods, new markets, new production methods, new sources of raw materials, and new types of organization. Drucker (1985) described three types of opportunities for product markets: the creation of new information/technologies, the exploitation of market inefficiencies, and the reaction to shifts in relative costs and benefits of alternative resources. More recently, Kim and Mauborgne (1997) have analyzed radical value innovations by firms that challenge an industry's conditions and look for total solutions for customers.

Though inherently difficult and risky, it is always possible to disrupt the market and innovate. The perception that everything has already been invented was already popular in the late nineteenth century and it was obviously wrong, though not all areas are equally susceptible to innovation. The alternatives for innovation are ultimately associated with the possibilities for value creation that were described in the

---

[15] See for instance Kirzner's (1997) criticism to the mainstream notion of equilibrium and his analysis of entrepreneurial discovery.

previous chapter: (a) introducing differentiated, better, or totally new products; and (b) reducing total costs for producers and customers. Only through innovation can new value be ultimately created and, thus, value-creating innovation is another antecedent of profits.

Innovation is a contextual condition that is closely associated with some types of profits, but it is not its only explanation. In other words, profits are not merely compensation for innovation and they do not always go to the innovator, even though the search for profit may drive the process of entrepreneurial discovery. In this sense, Teece (1987) has argued that profits from technological innovation may go to those firms that own complementary resources to exploit the innovation, rather than the innovator as such. First-mover advantages certainly exist for many innovators, but late-mover advantages could actually be greater in many cases.[16] However, innovation is a necessary contextual requirement for profits to arise, regardless of who keeps its benefits, e.g., the innovator, the followers, some complementors, or the customers.

Specificity

There is one additional contextual condition for profits to emerge that often remains implied, but we should make explicit and study its implications for value. It is heterogeneity of resources and the value that they may create. Drawing from Penrose, RBV scholars Barney (1991) and Peteraf (1993) stressed that competitive advantage for some firms cannot exist if there is homogeneity across the resources that comprise firms: heterogeneous and rare resources are required for a firm to enjoy superior performance. They claim that there cannot be differences in performance without some heterogeneity across firms and the resources that they comprise.

However, the key point is not that firms and resources are heterogeneous in their nature, but their heterogeneous potential to create value. Even if we assume that all firms are indeed different because they comprise different sets of resources, their performance would not be different if these resources are fully compensated at their contribution to firm value. For a residual profit to exist, the resources must be

---

[16] See Lieberman and Montgomery (1988) for a review of first-mover advantages and disadvantages.

able to contribute more to value creation than they are compensated for. Given that there is an externally driven market value for resources and their compensation, profits or losses would emerge if they do not make exactly the same contribution across firms.[17] This can happen because there is uncertainty and innovation as explained earlier, but also when the actual value that a resource creates is specific to the bundle of resources in which it is included, i.e., the firm strategy. In other words, profits may arise when the value created by resources actually depends on which other resources are used as well. For instance, a brilliant expert in heart surgery cannot create much value in a poorly endowed hospital, and far less working on a farm. Some specific hospitals may be able to help the surgeon generate more value than the market salary he or she demands and in that case the hospital can generate some profit.

Barney (1986) and Peteraf (1993) had noted that a competitive fight among firms to acquire strategic resources could bid up their prices so much that the benefits of their possession to the firm could be fully offset by their costs. Ex-ante limits to competition for acquiring these resources must exist, which create imperfections in strategic market factors, so that some profits can be kept by the firm and not by the resource owners. In our example, hospitals could bid up the surgeon's salary to attract him or her to their organizations. However, if there is some value specificity, not every hospital can offer equally high salaries to the doctor. The hospital in which the doctor can create most value (because of the other resources that it has available) should be able to pay a higher salary and even keep part of the extra value added generated by the surgeon's expertise for itself.

Thus, to the extent that different combinations of resources can create different value, we may observe that there are better or worse combinations. Without value specificity resources would always create the same marginal value and they will probably obtain full compensation. To the contrary, different levels of profits can be achieved depending on which specific resources are gathered within the firm strategy and the appropriability regime of the generated value, which is distributed between the resource owners and the firm.

---

[17] If we assume that resources are compensated at their opportunity cost, i.e., the marginal value created in the next best possible use of the resource, some profits will be kept by the firm as long as the resource's contribution to the firm is larger than the contribution it could do in its second use.

The profit-earning potential of resources

Grant (2005) develops further the traditional analysis of resources in the RBV of the firm and discusses the potential of resources to generate economic profits. He argues that the profit-earning potential of resources is determined by its characteristics, which can be summarized in the following analysis.

a) The extent of competitive advantage from the resource.
  - Relevance: they must be linked to the key success factors, so that they can assist the firm in creating value or surviving competition.
  - Scarcity: to be able to generate economic profits (rents or profits above the minimum required to compensate internal capital providers), the resource must not be widely available for all competitors.

b) Its sustainability through time.
  - Durability: long-lived resources like reputation can be sustained through time, as opposed to temporary technological advantages, for instance.
  - Transferability: resources that are more difficult to move and transfer between firms, e.g., through acquisitions, are more sustainable.
  - Replicability: they should also be difficult to replicate or be fully substituted for by an alternative resource.

c) Its appropriability by the firm.
  - Property rights: when ownership is not well defined, the returns from a resource may not be entirely appropriated by its provider and be kept by the firm.
  - Social embeddedness: resource providers that are socially embedded may also be less likely to obtain their marginal contribution, such as specialized human resources that interact and work together in complex settings.
  - Relative bargaining: in these cases of weak property rights and high social embeddedness, relative bargaining will determine who keeps the extra returns from the resource, its owner or the firm.

This model is quite similar to those of Barney (1991) and Peteraf (1993), but expands the analysis of resources beyond value and uniqueness as bases for sustainable competitive advantage. Grant's model explicitly identifies and places greater emphasis on the appropriability of the returns by the resource owner as opposed to the firm, which is only partially discussed in Peteraf's (1993) ex-ante limits to competition. However, just like in the other models, the analysis of resource value remains underdeveloped and this model still focuses in uniqueness, sustainability and appropriability rather than the resource's actual value creation.

Profit generation through resource combinations

The three contextual conditions make possible the emergence of profits. However, only uncertainty can be regarded as the strictly necessary assumption for profitability. Only in an uncertain world with some things yet unknown can there be recombination of existing resources and innovation, so that uncertainty is a prerequisite for both conditions and sufficient on its own for profits to exist. Similarly, there would be no innovation, uncertainty, nor profits, if no matter how resources are combined they created the same value; it is actually value specificity that allows innovation through new resource combinations, which also requires some uncertainty in parallel.

These contextual conditions are not all equally important across firms and circumstances. Different firm strategies may build on each of these three sources of profitability and they could lead to different types of profitability with increasing levels of complexity and even sustainability.

The most basic type of profits can be associated primarily with exploiting uncertainty. As we discussed earlier, even very simple combinations of resources may result in profits or losses when there is some uncertainty about the value that they may create. Such uncertainty may result accidentally from purely external shocks or be actively brought on by entrepreneurial actions. In this sense Barney (1986) stressed the role of luck in obtaining superior returns as well as the possession of private information about the returns that resources may generate. He also argued against environmental analysis based on publicly available information, which would ultimately be incorporated in the market price of resources.

Uncertainty driven profits explain the temporary existence of profits and losses for specific firms, but not the existence of either one on the aggregate. In other words, there is no reason to believe that future expectations about the contributions of resources are biased in an optimistic or pessimistic direction, so that on the aggregate there will be no profits or losses if the expectations are correct on average. Knight believes that the number of entrepreneurs should determine whether there would be profits or losses in the aggregate. He argues that if there are few entrepreneurs or, equivalently, if they consistently underestimate the prospect of their business, then we should observe more profits than losses on the aggregate because all opportunities for business would not be exhausted. However, aggregate losses could also be possible. In either case, it is how people deal with uncertainty and their proficiency in doing so that generates this type of profits for a specific entrepreneur.

In addition to uncertainty profits, value specificity associated with resource heterogeneity may also produce profit differentials. The value specificity of resources makes it even more difficult that resource providers will be able to obtain as compensation their marginal contribution to the firm. When this marginal contribution changes depending on the presence of other bundled resources, there is no fixed market price for a resource but a distribution of prices that it may get in different firms. Thus, for those resources with higher value specificity, there is greater potential that a firm can attract a collection of synergistic resources that reinforce each other's value creation potential. This extra value added will be divided between the resource owners and the firm, which controls access to the rest of the resources. Most likely, this bargaining about the appropriation of the specific value will result in a substantial profit for the firm and the rest will be kept as extra compensation for the resource owners slightly above their next best opportunity available to them. Thus, the firm that can gather the most effective combination of value-creating resources will be able to obtain greater profits.

As long as a firm is able to gather cospecialized resources and bundle them together, it should be able to extract some profits because of the greater value that they can generate. However, profits should decrease when value specificity is reduced and the resources become commoditized in terms of generating similar marginal value across firms. In that case, their compensation will become standard in line with its market value and specificity profits would disappear.

Finally, there is a third mechanism for resources to be bundled within a firm, but their value to not be appropriated by the initial resource providers. As we discussed earlier, firms may innovate and look not only for new ways to combine resources (i.e., specificity profits based on Schumpeterian entrepreneurship), but develop entirely new resources that are added to the pool of initial resources that comprise the firm. Different combinations of resources generate through time new resources that are separable from the initial set of inputs that went into their creation, like brand name and organizational capabilities. These are firm-level resources, the development of which requires substantial innovation beyond the mere recombination of existing resources.

RBV scholars Dierickx and Cool (1989) have explained how firms accumulate asset stocks through time. Some of these assets are non-tradable because of their idiosyncratic and socially complex nature. These are the critical strategic assets responsible for these types of profits. They are developed slowly through time and this process of accumulation is facilitated by the possession of an initial large stock of complementary assets. In addition to their value creating potential, the key feature for these strategic assets to generate profits is that they need to reside at the firm level, so that their returns are kept by the firm's owners and not by any resource providers.

These three types of profits rely on an increasing level of complexity in how resources are combined within the firm strategy and the value that they create. Uncertainty profits are the most simple because they are based primarily on not knowing the value that a given recombination of resources can eventually produce, which makes it the necessary and sufficient condition for profitability. Specificity profits add greater complexity because they are built on gathering within one firm strategy specific resources with synergistic effects on the value that they create at a given moment in time. Finally, organizational innovation profits are probably the most complex because they rely not just on the recombination of existing resources, but on the creation of entirely new firm-level resources, such as new technologies developed by the entire firm, the value of which can change through time.

The sustainability of profits through barriers to competition

One of the key ideas in economics since its early days is that competition should drive profits down as new firms enter an industry in the search for economic profits. Any extra returns to a firm's bundle of resources above the compensation that they require should eventually disappear. However, empirical research shows that indeed profits tend to disappear over the long term, but they do so at quite a slow pace. For instance, Mueller (1986) has shown that, though there is evidence of slow convergence towards the mean, there is a relatively stable ranking of firms in subgroups through time and the sustained differences in profitability across firms do not result from different levels of risk or industry membership.[18] More important for strategy, Jacobsen (1988) has provided empirical evidence that firms can actually influence the level of profits and their sustainability through their strategic choices, including vertical integration and marketing expenditure. Despite the tendency for profits to disappear over the long run that classical economists predict, profit differentials among firms do exist for long periods of time driven by the strategies that firms follow.

To be able to sustain superior profitability, there must be some barriers to competition that prevent existing and potential competitors from gathering a similar set of resources and, thus, replicate the firm's strategy. Barriers to competition are the key necessary condition for profits to be sustained. They were first studied at the industry level as barriers to entry (Bain, 1956), later on at the level of strategic group as mobility barriers (Caves and Porter, 1977), and finally at the firm resource level as isolating mechanisms (Rumelt, 1984).[19]

Though there is a divergence of opinions about what exactly constitutes a barrier to entry,[20] most definitions revolve around two ideas: (a) any factor that makes new entry into an industry difficult, and (b) higher relative costs for incumbents than for possible new entrants.[21] This second conceptualization provides a more strict definition over the first one, leaving out capital requirements, for instance, if both incumbents and newcomers have to face the same capital investments but at different moments. From our perspective, any resource that gives the firm the potential to provide greater customer benefits may also be regarded as a barrier to entry as long as newcomers cannot replicate

[18] See also Cubbin and Geroski (1987).
[19] For a review of the economic literature about barriers to entry, see Geroski *et al.* (1990).
[20] See Demsetz (1982).
[21] For instance, Bain (1956) stressed that barriers to competition allowed firms to enjoy superior profitability "without inducing potential entrants to enter the industry," while Besanko *et al.* (2004: 301) define it as "those factors that allow incumbent firms to earn positive economic profits, while making it unprofitable for newcomers to enter the industry."

it effectively. This broader definition includes any defendable resource that generates enhanced customer benefits to the incumbent and not just lower costs. For instance, any first-mover advantages may become effective barriers to competition, even though they may not represent higher costs for newcomers, like a research and development headstart or a better location.

Potential barriers to entry are very diverse. Bain initially identified three types of barrier: lower costs of incumbents associated with size (i.e., economies of scale), absolute cost advantages independent of scale (e.g., access to raw materials), and differentiation. Porter later specifically identified capital requirements, customers' switching costs to another supplier, access to distribution channels, and government regulation; he also included incumbent retaliation and limit pricing as strategic behavior that reduces potential new entry. Similarly, RBV scholars like Peteraf (1993) have stressed ex-post limits to competition, like imperfect imitability or substitutability of resources.

To analyze their impact on the sustainability of profits, we can group barriers to competition into three categories according to their effectiveness in preventing new entry, which depends on the extent to which the underlying resources can be more or less easily replicated by newcomers.

Barriers with perfect replicability

New entry typically needs to face initial investments and overcome hurdles that incumbents have already handled. These barriers include investment in fixed assets, licenses, and any kind of start-up costs to create a similar position in the market. In contrast to newcomers, incumbent firms do not have to face these costs, which are sunk for them. All firms have to obtain the same resources at the same costs, though they may do so at different moments in time. Marshall referred to them as quasi-rents, which give superior profitability to incumbents, though not in the long run; incumbents and newcomers would have similar performance in the long term.

Though they make entry more difficult than without their presence, high barriers with perfect replicability are not very effective in sustaining high profitability as financial resources are channeled eventually towards their most attractive use. In this case, incumbents do not have superior resources well protected from replication and any superior profitability is likely to be temporary. The type of barrier with perfect replicability is usually behind the simple resource combinations that generate uncertainty profits. The profits and losses associated with uncertainty should decrease as time goes by and the uncertainty is reduced, so that they are primarily a timing phenomenon.

Barriers with asymmetric replicability

For barriers to be really effective, they must have an asymmetric effect on incumbents and newcomers. Gathering the same resources should have been somehow easier (e.g., lower costs) for incumbents than for new entrants. For instance, with regard to start-up costs, newcomers would need to face higher costs than incumbents when they started. Otherwise, it is just a question of different timing without truly affecting the relative competitive advantage of new and existing firms in the industry. Similarly, product differentiation is an effective barrier only if newcomers can develop such a differentiation (e.g., based on advertising) with substantially greater costs than incumbents had to suffer, for instance, requiring more advertising expenditure to build a similar level of customer awareness. Stigler (1968) made this important point even for economies of scale, which cannot be considered an effective barrier to entry if they imply similar penalties for suboptimal production levels for both incumbents and new entrants. Thus, it is the asymmetry in replicating incumbents' resources that constitutes an effective barrier for newcomers.

This type of barrier with asymmetric replicability is closely associated with specificity profits based on the combination of synergistic resources. In contrast to simple resource combinations surrounded only by barriers with perfect replicability, this type of profit is more sustainable over time. Even if competitors try to replicate the set of resources of a successful firm, they cannot do so equally effectively when its success is based on highly specific assets. In this case, superior performance based on synergistic resources is more difficult to replicate and it can be done only partially, because not every firm will be able to generate the same value from getting an additional resource to its own unique set of resources.

Barriers with limited substitutability

In the last two decades strategy scholars have moved beyond cost asymmetries as the main reason to understand short and long term profitability.[22] From an RBV perspective, differences in profitability can only be sustained if there are some imperfections in the market for strategic resources, as Barney (1986) noted. If all resources are tradable, there would be perfect replicability and long term economic profits should eventually disappear. At the very least, access to these resources should be asymmetric to different firms to generate different costs and ultimate profitability. But the potential to actually replicate strategic resources is most severely limited and uncertain when there is no market for them at all. In particular, competitors may not be able to replicate some firm level resources, such as certain organizational skills and brand name. In these cases, only limited substitutability can be achieved with a somewhat equivalent but different resource. Causal ambiguity, for instance, is widely regarded as a highly effective barrier to replicate a strategic resource.[23]

Aside from the costs of trying to do so, it is unlikely that competitors may replicate a strong position based on firm level resources. Competitors would have to go through the entire path dependent process of developing such a resource and there is no guarantee that the newly developed resource (e.g., firm level competencies) will be able to adequately substitute for the original resource developed by the innovator. Thus, profits based on organizational innovation can be more sustainable to the extent that they are protected by barriers with limited substitutability.

In summary, the strategy field has drawn from economics the concept of industry barriers to entry as the key determinant of long-term superior performance and expanded its applicability to lower levels of analysis. This concept plays a critical role in the Porterian approach to strategy and strategic groups (mobility barriers) as well as in the RBV (isolating mechanisms), which has refined substantially the general idea of limits to competition.[24] Superior performance is sustainable if and only if competitor imitation is sufficiently disrupted. However, not all barriers have the same potential to protect a superior positioning based on a somewhat unique combination of resources. While some

---

[22] Mahoney and Pandian (1992) identify over thirty isolating mechanisms used in the RBV and the organizational economics literature.

[23] See Lippman and Rumelt (1982) and Reed and DeFillippi (1990) for further discussion of uncertain imitability and causal ambiguity.

[24] See Mahoney and Pandian (1992) for an analysis of the RBV that stresses the role of isolating mechanisms of resources (labeled as such by Rumelt, 1984) in the sustainability of rents.

Table 5.1 *A categorization of profits, resource combinations, and barriers*

Key contextual condition	Resource combination	Competitive barrier
Uncertainty	Simple combination of contributed resources	Perfect replicability
Specificity	Synergistic combination of contributed resources	Asymmetric replicability
Innovation	New resources at firm level (not contributed)	Limited substitutability

resources can be perfectly imitated, others have asymmetric replicability, and the most effective barriers have only limited substitutability. The different types of barriers to competition can be associated with the different types of resource combinations that we discussed in the previous section, as shown in Table 5.1.

Value analysis, profits, and competitive barriers

To capture value, firms have to create value for customers first. Profits are the residual income kept by firm owners after the other resources are compensated for their contribution to value creation, but their existence is not necessarily a temporary phenomenon. In a dynamic environment, the sustainability of profits depends on the presence of the three types of barriers to entry discussed above. These competitive barriers can also be related to the three contextual conditions that allow profits to emerge and with the value that resources jointly create in the first place. Let us analyze through one example how all of these factors, i.e., value creation, contextual conditions, and competitive barriers, are interrelated.

Profit sustainability of a new restaurant

Consider, for instance, a new restaurant in a recently developed business district. Quite possibly, an alert entrepreneur will see the sales potential for a restaurant in this new location and he or she may gather the necessary resources to build it, including the facility, equipment, licenses, employees, and any additional necessary resources, like the skills to prepare the food to be offered. Even if all of these resources are widely available, high profits may be produced if demand turns out to be sufficiently strong. High demand would probably induce the entrepreneur to increase prices rather than allowing long queues to form, an important nonmonetary cost to customers that serves to equalize the limited supply with the actual demand. However, as soon as the initially uncertain demand for the restaurant in the new area is observable, other entrepreneurs will try to capture the possibility for high profits and assemble similar resources. If they indeed have perfect replicability, extra profits should quickly disappear. In this case, the temporary profits would be due to potential entrepreneurs not having enough information about supply and demand conditions from the beginning. Eventually, the market would most likely be divided among potential firms when the compensation for necessary resources is similar to the returns that can be generated by a restaurant. If these resources are perfectly mobile, their market compensation will be very close to their marginal contribution and no extra profits will exist (i.e., above the minimum required to compensate the internal providers of capital). Uncertainty (i.e., luck or just shocks to the existing market conditions) is necessary and sufficient for this type of extra profits to occur, but perfect replicability will make the superior profits not sustainable.

However, restaurants are comprised of heterogeneous resources and they do not create the same value for all customers. Some restaurants are located in areas of more convenient visibility and access (non-monetary customer costs). They can offer different types of food (horizontal differentiation) and provide a higher or lower overall level of quality and service (vertical differentiation). Consequently, they may attract a different type and number of customers. They can also have different levels of internal efficiency. Thus, there can be differences in profitability driven by all of these factors associated with heterogeneity of resources. Some restaurants may be able to gather exactly those resources that reinforce each other's contribution to value. For instance, one restaurant may hire a good Japanese chef, buy higher quality inputs, use more luxurious decoration, and employ a larger number of skilled waiters in order to create a somewhat unique dining experience where customers may treat occasionally their business partners. The combination of all these resources may stress their specific characteristics, so that their effect on the customer's assessment of value (i.e., their willingness to pay) may be greater when these more unique resources are complemented by other cospecialized resources. In other words, unique skills of the chef and the waiters, for instance, can be better exploited when they are employed in this type of restaurant alongside each other and with all the other resources in this restaurant.

Cospecialization is behind the asymmetric value that certain resources can provide contingent on their surrounding context. It is not the scarcity of good chefs that may generate profits to the firm, but the extra value that the chef might create if he employs his skills in the right environment, i.e., along certain cospecialized resources. This synergistic effect can produce greater compensation for the chef as well as profits for the firm. The chef may be paid more in this restaurant to the extent that he can apply his skills better. Part of this extra value generated by the cospecialized resources may be kept by the entrepreneur as well. To the extent that these resources are rare rather than commodities (i.e., easy to obtain and assemble), the profits from the Japanese restaurant will be protected by barriers to competition with asymmetric replicability. When there is asymmetric replicability of resources, profit differentials can be sustained over time, as each firm would have to bear a different cost to create even similar value for customers, i.e., similar market positioning. In our case, new restaurants cannot perfectly replicate the Japanese restaurant's entire collection of resources and the value they jointly create, nor even extract the same marginal value from those resources that are similar; however, a new restaurant with even greater use of cospecialized resources could produce greater profits.

Finally, profits may also result from the possibility for firms to innovate and develop new resources that did not exist before. Like any business, restaurants can develop organizational level resources, such as a collective skill, certain reputation, and maybe a patented branded product. Though these new resources were dynamically developed by other specialized resources through time, the value that they provide will not be distributed to the resources that contributed to them and it will be kept by the owners of the firm. For instance, the famous Benihana chain could set up one of their Japanese restaurants in the new business area. Their powerful brand name and accumulated experience cannot be instantly replicated by assembling a set of cospecialized resources, even at an asymmetric cost. Any given organizational-level resource can only be substituted for another as opposed to being truly replicated. Thus, the possession of this type of resource (the Benihana brand name and accumulated experience) constitutes a very effective competitive barrier.

To a large extent, sustainable profits in the long run for the restaurants in the new area will result from a combination of all of these factors. Those restaurants that can deal better with the environmental changes and are faster to respond with adequate bets in the market may obtain some greater profitability, though they would need to keep doing it through time to keep above-average profitability (uncertainty profits). Similarly, the restaurants that have a clear strategy and assemble only those resources that best contribute to its basis for value creation may also obtain superior performance (specificity profits). Finally, those restaurants that have been able to build organizational resources with imperfect substitutability can also keep the extra value that these resources can generate (firm innovation profits).

PART II

Firm strategies

6 | *Business strategy*

Elements of business-level strategy

For the last several decades strategy scholars have tried to understand what determines firm performance. The basic premise is that something that firms do or have done in the past gives them a competitive advantage that results in superior performance. In essence, a firm's strategy presumably defines what the firm does, which may generate a somewhat unique competitive advantage that results in superior performance. Though there has been much debate about the planned or emergent nature of a firm's strategy, we are now interested only in the content of the strategy rather than its formation process.[1] It seems reasonable for researchers to try to categorize the different strategies that firms may follow in their own industry and to explore which ones may provide superior performance.[2]

Unfortunately, the search for a solid categorization of firm strategies across different industries has not been very successful, particularly with regard to their implications for performance. Michael Porter's categorization of three generic business strategies has been the most influential in the field. As discussed in chapter four, firms may follow either a cost leadership or a differentiation strategy, but if they try to achieve both, they may end up stuck in the middle with lower than average performance; as a third alternative, a focus strategy within a narrow segment of the market may define the strategy, alongside one of the two basic options. However, a meta-analysis of the empirical literature on generic strategies shows that, though firm strategies can be grouped into a reduced typology, there is no clear evidence of

---

[1] See Mintzberg (1978).

[2] In addition to the business-level strategy categories that we discuss in this section, Miles and Snow (1978) suggest an influential categorization of corporate strategy, including how firms develop and control new businesses in contrast to other competitors and possible changes in the environment.

differential performance effects.[3] In other words, researchers have not been able to empirically find any strategy inherently superior or inferior to others. Though other researchers have tried to refine and expand the basic categorization of generic strategies including other strategic alternatives, the search for a useful categorization of business strategies has not allowed us to move beyond a purely descriptive taxonomy.[4]

The limited success of generic strategies and other typologies is not really surprising. Firms are highly complex organizations that interact in different ways with their environment, including customers, suppliers, competitors, governments, and many other external factors. Any type of generic strategy broadly defined is likely to be an oversimplification of how firms compete, which can have a very limited effect on performance, if any at all. Only very general recommendations can be provided for a strategy defined as such a high level of generality.[5] We need to identify with much more precision the different elements of a strategy and the key challenges in each of them to make further progress in the field.

Hambrick and Fredrickson (2005) have suggested an interesting approach for strategic management that moves clearly beyond the idea of generic strategies. In their opinion, a firm's strategy is basically the answer to five major questions about (1) the different markets in which the firm may be active, (2) the modes of entry in them, (3) the company's differentiation from competition, (4) the speed and sequence of the strategic moves, and (5) the underlying competitive logic of the firm, implicitly referring to how the firm creates value. This approach provides a more detailed description of a firm's strategy than the existing broad typologies of strategy. However, it would be highly desirable for our analysis to have a stronger theoretical base for the identification of the different elements of a strategy that includes other important aspects, such as the management of barriers to entry. In this chapter we will use a fine grained description of the main strategic decisions that firms face and the key issues in each of them. It is this set of decisions that ultimately comprise a firm's strategy, presumably forming a reasonably coherent pattern through time.

---

[3] See Campbell-Hunt (2000).

[4] For instance, fast response. See Miller (1986) and Mintzberg (1988) for other broad categorizations of strategy.

[5] See Rumelt (1997) for general suggestions to evaluate strategy.

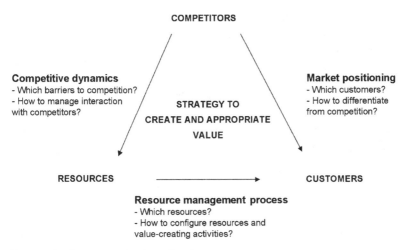

Figure 6.1 Elements of business-level strategy

A value perspective may help us identify which are the key issues in business strategy, link them to the existing research on content strategy, and examine their implications for performance. To do so, we can build from the ideas that we discussed in chapter three. The value-based model highlights the importance of dealing with resources, customers, and competitors as the main elements of a firm's strategy. From this perspective, the firm is essentially a collection of resources that compete with other firms to create value for customers and appropriate part of it. The interactions among the three corners in the model give rise to the three major types of decision that a firm has to make about its strategy. These main elements of a firm's strategy are shown in Figure 6.1, which are discussed in greater detail in the rest of this chapter.

Managing resources to create value for customers

How the firm manages its resources is a fundamental part of its strategy. Based on our discussion in previous chapters, we use a broad definition of resources, including owned tangible and intangible internal resources, inputs from suppliers, alliances, and complementary resources. Through their activities, firms somehow combine and transform resources into products and services that generate value for the customer. These activities constitute the foundation of the value-based model of strategy shown in Figure 6.1. Rather than focusing on the operational issues behind the activities of the firm, there are two main strategic decisions about how firms manage resources through their value-creating activities:

1. Which resources should be part of the value proposition of the firm to its possible customers?
2. How are these resources actually combined and linked interdependently to deliver value for customers?

We have addressed the first question in the previous chapters that draws primarily from the resource-based view of the firm and applies it to the analysis of value creation and appropriation. Basically, it is the value that resources can create that determines whether they should be part of a firm strategy or, instead, compete independently. Chapter three explains why resources competing together may create more value than as separate units under certain circumstances. This issue will be analyzed further in chapter seven when we specifically study corporate boundaries and the make-or-buy decision.

Now, we will concentrate on the second question: how are resources actually combined and managed to create value from a strategy perspective? As Drucker (1954) noted long ago, an enterprise is not just a mechanical assemblage of resources. He claimed that firms produce a "transmutation of resources," so that they should be able to produce more or better (for its customers) than all the resources that comprise them. It is how these specific resources are interdependently linked that ultimately creates value for customers.

There are many different ways in which value can be created that result in a large variety of products and services, each one with its own underlying technology and economic logic. Thompson (1967) identified three fundamental technologies that broadly categorize how firms may create value for customers: long-linked, mediating, and intensive technologies. By far, most work in strategy has focused on the long-linked technology that characterizes value chains, which is particularly useful for manufacturing firms. However, as Stabell and Fjeldstad (1998) noted, different ways to create value have their own strategic challenges and their unique configuration of its main activities, which may not always be well analyzed as a value chain. Let us analyze the strategic implications of the different ways in which products and services create value.

Value created by products

The traditional concept of the firm is based on the technological transformation of inputs into outputs carried out by manufacturers. Though the variety of available products is enormous, their competitive logic is quite similar.[6] For product-based firms, the customer acquires a physical product in exchange for the price paid. The customer may use or consume the product any way that he or she wants *after* acquiring possession of it, of course, limited by the existing laws (e.g., copyright limits on reproduction). Value is materialized through the transfer in the possession of a physical product, when each party presumably gains in the exchange.

The concept of the value chain has become the standard approach to the analysis of how value gets created by these firms.[7] As usually occurs in manufacturing firms, there is often a sequence of steps from the raw materials to the finished goods that the final customer consumes. Firms are basically links along a chain of value creating activities. The firm's primary activities are sequentially ordered from inbound logistics to after-sales services, each one presumably adding more value to the product than its costs. Secondary activities (like human resources management and financial control) add value only indirectly by facilitating the efficient functioning of primary activities. Each activity and their linkages along the value chain (including suppliers and buyers) should be actively managed to achieve the maximum overall capture

[6] Murphy and Enis (1986) identify different types of products from a marketing perspective. In addition to products and services, they include also ideas, which expands marketing to nonbusiness activities. All of them can be further categorized based on the effort and risk involved in acquiring them: convenience (i.e., no strong preferences exist for customers, e.g., commodities), shopping (carefully evaluated by customers, e.g., cars), and specialty (highly unique products and services, e.g., strategy consulting). Marketing strategies may change substantially across these types of products. They also include another category of preference products somewhere between convenience and shopping, when certain preferences exist for a particular brand, e.g., soft drinks, but not much effort is committed.

[7] See Porter (1985) for the concept of the value chain and its use to develop differentiation or cost advantage. Stabell and Fjeldstad (1998) provide an excellent analysis of the value chain and extend significantly the strategic implications of value creation to other possible configurations of activities, specifically professional service firms (shops) and network based firms. In this section we follow their analysis, which is inspired in Thompson (1967) and Porter (1985).

of economic value by the firm, i.e., the difference between revenues from customers and costs to the firm.

To a large extent, the entire organization is structured to facilitate the manufacturing process workflow. Thus, firms protect their technical core from fluctuations, including for instance buffering and forecasting to manage the interdependence of their own activities and also with the environment. The notions of productivity and distribution channels were initially developed for this type of firm, though they have been extended to services in a somewhat questionable manner. Productivity indicates the firm's efficiency in terms of its output, which depends on the level of standardization, economies of scale, and supply chain management, among other cost drivers.[8]

The value that the firm creates for the customer is embodied in the tangible and intangible features of the product.[9] Marketing techniques allow firms to detect the ideal combination of features for the customers that they target through their range of products, including the possibilities for differentiation. However, from a strategic perspective, the critical combination takes place at a higher level of abstraction than products or services, i.e., the resources that make them possible, though customer utility ultimately comes from products.[10]

[8] Porter (1985) identifies ten cost drivers broadly dealing with economies of scale, the management of relationships with other activities along the internal and external value chain, and the firm's context. They are scale, capacity utilization, learning, linkages, interrelationships, vertical integration, timing, firm policies, location, and institutional factors.

[9] Some products, however, may be affected by externalities. For instance, the value of design products associated with higher status is affected by who else owns those products. Similarly, products that are used as part of a network service (e.g., phone handsets) are also affected by the number of compatible phones. The effect of this type of network externalities will be discussed in greater detail later on. In general, externalities in the case of products may be regarded as an additional attribute of the product in this augmented conceptualization.

[10] In her book, Penrose insisted on the difference between resources and the productive services that the firm can obtain from them. To some extent, the knowledge to obtain more or different productive services from available resources can be regarded as a resource itself. For our analytical purposes, it is important to distinguish between the product-level analysis that concerns the marketing area and the firm-level analysis of resources that is the focus of strategic management.

Value created by professional services

The distinguishing characteristic of services is that they are not associated with a physical product whose possession changes from the firm to the customer. In contrast to products, a service is not consumed sometime after it has been delivered, but at the same time it is provided, like in a movie theater or a restaurant. The variety of services is so large that it is sometimes hard to distinguish them from products, and a comprehensive and meaningful categorization is virtually impossible. For instance, a company may produce frozen pizza sold through a supermarket, which is clearly part of a value chain.[11] However, if we eat a similar pizza inside an Italian restaurant, we would be using a service. Furthermore, if the food is highly standardized, like in fast food restaurants, it could be considered that these firms are essentially value chains. Similarly, consulting is clearly considered a professional service, but getting a packaged software solution made by the consultants could be considered either a product or a service depending on its characteristics, while a book that simply explains such a solution in detail, and sold through book stores, would be considered a product. Thus, the main characteristic is not really the nature of the firm's offering, but the competitive logic on which they build.

Hair salons, restaurants, hospitals, schools, and consultancy practices are examples of professional service firms which are associated with the practice of a given profession. These services share some key features in how they create value. Rather than exchanging a standardized physical product through spot market transactions, professional services basically depend on the expertise of the service providers to deliver a customized solution to its users. Thompson (1967) coined the term "intensive technologies" to describe those firms that bring about a change in some specific object, and who then provide important feedback with regard to how this change should take place. Elaborating on this idea, Stabell and Fjeldstad (1998) stressed that professional service firms, which they call "value shops," basically attempt to solve customer problems. The continuous interaction between firm's experts and the customer should not be treated as a sequential chain of

---

[11] Retailers can be considered as value chains that do not transform the product. They only carry out inbound and outbound logistics, which is basically inventory management.

value-creating activities, but a circular set of activities to define problems, find solutions, execute them, and usually redefine them.

Professional services have a very different competitive logic than firms that sell standardized products. The professional knowledge of the individuals within the organizations that provide the service is what characterizes how these firms create value.[12] Though all firms have more or less intensive relationships with customers, and one way or another help solve the problems of their customers, the value provided by professional service firms is created in the direct interaction between the customers and the firms' employees. For instance, restaurants are only as good as the expertise of the chefs and the surrounding context in which the food is actually eaten by the customer.

Building greater expertise in their human resources in a certain direction is the critical strategic challenge of these types of firms, which are only as competitive as their employees doing their professional activities in direct contact with the customers. The value provided by a car is determined primarily by the inherent and surrounding features of the car produced by the entire manufacturing firm. However, the value created by a consulting firm is only as good as the specific solution provided by the consulting team to the firm. Professional service firms do not standardize their processes to achieve economies of scale as much as manufacturing firms. Efficiency, though obviously important, is secondary to effectiveness. To the extent that the quality of the service is difficult to gauge by nonexperts, firm reputation becomes more important, which helps to attract better human resources and more sophisticated customers. For instance, with their greater reputation, top consulting firms attract the best talent, but also the most demanding customers with challenging problems. Having first access to these problems, the expertise of people in these firms is expanded, which contributes to sustain and enhance the reputation of their firms. In contrast to value chains, this is a very different way to create value for customers.

Value created by networks

There is another type of value creation that deserves to be studied separately from value chains and professional services. Stabell and

[12] See Maister (1997) for an applied analysis of professional service firms.

Fjeldstad (1999) call them "value networks," referring to firms that essentially mediate exchanges between customers. Thompson (1967) explored the mediating technology that makes it possible for these firms to have as their primary function the linking of customers that are somehow interdependent. The industries are characterized by the existence of important network externalities on their demand side. Examples of these firms include telecom operators, banking, transportation, and many organizations based on information exchanges through the internet, like eBay or Google.

Facilitating any sort of exchange is very different from manufacturing and selling a product, or offering a specialized service from professional experts to solve a unique customer problem. Rather than transforming inputs into outputs or delivering a specific service, value networks manage interactions among a set of points or customers. In a network customers are connected to each other by means of a physical infrastructure and the role of the firm is to facilitate possible interactions among the members of its customer set and with other networks. As exchange facilitators, they engage in three primary activities: (1) operating the network's physical infrastructure, (2) managing the relationship with each of their customers, and (3) providing the services that allow their customers to interact with one another through the network. These activities are carried out concurrently by the firm in contrast to the sequential activities in a value chain or the intensive technology between professional service firms and their customers.

To see how these firms actually create value through these three primary activities, we can consider one particular type of value network, such as mobile phone operators. Mobile phone operators have to establish and operate a physical infrastructure that links a set of customers or nodes within a network and with other networks. Their infrastructure includes antennas, switchboards, and other equipment that allows the physical transfer of digitized voice, data, and images. The relationship with each of the customers also needs to be managed, including attracting new customers to the network, invoicing, and contract management. On top of their physical network infrastructure, phone operators offer a variety of services that allow customers to interact with other people and exchange voice and data through different means, including traditional calls, voicemail, and access to other networks such as the internet.

When we look at these firms as value networks, some of their unique features are evidenced in the way that they create value through primary activities. Since the value of belonging to one network is directly dependent on the number of nodes in the network, any system that gains a considerable advantage early on may become the market leader in a battle where the winner often takes all. Network size and infrastructure management plays a key role in these firms, mainly because the marginal cost of one more transaction through the network is negligible, but fixed costs are enormous and need careful planning.

But value networks not only operate a physical infrastructure; they also have to manage their customer sets. Networks may grow horizontally by attracting new nodes or by signing interconnection agreements with other networks. Both mechanisms increase the value they provide for their customers who may then have access to more people. To attract and retain new customers, networks engage in promotion activities and customize available contracts. A variety of invoicing alternatives have allowed phone operators to target different customer groups. In addition, a fundamental aspect these firms use to manage their customer sets is the composition of the actual network. They try to build consistent customer sets that interact frequently with other members of their own network.

Finally, value networks also have the possibility to grow vertically by adding layers of services on top of their infrastructure so that their customers can use them to interact with each other in new ways. Providing a new service either in-house or coproduced with another network, a network firm can create value in two ways: it may attract new people to the network or it may generate more demand for underlying services. An example of a value-creating service is the voicemail service of mobile phone operators. On the one hand, offering this service may attract new users to the network if their competitors do not provide voicemail. On the other hand, voicemail actually increases the use of the basic phone service, since the caller is actually charged for making the unanswered call and the receiver often returns the call.

The value that customers receive from network based firms is not embodied in a product or a customized solution developed by the professional experts. The value comes from being part of a network, which provides access to other customers. In this sense, the value resides in the accessibility to other customers. Thus, customers typically pay a fixed amount for being part of the network (i.e., having access to

Table 6.1 *Configurations for value creation*

	Product	Professional service	Network
Object	Supplying a product, by managing inputs	Providing a solution, based on the expertise of employees	Facilitating exchanges, by managing a network
Key firm costs	Standardization and economies of scale	Attract, train, and retain human resources	Network capacity and use
Nature of customer value	Product features	Solution effectiveness	Connectivity to others

a mobile phone service) plus actual use of the network (i.e., use of the phone). This is so because connectivity, i.e. being reachable, has value on its own for customers, even if they do not use the service frequently.

Based on Stabell and Fjeldstad (1998), Table 6.1 summarizes the comparison among the three basic technologies that create value for customers. Depending on the economic logic of its way to create value for customers, the strategic challenges of firms may be very different. Costs and product features are critical for manufacturers, human expertise and firm reputation for professional service firms, and externalities and network management for network based firms. Strategy researchers have a full agenda if they want to identify and understand the main strategic decisions about using and combining resources through these underlying technologies and new ones that may deserve their own analysis.

To complicate things further, firms often cannot be categorized into only one of the three technologies. For instance, a bank, though it is essentially a mediator of financial funds, may provide highly standardized financial services that outsources from outside (e.g., house insurance), while also providing financial advice to its customers; thus, it has elements of a value chain and a professional service firm in addition to managing a network. Sometimes it may make sense to divide the firm into different units, each one with its own competitive logic. If they do not really support each other's value creation potential, the organization may break into different firms, like the breakup of AT&T

in the eighties into a product based firm (AT&T Computer Systems), a professional service firm (Bell Labs-Lucent), and several network firms (long distance phone service and the regional Baby Bells).

Market positioning

Firms essentially manage resources to create value for customers in competition with other firms. Direct competitors and substitutes, both direct and potential, play an important role in how much value a firm can create and appropriate. Customers compare available products and services to decide which ones they decide to buy. This interaction among customers, competitors, and the firm itself determines its market positioning, which corresponds to the right side of the triangle in Figure 6.1. Two basic questions summarize a firm's market positioning versus its competitors:

1. Which customers does the firm target with its products and services?
2. For the targeted market segments in which the firm competes, how are the firm's products and services different from those of the competition as perceived by the customers?

The first question is basically an issue of market segmentation while the second one deals with product differentiation. Segmentation and differentiation constitute the main strategic decisions of the firm with regard to its positioning in the market. They are key elements of marketing strategy, but also have broad implications for the entire organization and its competitiveness.

Probably because they are so intimately connected, there is some confusion between both terms.[13] Some authors, like Wendell Smith, regard them as alternatives, but others, like Michael Porter, consider differentiation as a means of implementing market segmentation. In his classic article published in 1956, Smith defines differentiation as an

---

[13] See Dickson and Ginter (1987) for a clear conceptualization of both terms and the strategies associated with them. They argue that both concepts are highly related and they are not alternatives. For them, a market segmentation strategy also requires the pursuit of differentiation, but firms may have a differentiation strategy with or without segmenting the market. However, we actually observe commodity-based industries, like in construction materials, where the firms offer a wide array of products for different segments, though the products are not differentiated versus those of competitors.

attempt to shift or change the slope of the demand curve, so that the outcome is more favorable to the seller, usually through promotion and advertising. He also defines segmentation as demand disaggregation that brings about the recognition of different demand schedules, so that supply adjusts to demand in such a case rather than vice versa. In contrast, for Michael Porter, differentiation is based on physical or nonphysical product differences that result in a lower degree of cross-price elasticity among competitors, so that it is basically a complement to a market segmentation strategy. Aside from the type and the extent of differentiation, the firm would need to make a decision about targeting a broader or narrower part of the market.

Segmentation and differentiation represent two highly related concepts and often complement each other, though they address two distinct questions that are truly orthogonal. Market segmentation refers to analyzing how much heterogeneity exists among possible customers and choosing a larger or smaller set of customer segments to focus on. It is essentially a demand-side concept that is equivalent to product variety on the supply side. In contrast, differentiation deals with how the customers perceive the product or service in contrast to those available from other competitors. Firms frequently segment the market to develop products with unique features for the targeted segments, but they may or may not be different from those of competitors in such segments. Thus, there may be firms with a wide range of products for different segments, but no product differentiation from competitors that all may offer commoditized products for each segment, so that there could be segmentation and no differentiation. Equivalently, there may be differentiation without segmentation, when the product is perceived as different and superior to others from the customers' point of view across an entire homogeneous market, i.e., a broad differentiation strategy in Porter's typology. Let us briefly discuss the two key aspects of a firm's market positioning.

Segmentation

From a value perspective, the segmentation strategy of a firm deals with defining the customers for whom the firm intends to create value. Obviously, there are many differences across people, including their individual preferences, their demographic characteristics (which can be

used to infer preferences), their physical location, and their wealth.[14]
Market research is often used to uncover the existing differences among
potential customers with the ultimate goal to understand what different
subsets of people value with regard to the product or service. For each
segment the firm may develop a tailored product specifically adapted to
the existing needs of this type of customers. In addition, firms may even
try to actually influence consumers directly and what they value, as
opposed to merely detecting and accepting existing differences across
customers, which has been called a segment development strategy.[15]

All the activities related to identifying, adapting to, and creating
different types of customers comprise the segmentation strategy of a
firm. The options for segmentation range from a single strategy to cover
the entire market (basically no segmentation, like some utility firms) to
covering some or all of a market through a wide range of products for
each segment, and even to having a very narrow strategy that focuses
on only one small niche market. It is somewhat surprising to see that
there is not much research in strategy about market segmentation. For
instance, Michael Porter argues that the main issue is the extent to
which a firm could use a focus strategy in one specific segment or
follow instead a broad strategy.[16] But even this segmentation decision
is later on qualified by the choice of a generic strategy within the
chosen segment, usually either cost leadership or differentiation, which
constitutes the two fundamental alternatives for competitive advantage
in his model.

Ultimately, the focus strategy involves a critical trade-off between
increasing margins, presumably driven by the greater attractiveness
of a product adapted to customers with unique needs, and reducing
potential overall sales, because the market has been limited to a smaller
subset of customers. It is, therefore, an issue of choosing the arenas in

[14] See Day *et al.* (1979) for different ways to identify market segments.

[15] Dickson and Ginter (1987) consider this type of segment development strategy
as a particular form of demand function modification, which is inherently
different from the mere disaggregation of demand into existing subsets or
segments.

[16] In contrast to the other two generic strategies, Porter does not really discuss
the focus strategy in his book published in 1980 in much depth, though he
included a chapter in his book published in 1985 on segmentation dealing with
bases for segmentation (i.e., product variety, buyer segment, distribution
channel, and geographic buyer location) and the attractiveness of different
segments from a five forces perspective.

which the firm will be present, though it has implications for the entire value chain and the broader versus specialized resources that need to be developed. How to deal with customer heterogeneity is a critical element of a firm's strategy and, more precisely, its market positioning.

Empirical research in marketing strategy has studied the benefits and costs of a broader product breadth, but there are mixed results about the often presumed superiority of a broader product range (Kekre and Srinivasan, 1990; Sorenson, 2000; Cottrell and Nault, 2004). Somehow the overall value for customers of having more options needs to be assessed, including any additional costs for the firm and its customers that it could require. Ultimately, a firm's product diversity should probably reflect customers' heterogeneity in the market. Thus, in industries with substantial differences across different types of customers, that is, highly segmented, a larger product variety is likely to develop. In this sense managing market segmentation is virtually equivalent to managing product variety as its flip side.

Economists have studied the conditions that facilitate the emergence of excessive or insufficient product variety in contrast to the social optimum.[17] This literature has provided interesting insights that can be useful for strategic management. The optimum basically depends, on the one hand, on the increased benefits generated to consumers by having greater choice that can better satisfy their somewhat heterogeneous preferences. On the other hand, the greater overall costs that this greater product variety can create should also be considered, i.e., loss of economies of scale of fragmenting production. This trade-off determines how much product variety exists in the market and it is essentially a question of value analysis.

The existing theoretical literature on product variety in economics argues in different directions towards excessive variety (Chamberlin, 1933), insufficient variety (Dixit and Stiglitz, 1977), or both possibilities depending on the circumstances and the different parameters in the models (Spence, 1976; Hart, 1985). However, most models agree that there will be a greater variety of products, each one for a specific segment of the market, if there are (a) lower degrees of substitutability between products (i.e., if the consumers essentially believe that products are very different from each other), (b) smaller economies of

---

[17] For a review of the economic literature on product variety see Lancaster (1990).

scale and fixed costs, and (c) greater competition among firms (i.e., monopolies would have less variety than markets with monopolistic competition, especially when they are more protected from potential new entrants).[18]

Differentiation

While market segmentation refers to how the firm deals with customer heterogeneity, product differentiation results from the contrast between the firm's offering and that of competitors from the perspective of the customer. Chamberlin (1933: 56) provides a very clear definition:

A general class of product is differentiated if any significant basis exists for distinguishing the goods of one seller from those of another. Such a basis may be real or fancied, so long as it is of any importance whatever to buyers, and leads to a preference for one variety of the product over another.

Broadly considered, some differentiation needs to exist for firms to have unequal market shares. If all customers see the available products as totally equivalent, including their features, prices, and other customer costs required to have access to them, they would have no preferences for either one and we should expect all firms splitting the market in equal shares. In this sense, all strategic decisions ultimately deal to some extent with the possibility to create differentiation as the basis for switching customer preferences and influencing the final decision to buy a firm's products or services.

It is important to note that differentiation versus cost leadership are not incompatible alternatives for strategy from a value perspective. Either differentiation or lower costs (for the firm and the customers) may result in superior firm performance because both actually contribute to create value. Both can perfectly coexist and there is no need to choose one to avoid being "stuck in the middle," as Porter (1980) suggests for most circumstances. Furthermore, cost leadership is frequently used to create a unique position in the market as the low-price provider (the usual price-based competitors like Wal-Mart), so that price becomes the differentiator factor that switches customer preferences for products and both differentiation and cost leadership become

---

[18] These are the main conclusions from the survey done by Lancaster (1990).

parallel concepts in the demand and the supply sides respectively. As marketers know well, price is another feature of the product and customers make their final purchasing decision after considering the entire set of product features and costs. All of them can be the basis for product differentiation.[19] Empirical research in strategy shows that firms can combine successfully both generic strategies, though they seem to be less compatible at the product level.[20]

Certainly, firms could have differences in profitability if their costs differ even without product differentiation that is directly observed by the customer. In this sense, Porter is right that cost leadership is a different type of competitive advantage than differentiation. As we discussed in chapter four, lowering costs is one way to create value. Relative costs determines relative profits versus those of competitors. However, only by charging lower prices can a cost leader achieve a superior market positioning, whose attractiveness would depend on the value that customers give to the price differential in contrast with other possible differences across products. These differences that are considered by the customers to form their preferences are just sources of differentiation. It is ultimately differentiation including price differences that determines the relative competitiveness of firms in the market and their ability to attract customers, though differences in costs need to be considered to understand overall profitability.

From a value perspective all firms compete in both: enhancing customer benefits and reducing total costs (the firm's plus customers' costs). They may stress either possibility or both at once in their strategy and the resources that they need to assemble and develop further. Only by providing a better value for at least some customers can a firm achieve greater competitiveness, including having a product with higher quality, greater ease of use, lower price, or an appropriate combination of them. Otherwise the nondifferentiated firms would split among them the part of the market that is not covered by differentiated players. Thus, a firm's positioning is primarily determined by how its

[19] This is the view of Mintzberg (1988), who sees low cost/prices as an alternative way to differentiate the firm's product. See also Fulmer and Goodwin (1988).

[20] Dess and Davis (1984), and Calori and Ardisson (1988) show empirically that firms may follow a combination of cost leadership and differentiation and still have high performance. In contrast, Nayyar (1993) claims that firms may combine them across different products in their portfolio, but that they are incompatible for specific products, which should be based on either costs or differentiation.

products and services differ from those of its competitors, including the prices that it may charge. Of course, the final value appropriated (or lost) by the firm will also depend on the costs of the firm to deliver the product with its set of features, e.g., quality, user-friendliness, and price. To compete on price, cost efficiency becomes particularly important, just like research productivity is particularly relevant for companies that compete through innovation. However, competing through costs to differentiate through lower prices does not imply a different type of generic strategy, but is just one way to differentiate (by low prices) that requires specific resources (cost efficiency), analogous to other sources of differentiation (e.g., a high performance product) that requires the right types of resources (research and development superiority).

Greater ability to attract customers, thus, requires some differentiation, though cost differences on their own also affect relative profitability. Firms fight to create value for customers, which includes attracting as many customers as possible and increasing their willingness to pay higher prices. For these reasons, the main strategic goal is to create a customer preference for the firm's products and services rather than just increasing operational efficiency as such.[21]

Given the importance of differentiation for building a competitive advantage, there is abundant research on economics, marketing, and strategy about the sources of differentiation and its effect on performance. Economists have investigated, usually through mathematical modeling, the two main types of differentiation (vertical and horizontal, briefly discussed in chapter four) and the characteristics of the market equilibrium.[22] The traditional approach is based on the theory of monopolistic competition from Chamberlin (1933) as a new type of industry structure between monopoly and competition. In this approach, there is one representative consumer, that is, all firms compete equally for all customers.[23] A new entry with a differentiated product takes customers equally from all existing products in the industry, which is based on questionable assumptions about symmetry in

---

[21] This is also discussed in Porter (1996), who tries hard to make consistent his early ideas about cost leadership as a generic strategy with the claim that trying to increase operational efficiency is not a strategy.

[22] For a review of this literature, see Beath and Katsoulacos (1991).

[23] Authors like Spence (1976), Dixit and Stiglitz (1977), and Perloff and Salop (1985) explore this representative consumer approach.

customer preferences. The main features of this model are probably that in the long run new entry drives profits to zero, though all firms remain differentiated, and there can be too few or too many brands depending on the assumptions in the model.

In contrast, the spatial differentiation models view each firm's product as having one particular location in product space, though it can be expanded to different sets of characteristics.[24] Firms compete more intensely with other firms more closely situated to them, so that there is no assumption of symmetry among customer preferences. Inspired in Hotelling's (1929) seminal paper, firms locate somewhere along a line or a circle and we can study how they may choose their location, the prices that they set, or both. Customer preferences with regard to the available products are usually modeled through some sort of distance, e.g., transportation costs, from the customer to the location of the firm's product. In Hotelling's original study firms choose to set their store somewhere along one street with limited length. Customers are supposed to be homogeneously distributed along the line, though each one has to bear some transportation cost to move to the point where the stores are located. If prices are given, the solution indicates that two firms would locate in the middle of the line, thus resulting in minimum differentiation between them. However, the conclusions change radically if we have more than two firms, if the physical space is a circle instead of a line, or if the firms can change both location and prices. Under many other assumptions, the firms should choose maximum differentiation instead or there may be no equilibrium.[25] Thus, economists have explored a large number of possibilities that result in very different conclusions depending on the specific assumptions about the choices for modeling the problem.

Empirical research has uncovered some of the possible types of differentiation that may be pursued. For instance, industrial organization (IO) economists Caves and Williamson (1985) showed that there are

[24] See Lancaster (1990) and Rosen (1974) for different approaches to modeling product differentiation as a combination of different product attributes.

[25] See Salop (1979), who reached the opposite conclusion from Hotelling using a circle rather than a line. In this case, firms choose to locate as far apart as possible. In contrast to models based on representative consumers in which there could be too many or too few differentiated brands, there are always too many differentiated firms in this model. d'Aspremont, Gabszewicz, and Thisse (1979) explore the assumptions behind Hotelling's spatial model and the circumstances under which there would be no equilibrium.

two sources of product differentiation that may result in the imperfect substitution between competing brands that characterize individual negative sloping demand curves: product attributes and information costs to the buyer. Miller (1992) showed that firms could compete through the emphasis in different dimensions of competition, including lower costs and prices, pioneering (new products and patents), selling (sales promotions and advertising), and quality (superior products). Kotha and Vadlamani (1995) found support for Mintzberg's typology that firms can differentiate through quality, image, design, support, or price. Thus, there seem to be many alternatives for differentiation, which sometimes deal with the benefits that customers perceive in the product and their associated costs, including both monetary and nonmonetary costs. The set of choices for differentiation ultimately depends on what the customers value in each specific industry.

Firms compete alongside a reduced number of product dimensions for which there may be heterogeneous preferences among customers, which gives rise to various horizontally differentiated products. After choosing a given location in product space, there may be a race among competitors to provide greater value along the chosen set of dimensions, which becomes a question of vertical differentiation. It is interesting to note that this strategic race has usually been acknowledged for cost competitors (i.e., cost leadership), but not for other dimensions of differentiation for which a race may also exist (e.g., quality). Firms make their market positioning decision taking into consideration both customer benefits and total costs, while trying to find a broader or narrower segment on which to focus. Having defined its market positioning, that is, its strategic choices for segmentation and differentiation, the level of vertical differentiation along possible dimensions of value for customers determines the competitiveness of the firm in the market, i.e., its share in the market and its ultimate profitability. Achieving a certain differentiation requires an adequate management of resources, so that market positioning and resource management are both important interconnected elements of business strategy as well as critical determinants of firm performance.

Competitive dynamics

Strategic decisions about resources and positioning are taken in markets where competitors can also anticipate or respond to the actions of the firm. We need to analyze the interaction among the resources that the firm manages, the firm itself, and its competitors in the market. The left side of the triangle in Figure 6.1 represents how the firm develops and protects its resources versus competitors as part of its strategy. Two questions capture the main elements of a firm's strategy versus its competitors, i.e., its competitive strategy.

1. How does the firm manage its dynamic interaction with competitors in the market?
2. In particular, which barriers to competition can the firm build around its strategic resources?

The second question deals with barriers to entry as a critical concept in strategy, which we already studied in chapter five. A firm is basically a collection of resources that compete versus other players in the market to create value for customers and capture part of it for itself and its resources. Superior profits can only be sustained if the firm can prevent imitation from competition by building some barriers around its critical resources. Creating barriers to competition and managing them are key elements of a firm's strategy, which determine the overall profitability of the industry and its players. Without any barriers, potential and current competitors could develop similar resources, so that they would replicate a firm's positioning in the industry and eventually split the market and profits. We discussed in the previous chapter how different types of barriers to competition can hinder a competitor's potential replicability of strategic resources to a different extent.

All players within an industry try to develop strategic resources and build barriers around them in order to achieve a superior positioning in the market, i.e., one that provides greater value to the targeted customers. Let us now address the first question regarding how firms manage their market interaction with competitors, including the actions and responses that they take and their effects on performance.

The formal analysis of competitive interaction has grown enormously through the use of game theory. Game-theoretic mathematical modeling has taken over industrial organization economics, which has become the standard method for developing theory.[26] Given certain

---

[26] See Tirole (1988), for instance. See also Saloner (1991) and Camerer (1991) for their analysis of the contributions of game theory to strategic management. Fisher (1989) also makes some interesting points against the use of game theory in economics, defended by Shapiro (1989).

assumptions that determine the rules of the game, particularly about the pay-offs for each player's combination of strategies, the order of moves, and the information that each player has about the others, at least one (Nash) equilibrium can always be obtained, so that no player has an incentive to deviate from the strategy that it chooses to play. The analysis of the possible Nash equilibria in the game and the effect that changes in any assumption in the model has in the equilibrium provide a very rigorous approach to develop "no-fat modeling" (Rasmusen, 2007). Thus, game theory has been applied with great success to the conceptual analysis of first-mover advantages, commitment, credible threats, unpredictability, cooperation, and almost any kind of interaction among firms.[27]

Unfortunately, despite its rigor in theory development, game theory has important limitations. For instance, experimental evidence shows that the equilibrium is very often not played by people in a game. Also, it makes very strict assumptions, particularly about information, which lead to radical changes in the solution with even small variations. Almost any kind of solution can be devised changing some assumptions. Furthermore, there are often too many possible equilibria. However, the most important problem of game theory for strategy is probably in the notion of equilibrium itself. Though this concept is useful to understand an entire economy with many players in a long term horizon, its use is questionable for games that are played between a very reduced number of players in situations that will probably not repeat themselves in the future in the same conditions, like most strategic decisions are.[28] It is a very solid approach to investigate different competitive situations and even develop propositions, but it is ultimately empirical research and broader strategic analysis that looks beyond highly stylized situations that ultimately determines the validity and usefulness of its propositions for strategic management.

---

[27] See Dixit and Nalebuff (1991) for a great discussion of game theory applied to business decisions.

[28] Camerer argues that introspection, communication, adaptation, and evolution may provide the basis for producing the equilibrium in real life. However, he also notes that the goal of game theory is analytic, rather than normative or descriptive. Even if game theory cannot be used to provide specific recommendations in a real world situation, its true goal is helping us understand what may occur.

In contrast to the theory building focus of game theory, competitive dynamics has also been studied from a more applied perspective, including a large literature on first-mover advantages and disadvantages in strategy, marketing, and economics. In their review of the literature, Lieberman and Montgomery (1988) identify three major types of first-mover advantages: technological leadership, preemption of scarce assets, and buyer switching costs. First-mover disadvantages can also be interpreted in terms of differential costs and benefits of incumbents versus new entrants with regard to building resources and resolving market uncertainty.

With regard to specific competitive actions, Porter (1980) discussed different types of competitive moves and he expanded his analysis of defensive strategies and ways to attack an industry leader in a later book (1985). More recently, strategy researchers have begun studying the interaction between competitors, particularly the analysis of actions and responses.[29] This literature looks at specific characteristics of actors and responders (e.g., demographics, size), the actual actions and responses (e.g., likelihood of response, type of action), the context in which they compete (e.g., market commonality, industry structure), and its performance effects for the firms. For instance, actions that target more directly and heavily the customers of rivals (i.e., greater attack intensity and action threat and centrality) meet a higher number of competitive responses.[30] Ferrier *et al.* (1999) also found out that market leaders are more likely to be dethroned or lose market share when their actions are less aggressive and carry out simpler repertoires of actions and more slowly. Though they are not always evident, the competitive actions always have important effects on the players' resources and market positioning in order to have consequences on firm performance.

A firm's competitive strategy also includes its cooperation with other firms to jointly develop and exploit resources. Cooperation and complementary resources are particularly important for learning and innovation. Firms both compete and collaborate dynamically in the market.[31] The management of alliances, thus, becomes a central part of a

---

[29] See Smith *et al.* (2001) for a review of this literature.
[30] See Chen and Miller (1994) and Smith *et al.* (1992).
[31] See Brandenburger and Nalebuff (1996) for an analysis of what they call "co-opetition" based on a game theory perspective.

firm's strategy, which has grown to be a very large area of research in strategic management.[32]

The interaction among the different elements of strategy

We have briefly introduced the three main elements of a firm's business strategy. Most research in content strategy may fit into one of the three elements that we have discussed: competitive dynamics, market positioning, and resource management. A critical feature of the model presented in Figure 6.1 is that all the elements of a strategy are interrelated. They form a system that defines how the firm relates to its customers, resources, and competitors. These strategic decisions are not related for normative reasons, like the match between the environment and the firm's strategy through the industry's key success factors, or, similarly, the alignment among the different aspects of a strategy pointing into one direction that presumably gives consistency and coherence. These elements are necessarily linked and jointly defined as a result of the interplay among the three angles in the triangle formed by competitors, customers, and resources. In this sense, the firm's positioning, the configuration of its activities to create value, and the barriers to entry around its main resources, are all interdependent. In other words, where one starts to define the strategy does not matter, because all three elements are interrelated and defined by their relationship with the others.

This view of strategy solves to some extent some of the controversy around the relevance of superior industry positioning versus internal resources as the basis for competitive advantage, defended by traditional IO and resource-based view (RBV) scholars respectively. For Porter, industry membership and market positioning are the main determinants of firm performance. The main strategic decisions are, therefore, choosing an attractive industry and jockeying for a superior market position that isolates the firm from the effect of competitors, primarily through the creation of barriers to competition. Thus, a firm's strategy is presumably set from the outside to inside the firm.

In contrast to Porter's focus on market positioning, Barney (1991) defends the analysis of internal resources as the key to understanding

---

[32] See Inkpen (2001) for a review of some of the major topics covered by this stream of research on strategic alliances. We will discuss collaboration and alliances in the next chapter on corporate strategy.

firm strategy and profitability, which we described in chapter three. He criticizes the emphasis on barriers to entry of Porterian models, which are based on a static and defensive model of strategy. Industry analysis and membership becomes secondary to the development of unique resources and core competences that can be used in different arenas. Though certainly more ambiguous than the Porterian analysis, the RBV provides a more dynamic approach to the analysis of competitive advantage that starts from internal analysis and moves outside the firm.

Porter (1991) has also questioned the usefulness of the RBV by directly comparing it with the detailed analysis of the value chain activities within his model more heavily based on market positioning. In his opinion, the analysis of activity drivers, defined as structural determinants of differences in the costs or value created by activities, provides greater precision in identifying what a firm does and the basis of its competitive advantage in the market. Because resources, especially skills, are developed and maintained through the activities that a firm carries out, the analysis of activities suffices and it can be done with greater precision based on value chain analysis. From this perspective, competitive advantage must be based on how firms are positioned at the market level and the analysis of activities (i.e., their cost and differentiation drivers) may be more useful than the more ambiguous analysis of resources.

From a value perspective, this debate is not very productive and it possibly does not even represent a choice at all. Superior market positioning is based on unique resources as much as vice versa. If there are not unique resources defendable from competitor's imitation, there cannot be a superior positioning in the market. Resource management, barriers to competition, and market positioning all result from the firm's interaction with resources, competitors, and customers to create and capture value. Thus, changing how one deals with any of these critical stakeholders will necessarily affect the three sides of the triangle because they are all connected.

The influence of the industry and the top managers on business strategy

By definition, business-level strategy is set within the context in which a business unit competes, that is, its industry and its surrounding environment. Though the boundaries of an industry are hard to define precisely, presumably all players within a given industry compete by managing their activities to create customer value in a somewhat similar way. It is the extent of substitutability among their products and services that ultimately determines whether they compete in the same industry. The cross elasticity of demand between products indicates the extent to which two products compete with each other and when they can be considered part of the same industry at some level of aggregation.

To analyze a firm's industry and its environment, we essentially need to study its possible interactions with competitors, customers, and external and internal resource providers, which constitutes an industry's structure. The structural characteristics of an industry have been studied by industrial organization economists since the early work on the structure-conduct-performance model, inspired in Mason (1939) and further developed by Bain (1956).[33] These structural characteristics can be summarized into the well-known five forces model proposed by Michael Porter (1980). The nature of the industry and its structure, including also its stage in the product lifecycle, are the critical determinants of the competitive behavior of firms in the industry and their average profitability.[34] In Porter's model the intensity of rivalry, really the pressure over margins, is driven by several critical industry characteristics (like the number of competitors and industry demand growth), as well as by other surrounding "forces" that also exert pressure on prices: the bargaining power from customers and suppliers, the existence of barriers to entry, and the pressure from substitute products in related industries.[35]

Empirical research has attempted to measure the relative impact of both factors, the industry and the firm's positioning, on firm performance. Though the estimates differ substantially, studies of components of variance of firm performance tend to show that industry

[33] See Scherer and Ross (1990) for a great textbook review of this large literature, mostly empirical across different industries, which has been substantially replaced by the more recent game-theoretical literature of the new IO economics, like Tirole (1988).

[34] See Anderson and Zeithaml (1984) for an analysis of how the product lifecycle affects firm strategy. Most textbooks and manuals in strategic management, like Grant (2005) and Porter (1980), discuss strategy in different contexts, such as in high growth or mature industries.

[35] Complementors could be included as well.

effects are close to twenty percent of performance variability, while firm effects stable through time account for about twice as much.[36] Even though industry membership substantially affects a firm's performance, its positioning within the industry seems to matter much more.

A firm's strategy and the resources that are more critical for success depend on the characteristics of the industry, though industry structure is also endogenously driven by the actions of its players. Since the early work in strategy of Andrews (1971), key success factors at the industry level are supposed to explain the greater performance of those firms that manage to do better along these factors.[37] These factors ultimately refer to superior resources whose ownership gives a firm an advantage over competitors in its industry. From a value perspective they represent strategic races among competitors to achieve a superior and defendable resource profile.

Effects of industry structure on profitability

Porter's (1980) model of the five forces is certainly the best known tool for industry analysis. The critical concept in understanding industry and firm profits is rivalry. As explained by industrial organization economists and the structure-conduct-performance model, high average profitability can be observed in industries with lower rivalry, i.e., gentle nonprice rivalry. It is the level and type of rivalry that exists in an industry that determines its profitability. For instance, industries with few players and high demand growth should produce less pressure on margins and allow greater profitability. In contrast, perfectly competitive industries should be associated with intense price competition and low profits for all competitors.

The extent of rivalry in the industry primarily depends on its structural characteristics, which can be grouped into five forces.

---

[36] See Rumelt (1991) for an early piece of this research stream and Bowman and Helfat (2001) for a later review. McGahan and Porter (1997) showed that the industry effect varies substantially across different types of industries, though its average impact is about half of the firm (business-level) effect.

[37] See Vasconcellos and Hambrick (1989) for an empirical analysis of key success factors in industrial markets. Amit and Schoemaker (1993) provide some refinement of these ideas from a resource-based view perspective.

The intrinsic characteristics of the industry (such as concentration, demand growth, and cost structure) are the primary determinants of industry rivalry. However, the potential of new entrants (i.e., the existence of entry barriers), the pressure from substitute products, and the bargaining power of suppliers and customers versus the firms in the industries (and the prices they pay and charge) also determine the level and type of rivalry within the industry. Though some rivalry among competitors will always exist, it is only destructive rivalry on prices that destroys margins as opposed to differentiation-based rivalry that increases customer insensitivity to prices and allows higher prices and margins, like Coke and Pepsi in the soft drinks industry.

The effects of rivalry in industry profits are well known since Adam Smith and Cournot. Porter has taken traditional economic analysis and turned it into a powerful tool for strategic management. From this perspective, the capability of the firm to build a strong position that isolates it from the effect of competitors in the market should ultimately determine the final profitability of a given firm within its industry. Thus, differentiation and barriers to competition emerge as the main strategic variables that allow firms to reduce their exposure to the actions of current, potential, and indirect competitors and their bargaining power over suppliers and customers. Choosing the right industry can be as important for high profitability as building a strong position that is difficult for competitors to attack. In this sense, Porter has defined strategy as jockeying for position in the industry context defined by the five forces.

Value analysis at the business level

We have analyzed firms as strategically independent competitive units whose major role is the creation of value for customers, so that the firm may appropriate some of this value for its owners. The competitive units that we call "firms" are comprised of a variety of resources, including firm-level resources, which should be able to produce more value as part of the firm's strategy than as separate entities, because otherwise these resources would leave the firm. Below we will analyze some examples of how the emergence and the specific boundaries of a firm will be determined by the value that it can create through its business strategy.

Why do schools exist, but not firms for long-term secretarial services?

Just like business firms, schools and universities compete against other institutions to gather knowledge and other resources in order to attract customers, i.e., students. Universities are more than the mere aggregation of separate administrative staff and teachers: they compete as one entity comprised of lower-level entities (schools, departments, and professors) within one overall strategy to deal with external and internal resources, customers, and competitors. Different elements of the strategy around their resources are defined at different levels of aggregation. They exist as organizations because they can provide more value than its separate entities could independently.

As far as strategic management is concerned, we could probe into the reasons why professors as a critical resource may find it better to compete as part of a school in a university instead of following their own strategy as independent competitive units. To compete independently, professors would have to gather relevant resources and attract students, while fighting in the market with other schools and professors. Certainly, there are large economies of scale and learning in teaching, so that a university as a collection of different professors and other staff facilitates knowledge specialization and division of labor. However, following a contracting rationale, we can ask why markets do not usually act as the coordination mechanism of professors and other support staff, which could be potentially tied to each other and to students through contracts.

It is worthwhile to note that in most schools and universities, besides administrative and support staff, there are tenure-track professors, visiting faculty, semi-permanent contracted teachers, and part-time adjunct faculty, as well as outsourced teaching carried out by external professors and even specialized firms for very specific noncore activities.[38] The variety of these contractual relationships is very large ranging from employment contracts to fully independent professors

---

[38] Some business schools, for instance, sometimes hire the services of outdoor training firms to provide this kind of specialized training.

that usually do some occasional teaching. The nature of these contracts becomes secondary as far as strategy is concerned. The strategy for an educational institution essentially combines a set of internal and external resources, including all of these types of professors and administrative staff, which are perceived by customers as part of the university that they may attend. Graduates get a formal degree from the university and not from a collection of specific professors, regardless of whether or not they are on the payroll. While the individual professor is carrying out his or her activities, regardless of the specific characteristics of the contract, he or she is acting on behalf of the school in dealing with internal and external resource providers, such as library services and book suppliers respectively. More important, the professor does not have to fight with other professors and schools in attracting students, and he or she delivers her teaching as part of a school's program.

From a value perspective, the school emerges as an independent competitive unit with one overall strategy to facilitate resource coordination and development (resource management) and to attract a certain type and number of students (market positioning), while competing with other schools as collections of professors (competitive dynamics). Excellent professors can exploit their superior skills if they work in an excellent university with a high reputation, better than they could do on their own or in a lower quality university. Being part of a high quality establishment allows them to dedicate more time to research and less time to administrative and marketing duties, so that the professor's superior skills are reinforced and developed further. A professor can usually create more value for students by being part of the collection of resources (i.e., university) and, thus, appropriate more value for him or herself than by being a freelance professor, as we can see in the higher salaries for tenured versus adjunct faculty. Similarly, the professor with high quality teaching and research also contributes to the value created by the university and its reputation as an institution of knowledge. The value jointly created by the collection of specific resources is shared between school owners and resource providers.

In this example we can see how collections of professors under one university umbrella may create more value than those professors could on their own. This is the reason why universities have emerged as professional service firms and they have replaced individual professors.

However, being part of a collection of resources does not necessarily create value for the resources. We may observe how some forms of art, for instance, are based primarily in the work of single individuals, like painting or writing, where most artistic value can be created by one person. In this type of activity, a collection of individuals does not create more value than a person can individually.

The importance of value creation on the emergence and boundaries of organization is particularly clear in the case of secretarial services. Ever since secretarial services were performed inside organizations, firms have usually hired their own secretaries. It is interesting to see that there are no firms that provide long-term outsourcing of secretarial services, but there are temporary agencies that offer secretarial services to firms. To understand the existence of this type of temporary secretarial services, but not permanent outsourcing, we should analyze how the firm as a collection of secretaries in this case may offer value over the services provided by one secretary.

First, it is important to notice that secretarial services are relatively low skilled and highly specific to the organization. A good secretary needs to know the formal and informal procedures of the firm as well as the preferences of her boss. Taking into consideration the initially steep learning curve, rotation among secretarial posts is limited, and fixed assignments are usually preferable.

It seems reasonable that some firms which may provide temporary secretarial services exist. Very often, they provide a substitute for one secretary that takes a short leave of absence, for instance, due to personal reasons. Though the effectiveness of the temporary worker will certainly be lower than the person being substituted, the negative effect on the organization's processes of the missing secretary will be reduced with such a temporary replacement. However, hiring and training one person for a short period as a substitute has important transaction costs. A specialized firm that provides this kind of service would be more efficient than the occasional need that may arise inside organizations for managing this type of replacement. Large firms may have their own staff of secretaries for temporary assignments, if the number of such needs becomes sufficiently large.

Transaction costs economizing is, therefore, critical for understanding short-term secretarial services, though paradoxically they are not really associated with contracting issues. It is interesting to note that the contract between the temporary worker and the permanent

secretary are exactly the same, except obviously its duration.[39] Regardless of the features of the contract, the firm hiring the temporary work
agency saves on the transaction costs of finding the right person for
a temporary assignment, though they have to pay a substantial com-
mission to the agency that frequently exceeds thirty percent of the
secretary's salary. On the other hand, the work agency has to bear the
entire transaction costs of having the right type of temporary workers
on the list, but they can spread this cost over a larger number of jobs,
as they rotate these workers among different companies until they are
hired permanently in one (thus, also providing hiring services in addition to replacement services). Finally, workers also benefit from having
less transaction costs on their side and greater likelihood that they will
find a job, a temporary one that may become permanent. Thus, the
value created by the work agency is divided among the three involved
parties. This value comes primarily from transaction costs economizing associated with a mediation service for finding a person/position
fit to fill a temporary job.

Why does this type of service exist only for temporary secretarial services, but not for long-term secretarial firms? Long-term professional
service firms exist for legal counseling or accounting, for instance,
but not for secretarial services. Value analysis can help us understand
why. These services are less specific to a given position and more highly
skilled than those carried out by secretaries. In these cases of value creation, specialized firms can take advantage of economies of scale and
greater competence development in their area of expertise, so that they
provide the service for lower cost than a customer firm could do internally. An accounting or legal firm creates value through economies of
scale, specialization, and learning. These firms may also develop a positive reputation that benefits all employees via higher salaries, which
they may not have as individual accountants and lawyers.

To the contrary, this is not the case for secretarial services, which
are essentially an individual activity. The key is that the quality of
the services of a secretary does not depend on whether it is part of a
larger organization of secretaries. Being part of such an organization
would not increase the level of competence or efficiency of the secretary

---

[39] It is mandatory by law in many countries with high levels of social protection
like Spain that the conditions for temporary workers need to be the same as for
people in the permanent payroll.

performing the job inside a certain firm. As a result, there is no reason for firms of long-term secretarial services to exist. Because they do not create any extra value in the long term, firms are not usually willing to pay extra for a secretary that belongs to a secretarial services firm, though they may benefit from temporary secretarial services and pay extra for it.

In summary, organizations emerge as collections of resources for the sake of value creation. Being part of a resource bundle may allow such resources to create and appropriate more value than they could do otherwise. This is done through the firm's strategy to deal with internal and external resources and customers versus other competitors in the market, that is, their collective strategic choices about resource management, market positioning, and competitive dynamics.

7 | *Corporate strategy*

Value creation at the corporate level

Strategic decisions are usually categorized into business versus corporate strategy based on the specific level at which they take place within the firm. Business strategy decisions are concerned with how the firm competes within a particular industry or product market. In the previous chapter we discussed the main strategic issues at the business level and how the firm deals with a particular set of customers, resources, and competitors. In the following three chapters, we will turn to corporate strategy, including key questions about diversification, internationalization, and the broader social strategy and responsibility of the corporation. This chapter focuses on the industrial scope of the firm and issues like diversification, vertical integration, mergers and acquisitions, and alliances.

The distinction between business and corporate strategy is really a matter of analytical convenience. Strategic decisions at both levels are necessarily connected and they cannot be fully separated. The corporation is indeed an aggregate of lower level organizational units with potential presence in different industries, geographical markets, and even social activities, which constitute the boundaries of the firm. Corporate decisions can only create value through its effect on how the firm deals with resources, customers, and competitors at the business level. Corporate level management affects the competitiveness of its business units, but there cannot be corporate strategy without business units. Similarly, even the simplest firm comprised of only one business unit will have some corporate strategy issues to deal with, such as its degree of vertical integration. Thus, the intimate connection between corporate and business strategy cannot be neglected and both jointly comprise the firm's strategy.

Though corporate and business-level decisions are connected, we will now concentrate on corporate management. Through its activities and decisions, the corporate office may have a positive or a negative effect on the competitiveness of its lower level business units. There is clear empirical evidence that part of the variance in firm performance can be attributed to corporate factors, in addition to any possible industry and stable business level effects.[1] Corporations as a whole are responsible for about ten percent of firm performance according to most studies, though they can be as low as zero, and eighteen percent or even higher in some studies. The corporate office can have a substantial effect on the performance of their business units, but its influence varies considerably depending on the particular industries and geographical areas in which the corporation has presence.

Among other strategic decisions, the corporate office is responsible for setting and managing the boundaries of the corporation as a whole. These decisions include the options for horizontal diversification into new businesses and vertical integration. In this chapter we will also explore mergers and acquisitions as well as the management of strategic alliances and inter-firm cooperation.

Corporate activities for value creation

Goold *et al.* (1994) argue that parent companies can basically engage in four types of activities at the corporate level and, most frequently, they end up making their businesses less competitive and destroying value.

- Stand-alone influence. Corporations can directly influence their business units as stand-alone profit centers through their direct involvement in setting strategic goals and planning, human resource management, approving capital expenditures, controlling business units, and so on. Unfortunately, these decisions may destroy value as corporate managers dedicate only part of their time to business-level issues, which are run by managers that have direct connection and full dedication to their resources, customers, and competitors.

---

[1] Bowman and Helfat (2001) provide a review of the literature on the corporate effect and conclude that most studies show a significant corporate effect, thus supporting the ideas that corporate strategy does matter and it should be studied, though some early empirical analyses found a negligible corporate effect (Rumelt, 1991).

- Establishing linkages. Business units that share a common corporate umbrella may also benefit from the linkages that can be established by the corporate office among the units. These links can foster cooperation and synergies among businesses, so that they may take advantage of economies of scale, transfer of best practices, and cross-selling to common customers, for instance. However, just like forced marriages, linkages established by a corporate office are not likely to work if there is not clear self-interest in the units in being part of such relationships. In addition, alliances may be a good alternative to take advantage of any potential benefit of occasional linkages.
- Centralized functions. When similar activities are performed across business units, centralized support functions can produce economies of scale by moving these activities to the corporate level. While this type of activities can create value for the business units, particularly through potential cost reductions, they may also generate excessive overhead, delay decisions, and ultimately result in inadequate support. Furthermore, if these activities can be removed from the control of the business units as a cost center without an impact in the unit's competitiveness, full outsourcing may be an even more efficient alternative.
- Corporate development. The corporate office may contribute to managing acquisitions, divestments, alliances, new ventures, and other activities of corporate development. Having the support of a competent corporate office may be an advantage for the business units that need to engage in such activities. However, the continuous buying and selling of businesses promoted by some corporate offices may interfere with the competitiveness of their business units. Furthermore, there is an efficient market for corporate control and, as far as value creation is concerned, the corporate office would need to somehow perform these tasks better than the market itself, i.e. better than other specialized players in corporate development.

The value created (or destroyed) at the corporate level is contingent on what the corporate office can specifically contribute to its business units to make them more competitive. Campbell *et al.* (1995) call this potential for a given corporate office to contribute to its business units its "parenting advantage." In this sense, the appropriate fit between the parenting advantage and its business units' competitive requirements and characteristics determines whether or not they benefit from being under its corporate umbrella. Thus, the boundaries of the firm cannot be set independently of the specific businesses under study and their fit with the skills at the corporate level.

Horizontal diversification into new businesses

How far should a firm go in putting different units under its corporate umbrella so that it may create value through adequate corporate management? This is the critical question in corporate strategy about the boundaries of the firm that we already began to discuss in chapter three with regard to their effect on the value created by internal resources. We will now probe deeper into this question applied specifically to diversification decisions that deal with entire business units rather than single resources. Diversification decisions have important implications for how the firm creates value through the different units that they manage. Let us analyze the potential benefits and costs of diversification as well as its ultimate effect on firm performance.

The benefits of diversification

The existing literature has identified several key benefits that may drive diversification decisions, which can be associated with how the firm deals with resources, customers, and competitors.[2]

---

[2] Evidently, this is not the only way to categorize the possible benefits of diversification. For instance, Grant (2005) in his textbook identifies three major competitive advantages that can be obtained by diversifiers: market power, economies of scope, and economies from internalizing transactions (also including the advantages of the diversified corporation as an internal market and its informational advantages over external markets). Jones and Hill (1988) identified three major types of benefits for different types of diversification: economies of integration (for vertical integration), economies of scope (for related diversification), and economies of internal capital markets (for unrelated diversification). The categorization in this chapter follows the same structure that we have used before, so that we may push further the idea that the core strategic decisions ultimately deal with the management of resources to create value in the presence of competitors.

Implications for resource management

Operational efficiency can be improved when some resources are aggregated so that the entire firm can take advantage of any possible economies of scope among its lower level units. Transaction cost economics (TCE) scholars stress the need for transaction costs to exist for these efficiencies to be actually realized only within the organization and not through market exchanges, though we questioned in chapter three that transaction costs are always a necessary prerequisite for diversification.[3] A multiproduct firm may arise to integrate the common and recurrent use of a specialized and indivisible physical asset in different businesses, which can then benefit from lower costs. Operational efficiencies, including both lower technology and administration costs obtained by merging related businesses, are a critical reason for a firm to diversify its operations and to aggregate within its corporate boundaries different types of resources to conduct activities in multiple arenas. These operational efficiencies constitute the traditional economies of scope behind related diversification.

In addition to the potential to increase operational efficiency, *knowledge and innovation* can be substantially affected by putting different units under the same corporation. This is the key idea behind the knowledge-based view of the firm (Grant, 1996; Kogut and Zander, 1993), though it has also been acknowledged from a TCE perspective by Teece (1980). The transfer of knowledge among business units has been regarded as a fundamental motivation for diversification in the existing literature, for instance, the general management skills that facilitated the emergence of conglomerates after the second world war and the more recent notions of dominant logic and core competence.[4] Furthermore, innovation and dynamic capabilities can be facilitated by putting different resources under the same corporate umbrella, which may increase the firm's absorptive capacity and its potential to develop new knowledge. In fact, firms often get into areas, either through

---

[3] The mainstream TCE approach to diversification is discussed in Teece (1980; 1982a).

[4] These two concepts were coined by Prahalad and Bettis (1986) and Prahalad and Hamel (1990) respectively. See Goold and Luchs (1993) for a review of the literature on diversification in management.

internal development or acquisitions, to improve their stock of available skills and technologies so that they may achieve further growth.[5]

The literature also discusses several *financial reasons* as a potential source of value creation for diversification. It has been argued that even unrelated diversification may result in financial benefits such as lower cost of capital, better allocation and control of financial resources, and reduced risk.[6] These motivations for diversification are valid as far as they may allow greater operational efficiency and information management. More specifically, financial resources are just one type of resource that firms need, whose management may produce some economies of scale. To the extent that a larger firm can obtain internal and external funds in better terms than a smaller unit, diversification can result in lower costs, analogous to the economies of scope for any physical resource usable across different businesses. The possible informational advantages that a corporate office enjoys over external capital markets are part of the operational benefits that firms may have over markets. The logic of internal capital markets is ultimately an efficiency based explanation, probably the best one for unrelated diversification.[7] As we will discuss later on, both the relative benefits and costs of internal versus external financial control would need to be assessed for each corporation. These financial motivations for diversification associated with cost of capital and internal capital markets seem to be solid, though possibly more difficult to gauge than the effect of operational efficiency and knowledge considerations in driving diversification decisions.

In contrast, *risk management* as a distinct rationale for diversification has been put into question.[8] More stable cash flow can result from shifting operations from one business to another in response to

---

[5] See, for instance, Kim and Kogut (1996) for an analysis of the technological trajectory of firms and its relationship with knowledge and diversification.

[6] For instance, Barney (1997) identifies three possible reasons for unrelated diversification: better capital allocation, risk reduction, and tax advantages.

[7] See Besank *et al.* (2004). Williamson (1975) analyzes in depth the advantages and disadvantages of internal capital markets.

[8] Amihud and Lev (1981) study the managerial reasons for diversification based on risk reduction. See Hill and Hansen (1991) for an empirical analysis that shows the negative effect on performance of those firms that diversify exclusively to reduce risk. Barney (1997) summarizes the key arguments against reducing risk as the sole motivation for diversification.

changes in industry cycles, but it is the operational benefits that produce the advantages of diversification in this case, not risk management on its own. Actually, it is unlikely that corporations may generate any advantage by making overall cash flows more stable without some connection among their business units. Reducing risk without any positive effect on operations or lower cost of capital does not add value and it does not make the firm more competitive or profitable. Stockholders could potentially benefit from having lower risk, but they can actually diversify their portfolios on their own, so that diversification to reduce risk does not really create value for stockholders. In fact, they can do so better than corporations can do for them without paying a premium to buy stock in other firms and based on their specific risk profile.

Implications for customer relationships

In addition to these potential benefits of diversification for the improved management of internal resources, diversification also affects the relationship between the firm's units and their customers. A diversified corporation may achieve synergies on the demand side by managing partially overlapping sets of customers in a coordinated manner. We will now consider not the synergistic effects of diversification in the management of resources by the firm, but in the customer's perspective and the greater value that they may obtain from diversified corporations, particularly through lower customer costs.

A diversified corporation may *reduce the nonmonetary costs of customers* because its units may share and better exploit its common interface with the customers. This is evident in the case of a brand name that can be used across a bundle of related but different products, thus strengthening their recognition and reducing information costs of customers. Also, cross-selling among the different products of a diversified organization encourages sales by facilitating customer accessibility to the products. Products can also be redesigned to take advantage of joint use, so that ease of use is improved through product bundling.[9] Even the mere size of a larger diversified corporation could have a positive effect in attracting customers, if customers perceive that

---

[9] A good example of this is Apple and its integration of hardware and software, particularly in the iPod and the iPhone, for which customers benefit most from their user-friendliness.

the reliability of the product, the post-sales service, and the capability to absorb potential legal penalties could be greater for an aggregate of business units, which share at least part of the corporate reputation and legal obligations.

Implications for competitive dynamics

Finally, diversified corporations may be better prepared to deal with the pressure from competitors over resources and customers than their business units could do on their own. By putting different units under the same corporate umbrella, the firm may achieve greater *market power* that could result in lower cost of inputs and greater prices for customers. The bargaining power of the units versus suppliers and buyers would increase as long as there is sufficient overlap in their resources and target markets. In this case diversification would not create greater value for society as a whole, but it would allow greater value appropriation for the firm and its internal resources. This collusive effect is also affected by multipoint competition.[10]

The costs of diversification

So far, we have analyzed how the diversified corporation may have certain advantages over independent units with regard to how they deal with their internal and external resources, their customers, and even their relative market power. However, greater diversification is not always better, because it also generates costs that need to be compared to its potential benefits discussed above. The literature has identified different types of costs associated with the two main levels of a diversified corporation.

Corporate-level costs

Diversified organizations have a corporate office of greater or smaller size in charge of managing the portfolio of business units. This corporate level necessarily has some costs. These corporate layers generate at least some labor costs and, more generally, overhead costs of managing information and coordination of the activities of the business units. Having a corporate office may reduce the competitiveness of the business units even beyond the directly observable overhead costs, for

[10] See Gimeno and Woo (1999) for an analysis of multimarket contact.

instance, delaying decision making. These are examples of administrative or *bureaucratic costs* of running the corporation as a system for allocating and controlling resources, which could be done by markets instead, as TCE notes. If the units competed independently in the market, the costs of organizing those activities through markets would be different and maybe not exist at all in some cases. These bureaucratic costs of managing transactions internally in contrast to market governance are primarily driven by the characteristics of the exchanges that are internalized within the corporation. Complex exchanges between closely interconnected units should presumably require greater administrative costs than the loosely connected businesses of conglomerates.

Beyond general transaction costs, the specific characteristics of the corporation and how good it is in managing certain businesses also matter. Corporate managers may become overloaded with information from businesses about which they have limited direct contact and, thus, less knowledge. Some corporations can be better than others at dealing with this challenge that diversification creates. This effect will become more important as the degree of diversification grows, particularly in a large number of unrelated businesses. By spreading their knowledge too thinly and imposing their decisions across different businesses, the corporate office may have a negative influence on business units in the pursuit of synergies, which are often overestimated. Corporate managers can exert too much influence, centralize activities that are critical to the competitiveness of the units, and manage the development of their business units less effectively than other corporations could, or than the units could do on their own. These are *additional costs specific to each corporation* that also need to be taken into account in the analysis of diversification, in addition to the more general bureaucratic costs of managing transactions inside the hierarchy.

Business-level costs

Besides general transaction costs and corporate-specific costs, business units may generate new costs when they become part of a diversified corporation. Business unit managers may try to influence corporate decisions in their favor versus other managers within the corporation.[11] These are called *influence costs*, referring to a wide range of activities

---

[11] See Milgrom and Roberts (1992), particularly chapter six.

of managers to influence the distribution of costs and benefits across different managers and units within the organization. Managers, particularly in large, diversified corporations, may fight against each other for individual promotions, more resources, greater power and higher salaries, thus engaging in rent-seeking behavior that distorts decisions and increases costs. Just like companies may spend heavily to obtain a monopoly from the government without creating value for society, managers may dedicate time and resources and manipulate information to obtain some privileges and resources from the corporate office. Influence costs would be eliminated if the business unit competed independently in the market.

Williamson (1985) has also noted that organizations provide *low-powered incentives* to managers in contrast to markets. For instance, business unit managers can expect greater forgiveness from the corporate office if a project suffers unexpected costs, though markets would be less forgiving and allow bankruptcy. In other words, managers feel much closer the pressure from the market if they do not have a corporate office above them that can protect them to some extent in case of failure. As a result, business units in diversified corporations may have somewhat reduced motivation and mitigated pressure to deliver high performance.

All of the benefits and costs of placing several businesses within a firm's corporate strategy determine the value that diversification may produce. The ultimate test of whether one business unit should be part of a larger firm or not depends on its relative competitiveness as part of one firm strategy in contrast to what it would be as a separate firm with its own independent strategy for value creation and appropriation. Broadly speaking, this is what Porter (1987) calls the *better-off test* for diversification decisions. This type of comparative test is the necessary and sufficient condition for the decision to diversify to generate value.[12]

---

[12] Porter (1987) also discusses the attractiveness of the industry and the cost of entry. However, these two tests do not seem necessary and the better-off test is sufficient to identify a possibility for value creation. Regarding an industry's attractiveness, much value can be created in presumably unattractive industries as Wal-Mart and Nucor, for instance, have shown. Industry attractiveness is in part determined endogenously and, furthermore, even in unattractive industry some firms can be very successful. Also, the cost of entry can be subsumed within the best-off test when it is a relevant variable (i.e., an incremental cost

The effect of diversification on performance

There is a large amount of empirical research that investigates diversification and its performance consequences. It is clear that the diversified corporation has become ubiquitous during the twentieth century in developed countries.[13] This evolution towards greater diversification seems to have occurred in waves of merger activity.[14] Apparently, the diversified corporation has some benefits over nondiversifiers, though diversification can go too far and it is often followed by "sticking to the knitting" policies.

The empirical research on the diversification–performance relationship in strategy is consistent with this interpretation, though the wide variety of results makes it difficult to reach solid conclusions. Many studies detect positive average effects of diversification, but others find a negative relationship and even curvilinear. One meta-analysis of the literature shows an inverted-U relationship between diversification and performance.[15] It seems that some diversification is good because firms may take advantage of synergies and knowledge transfer to more closely related businesses. However, as the corporation moves further to unrelated areas, the additional costs of diversification may start to exceed the potential benefits. Probably, the positive effect of businesses "relatedness" is the most widely accepted moderator of the diversification–performance relationship, such that only related diversification can be expected to produce positive results. In contrast, unrelated diversification is more likely to destroy value.[16]

that the entry could generate). In the specific case of acquisitions, the final acquisition price would merely determine who appropriates the value that may be created, but not whether the merger should take place or not (i.e., it would be a mere transfer of value between stockholders, but not an incremental cost of the merger).

[13] See Rumelt's (1982) analysis of Fortune 500 companies. The number of single business companies changed from 42 percent in 1949 to 14.4 percent in 1974. Santalo and Becerra (2008) find that 60 percent of all industries in their study of US public firms are populated exclusively by diversified firms.

[14] See Scherer and Ross (1990) for a historical discussion of mergers. The late nineties saw the last burst in merger activities followed by a period of refocusing activities after the technology bubble exploded in the early years of the twenty-first century.

[15] See Palich *et al.* (2000).

[16] Rumelt (1974) launched this idea that has received strong support, for instance by Chatterjee and Wernerfelt (1991), though other studies question it, such as

It is interesting to note that operational synergies are very difficult to achieve and empirical research has had trouble measuring its presumed positive effect on performance.[17] The practical difficulties in achieving synergies are probably due to the excessive managerial expectations from the corporate office about potential operational economies.[18] By forcing unwilling business unit managers to achieve unrealistic synergies, diversification often ends up making the business units less competitive and, thus, destroying value.

Whether diversification creates or destroys value has been the subject of much research in finance as well. There is abundant empirical evidence of a negative relationship between diversification and performance. For instance, Berger and Ofek (1995) find that US conglomerates are priced approximately fifteen percent below the market value than they would have as disaggregated independent businesses. The explanation for this fact is often based on agency costs associated with managerial personal interest in diversification and growth as opposed to pursuing stockholders' interests. However, more recent research argues that both diversification and performance are endogenously determined, so that firms with lower performance are the ones more likely to diversify; once this endogeneity is taken into account, the diversification discount disappears or even turns to a diversification premium.[19] In this sense, diversification does not necessarily destroy value, even if there is a negative cross-sectional relationship between diversification and firm market value.

From a value perspective, there are reasons to expect both positive and negative effects of diversification on performance as we discussed earlier. For different samples and in different moments in time we could expect one type of effect to be greater than the other. Santaló and Becerra (2008) show that there may be a diversification premium or a discount depending on the type of industries and firms included in the sample. There are clear reasons why either relationship could be

---

Bettis and Hall (1982) and more recently Park (2003) based on an endogenity argument.

[17] For instance, John and Harrison (1999) found no evidence that diversified manufacturing firms actually benefit from shared resources. Chatterjee (1986) also concluded from an analysis of acquisitions that operational synergies are smaller than collusive or purely financial synergies.

[18] See Goold and Campbell (1998) for an applied analysis of why synergies are so difficult to be obtained.

[19] See Campa and Kedia (2002) and Villalonga (2004).

observed, even after controlling for endogeneity. In industries with few diversifiers, specialists systematically perform better and diversification into them would be likely to decrease performance. The opposite conclusion can be obtained for industries dominated by diversifiers, which typically have greater performance in industries with few specialized firms. We should remember, however, that diversifiers are much more numerous in our economy and, thus, they tend to have more advantages than disadvantages in contrast to specialized firms.

Overall, it seems reasonable that the benefits of diversification may outweigh its disadvantages, particularly because diversified firms can do what Williamson (1975) calls *selective intervention*, that is, leaving divisions as virtually independent units when there are few benefits for greater integration (i.e., replicating market mechanisms of control and coordination), while exploiting the advantages of integration whenever they may exist. Though Williamson argues against the possibility for selective intervention to exist effectively, we have seen the number of diversifiers grow during the previous century probably for this reason, though they can go too far and start destroying value.[20] For each firm analyzing the possibility of diversification into a new business, the potential benefits and costs of such a move should be considered, which generally depends on the characteristics and skills of the firm, the new industry, and the relatedness between both in terms of resources and customers.

Vertical integration

One type of diversification decision has received special attention: vertical integration associated with make-or-buy decisions (and downstream integration). We can analyze value creation in vertical integration by looking at the different possible benefits and costs that we discussed above and applying them to this specific case.

First, vertical integration may result in operational efficiencies, both administrative and technological. The characteristics of the transaction should determine whether it can be managed more efficiently inside a hierarchy or externally through the market.[21] To be efficient, firms are

[20] See Grant *et al.* (1988).
[21] See Williamson (1975; 1985). Grossman and Hart (1986) provide a formal analysis of vertical integration from a property rights perspective.

likely to internalize those transactions that are more frequent, highly specific, complex, and surrounded with greater uncertainty. Most crucially, given the presence of opportunism and bounded rationality, the need to protect highly specific assets in market transactions may create high ex-ante and ex-post transaction costs for the firms. The presence of high specificity may lead firms to underinvest in these specialized assets, so that they could become less efficient than integrated players. This TCE explanation of vertical integration based primarily on asset specificity has received substantial empirical support.[22]

However, TCE is just one type of saving associated with lower administrative costs than vertical integration can sometimes provide, primarily in the presence of asset specificity. Overall, economies of scale and other purely technological reasons, in addition to transaction costs, also determine whether the market or the hierarchy is more efficient. Thus, the overall relative efficiency of the two alternative options, vertical integration versus market exchanges, needs to be taken into account. If the costs of managing the relationship between two units inside the organization or through the market are similar, technological reasons could even be the primary motivation for vertical integration.

In contrast, some authors inspired in the resource-based view (RBV) have stressed the knowledge implications for vertical integration.[23] Rather than choosing one approach, efficiency versus knowledge as the only rationale, it seems more reasonable to adopt an eclectic view because both can be regarded as different ways for vertical integration to create value. As we discussed in chapters two and three, a knowledge perspective can hardly be regarded as a full explanation for firm boundaries, neither contracting alone.[24]

In addition to the operational efficiencies and knowledge implications of managing vertically integrated resources, the literature has also

---

[22] See a review of the empirical literature by Shelanski and Klein (1995). There is wide support for the TCE explanation of "make or buy" decisions in economics (Joskow, 1987) and strategy (Pisano, 1990) as well as for downstream integration (Majumdar and Ramaswamy, 1994).

[23] For instance, Conner and Prahalad (1996). Richardson (1972) had already argued that the level of similarity and complementarity of the two firms' activities (more generally, their capabilities) would determine the boundaries of the firm.

[24] An eclectic or integrationist solution has been defended by scholars like Foss, Madhok, Mahoney, and Barney, for instance.

identified other benefits of vertical integration associated with market power. For example, Porter (1980) highlighted several advantages of vertical integration, including how it could assure supply and/or demand for the firm, offset bargaining power and input cost distortions, elevate entry and mobility barriers, enhance the ability to differentiate, and defend against foreclosure.[25] Indeed, vertical integration may have important effects on the firm's competitiveness and make it more or less competitive than other players. To the contrary, Williamson (1991) argued against making boundary decisions based on competitive dynamics and market power (i.e., *strategizing*). He believes that economizing, particularly on transaction costs, leads to the best strategy. This controversy triggered by Williamson resembles the older debate about the profitability of large firms between Bain (i.e., barriers to entry and industry concentration) and the Chicago school (i.e., greater efficiency and innovation). From a value perspective, both power and efficiency jointly explain firm profitability, though the former is primarily concerned with value appropriation and the latter with value creation. Both need to be taken into account to ultimately understand firm profitability and the performance consequences of strategic decisions like vertical integration.

Finally, the implications of vertical integration on customer relationships also need to be considered. The interface with customers of backward-integrated companies does not really change, but it does substantially for firms that integrate forward. To the extent that integration may affect the products and services offered to the customers and their nonmonetary costs, customer value can be created or destroyed. In some cases, vertical integration may facilitate the launching of new or differentiated products that stress unique high quality components, for instance. It also may provide better after-sales service with respect to parts and replacements, which can reduce risks for customers. Forward integration gives direct access to customers, which allows the firm to manipulate the accessibility of its products.

In summary, vertical integration affects how the firm deals with its internal and external resources as well as its customers. It also

[25] He also identified a variety of economies of integration (both technological and contractual); tap into technology, and enter a higher return business. This last point is not truly a benefit of vertical integration in a strict sense. It could be regarded as general good advice for any type of new entry decision, because it is obviously good for firms to be present in businesses with higher profitability.

influences how well the firm can fight for resources and customers *vis-à-vis* its competitors, i.e., its market power. Beyond a mere contracting issue for resource inputs, vertical integration is a major strategic decision that has the potential to affect how much value the firm can create for its customers and capture for its resource providers and stockholders. The acid test for the make-or-buy decision ultimately relies on relative value creation and appropriation.

Mergers and acquisitions

Mergers and acquisitions are another important corporate-level decision that deals with the boundaries of the firm. In contrast to internal development, firms may use mergers as a vehicle for internal growth as well as for horizontal diversification and vertical integration. To this extent, the analysis of mergers essentially overlaps with the issues that we have discussed earlier in this chapter. The same potential benefits and costs of firm diversification should also be considered for mergers and acquisitions. However, because there is a precise moment in time when a merger takes place, we can study with greater precision how the change in a firm's boundaries affects its market value, as event studies in finance and strategy often do.

Empirical research on mergers and acquisitions has investigated both the short-term effects on stock value and the long-term consequences on market value, usually one to three years after the merger took place. The short-term implications of mergers and acquisitions can be observed in the changes in stock price of the acquirer and the acquired firms, under the reasonable assumption that markets are efficient and reflect the consensus expectations of future cash flows to be generated by the firm for its stockholders. We can measure the change in both firms to see how much market value is expected to be created or destroyed in the future. The seller's stock price usually goes up between twenty percent and thirty percent while the acquiring firm's stock changes by around one or two percent on average, often insignificantly up or down, depending on the study.[26] Thus, on average the increase in the market value of the acquirer a few days before and after the acquisition is announced is substantially greater than the change in

[26] See the meta-analysis done by Datta *et al.* (1992). A recent review of the finance literature is done by Stein (2003).

the acquirer's value, even if we take into consideration the difference in size between both firms.

These results can be interpreted as strong evidence in favor of the positive effects of the market for corporate control for overall shareholders' wealth. In a process that resembles the survival of the fittest, better managed firms tend to acquire less well managed corporations. Acquired firms have typically underperformed the market during the two years before they were acquired and acquirers tend to have had above-average recent performance.[27] There is also evidence that more value is created when the merger takes place between firms in the same or highly related industries.[28] Defensive measures to prevent these acquisitions tend to destroy market value.[29] The expected value generated by mergers, however, tends to be virtually fully appropriated by the stockholders of the selling firm, probably because there is often a bidding war among potential candidates to acquire the firm.

However, the long-term consequences of mergers point in the opposite direction. There is clear empirical evidence that post-merger performance decreases substantially,[30] probably due to the problems of managing integration and its negative effects on innovation.[31] Jensen and Ruback (1983) concluded that most studies showed a decrease in market value around five percent one year after the acquisition; Magenheim and Mueller (1988) found a sixteen percent decline in the acquiring firm's stock price three years after the acquisitions took place. Scherer and Ross (1990: 173) conclude that, based on post-merger performance, "The picture that emerges is a pessimistic one: widespread failure, considerable mediocrity, and occasional successes." These negative consequences of mergers and acquisitions are not truly surprising to the extent that agency costs may induce managers to grow and

[27] See the summary provided by Scherer and Ross (1990).
[28] See Singh and Montgomery (1987), for instance. Morck *et al.* (1990) also report that stock prices of the bidding firm rise when they acquire other players in the same industry, but they fell with unrelated diversification.
[29] See Jarrell *et al.* (1988).
[30] See Ravenscraft and Scherer's (1987) detailed analysis of the economic effects of mergers.
[31] See the work of Michael Hitt and colleagues about the unintended negative effect of mergers on innovation. Haspeslagh and Jemison (1991) analyze the difficult process of post-merger integration.

acquire other firms, despite its possible negative effect on stockholder's wealth.[32]

The empirical evidence of short-term versus long-term effects of mergers on stockholder wealth constitutes an important controversy that still needs to be solved successfully. Apparently, actual and potential mergers are the key mechanism for the market for corporate control to create value for shareholders. However, even though mergers may create value when measured in terms of expectations, they actually end up destroying it. To some extent, this evidence is contrary to the efficient markets hypothesis, which has received strong support in many other contexts.[33] Drawing on post-merger performance, Scherer (1988) even questions whether mergers are indeed creating value by presumably transferring corporate control to better managers.

Though this controversy is particularly challenging for financial economists, strategy scholars are likely to be more comfortable with it. It does not seem unreasonable for mergers to be carried out based on overall positive expectations (particularly those of the managers, though they may be revised downward by financial markets). However, they may not achieve their goals because of the complex problems of integration. Strategy scholars have explored when mergers actually create value.[34] More or less value can be created under specific circumstances and there is no reason to believe that such a value can be correctly anticipated on average, including the estimates done by financial markets. But the existence of any possible aggregate errors does not imply that financial markets are not based on rational expectations that include all available information about the long-term consequences of mergers. They just do not have perfect foresight. Markets tend to overestimate the benefits of mergers, probably driven by the optimistic expectations of successful managers pushing the mergers.

Just like diversification, most empirical research has been concerned with the effect of mergers and acquisitions on firm value and the factors that moderate such an effect, primarily relatedness. However, there is far less research on how firms change their resource configuration and their interface with the customer after mergers. We need to move

---

[32] Jensen (1988) analyzes takeovers from an agency theory perspective.
[33] See the arguments from Jensen (1988) against the idea of myopic markets.
[34] See Hitt *et al.* (2001).

beyond pure measurement of market value and investigate the actual changes in strategy that mergers make possible as the underlying causes of value creation and its appropriation by stockholders.

Strategic alliances and cooperation

Resources may create and capture more value by competing as part of one firm strategy against other market players. Value creation and capture thus drive the boundaries of the firm, including the strategic decisions to diversify, integrate vertically, or acquire other organizations. However, firms also cooperate with each other.[35] They often do both, cooperating and competing with the same organization, often through some type of strategic alliances.[36]

Strategic alliances, including joint ventures and other forms of interfirm cooperation, are important corporate decisions and we should also analyze them as boundaries of the firm. Gulati and Singh (1998: 781) define strategic alliances as "any voluntarily initiated cooperative agreement between firms that involved exchange, sharing, or co-development, and it can include contributions by partners of capital, technology, or firm-specific assets." A critical question is why firms engage in this type of organizational form to manage their cooperation instead of relying on pure market transactions or full integration. The motivation behind the formation of specific alliances is very diverse,[37] but the literature can be grouped into three theoretical approaches: transaction costs, organizational learning, and strategic behavior.[38]

First, alliances are often regarded as an alternative governance mechanism for transactions, i.e., a hybrid organizational form between the hierarchy and the market.[39] To understand alliance formation, we should look for intermediate levels in the characteristics of exchanges

---

[35] See Smith *et al.* (1995) for a broad review of management research on cooperation.

[36] See Brandenburger and Nalebuff (1996) for an analysis of how firms do both cooperate and compete with other players at once.

[37] Inkpen (2001) provides a useful review of this large stream of literature. He highlights five broad categories of goals for alliances: increase speed, gain economies of scale by pooling resources together, reduce risk, increase legitimacy, and gain knowledge and learning.

[38] See Kogut (1988) for a review of these approaches to the analysis of joint ventures.

[39] For a TCE approach to alliances, see Hennart (1988) and Gulati (1995).

that drive internalization from a TCE perspective, such as asset specificity and uncertainty. Thus, alliances arguably develop when there are too many uncertainties to write a complete contract, but it is not effective to fully internalize the transaction either.

Second, alliances may be formed as a means for organizational learning.[40] Alliances can be used to learn from a partner, particularly tacit knowledge that is difficult to acquire without direct contact and observation. They can also be used to jointly create new knowledge by pooling complementary skills together. Despite the potential learning benefits for both partners, alliances create tension between cooperation and competition with respect to knowledge, so that allies may even engage in a race to learn from each other while trying to protect their own knowledge and competencies.[41]

Finally, alliances are often created to enhance the market positioning of the firm versus competitors, which Kogut (1988) broadly referred to as *strategic behavior*. This rationale, frequently collusive, goes from depriving competitors of raw materials to tying downstream distribution and stabilizing oligopolistic competition.

It is not surprising that these three theoretical approaches to alliance formation are closely related to the benefits of diversification and mergers that we discussed above. Alliances actually constitute partial integration across different firm strategies, so that they should be able to partially achieve the possible benefits of integrating different resources under one strategy. Thus, alliances have important implications for resource management (both with regard to efficiency and knowledge) as well as customer relationships and competitive dynamics (i.e., strategic behavior).

The rationale for alliances lies in the value creation potential of firm resources that are partially pooled together as well as its appropriation by the partners. Building from the RBV, Das and Teng (2000) have developed a powerful approach to alliances and their structural characteristics, which they compare to the traditional TCE perspective. They argue that, for alliances to exist, "The realized values of those resources contributed to the alliance must be higher than the value realized either by selling or by utilizing the resources in house" (Das

---

[40] See, for instance, the abundant research of Andrew Inkpen on this topic, for instance, Inkpen and Dinur (1998).
[41] See Hamel (1991), and Khanna *et al.* (1998).

and Teng, 2000: 38). This is basically the same rationale for the emergence of firms that we have explored in previous chapters, but applied now to strategic alliances. However, we still need to explain why only partial integration is the most appropriate organizational form.

It is important to note that the three theoretical approaches described above all view alliances as organizational forms situated in a continuum between full integration and market exchanges, although they point to a different reason why only limited integration is necessary: transaction costs economizing, organizational learning potential, or strategic benefits from competitive dynamics. For instance, the presence of medium levels of transaction costs, but not high enough to justify full integration, is presumed to justify alliances from a TCE perspective. However, such moderate levels of transaction costs between two firms would rather suggest the emergence of a loose hierarchy, probably using selective intervention from the corporate office when these transaction costs are greater. By changing the level of transaction costs (or learning and positioning benefits as well), we cannot explain the emergence of alliances as a new type of organizational form different from a loose organizational integration. Alliances make possible the integration of some elements of the strategies of two firms, sometimes very tightly, while keeping no integration at all in other areas. Thus, it is the dual feature of alliances that gives it its distinctive nature as an organizational form, rather than an intermediate level of integration.

From a value perspective, alliances are organizational arrangements that allow selective integration between the strategies of two firms to jointly create value. In some sense, they could be regarded as analogous to selective intervention in diversified corporations, but applied instead to independent firms that decide to integrate only a subset of their resources. However, an alliance between two independent firms is not equivalent to one firm with two weakly integrated divisions. While there could be benefits to integrating some specific resources, the full integration of the entire organizations may result in market disadvantages and actually destroy the value of those resources outside the scope of the strategic alliance. Even selective integration provides some reduced level of integration between separate units in a diversified corporation that could make them less competitive than they would be as truly independent units, at the very least the financial implications of being part of the same firm strategy. In other words, alliances may be the best option when there are benefits to integrate a subset of resources between two or more firms, while there are also drawbacks to even minimally integrating the rest of the resources. Both positive and negative aspects need to be present at once, rather than only moderate positive effects of integration.[42]

Value analysis at the corporate level

Corporate strategy is particularly challenging for management because it usually requires deep knowledge of different industries, organizations, and locations to be able to assess possible costs and benefits. For instance, an acquisition decision may take the firm into an entirely new ground in any of these arenas. It is sometimes very difficult to anticipate whether an integration of two businesses can indeed create value. The integration of channel and content in companies like Vivendi at the turn of the century provides a good case in point.

The integration of channel and content in Vivendi

Several powerful media conglomerates were created in the late nineties based on the presumed synergies between channel and content. This was the case in the acquisition of Seagram by Vivendi, of Endemol by Telefonica, and also to some extent by acquisition of ABC by Disney, and the TimeWarner–AOL merger. Though each of these mergers had its unique features, they are examples of vertical integration between content providers and channel network services. With the benefit of hindsight, we can see that these mergers failed to deliver the value that they promised in most cases and, quite likely, they have made the combined businesses less competitive than they would be as separate firms.

The example is particularly clear in the case of Vivendi, the French powerhouse in the water and public utilities sector, that went through a period of highly unrelated diversification in the eighties and nineties. Under new leadership in the late nineties, the firm refocused on the telecom sector, including businesses as mobile phone operators, TV

---

[42] This is a similar argument to, for instance, Hennart and Reddy (1997), when they argue that alliances are preferable over acquisitions when needed assets are mixed and indivisible from unwanted resources.

networks, press, and other network-based businesses. Vivendi's stock price reached a maximum price over €140 in March 2000 before the internet and technology bubble had begun to deflate. In the summer of 2000, Vivendi bought Seagram, which owned Universal Studios, music companies, and other content providers as well as some TV channel operations in North America. The acquisition price of $34 billion included a forty-six percent premium of $11 billion (about €10 billion). Vivendi's stock price went down approximately €20 from its value of €115 in the few days around the acquisition announcement, a decrease of €10 billion in market value. Apparently, the financial markets did not see much value creation or destruction in this merger and there seemed to be merely a transfer of value from Vivendi's stockholders to Seagram's owners. Two years later the price of the stock had fallen to around €15, much steeper than other firms in the telecom and media industries.

Mergers between content providers and channel companies were often justified in terms of overall synergies and improved market positioning of the channel firms. This backward vertical integration of channel into media could provide some improvements in overall efficiency that never seemed to be realized, as it is often the case for vertical integration. Probably more critical, channel companies could benefit from having access to unique content that could differentiate them. Thus, channel companies could set up barriers for their competitors and benefit from improved market positioning. However, this last argument was not correct. Any gains obtained by the channel company in setting barriers around its content operations would be fully offset by the losses to the content business of giving up its flexibility. In other words, there is no overall improvement in the joined market power of both units as one corporation, and the merger would only benefit one side, but equally damage the other side, just like changing transfer pricing between the units of an organization.

This merger is not likely to create much value and, furthermore, it may end up damaging the two businesses. Channel firms, particularly phone operators, and content providers are very different businesses that require radically different skills. Networks require heavy investment in fixed assets in a business based on technology and marketing; content providers are primarily constituted and managed by individuals with high creativity. Integrating these two activities may be counterproductive. Furthermore, the motivation of content developers to innovate and improve may be reduced if their content has a guaranteed channel to customers (i.e., low-powered incentives), just like channel firms may also be damaged if they are forced to deliver below-quality content produced in-house.

We need to assess the overall value that the business units as collections of resources can create inside and outside the corporate umbrella. This analysis includes any change in overall efficiency, positioning, and market power, as well as the capability to innovate and develop new products that better satisfies customer needs. In the case of content providers, it seems reasonable to believe that their creativity and overall competitiveness was hurt by integrating them with channel firms. Vivendi stockholders paid a heavy price for it, even beyond the high premium. In a similar move, the Spanish phone operator Telefonica bought the Dutch content providers Endemol for €4.8 billion in 2000 and sold a seventy-five percent stake in 2007 for the firm valued seven years later at only €3.5 billion. This is a clear example of value destruction. When the new CEO announced the decision to sell Endemol, he claimed that Telefonica could then negotiate with all content producers in a better position without being tied to one of them. Quite likely, Endemol also has the opportunity to thrive as a separate organization with its own firm strategy.

The possible benefits of integrating channel and content, even if they are doubtful and possibly very small, can probably be achieved through a strategic alliance without the need to integrate vertically both businesses. Full integration may damage those resources that should not be integrated, even with a cautious corporate office using selective intervention. The presence of both positive and negative effects of integration on different subsets of resources makes strategic alliances a better option to achieve whichever limited integration could be beneficial to the two businesses without suffering its drawbacks. In addition to important transfers of wealth between stockholders, some of these examples of vertical integration actually destroyed substantial value for society.

8 | *International strategy*

The theory of the multinational

Just as diversified corporations span their activities across different industries, multinational enterprises (MNEs) have a physical presence in several countries. The theory of the multinational explores why MNEs emerge to set and manage their international operations across geographical boundaries, and therefore can be regarded as a specific part of the theory of the firm. We now want to analyze why MNEs exist instead of managing cross-border interdependence of business activities through other governance arrangements such as exporting, licensing, or joint-ventures, which are often called *modes of entry* in international business literature.

Early approaches to the analysis of MNEs relied on the literature on trade.[1] Prior to 1960, there was not a theory of the MNE that could be considered sufficiently consistent and developed, though there were some dispersed ideas about the reasons behind internationalization. For instance, the existence and benefits of international trade had already been studied by David Ricardo in his theory of comparative advantage and later developments.[2] Ricardo showed that international trade would benefit two countries even if one of them was more efficient in manufacturing all types of products. Early trade theories focused on the MNE as one type of capital exporter, either of foreign direct investment (FDI) when the firm had control of foreign

---

[1] For a comprehensive review of early theories of the multinational, see chapter three in Buckley and Casson (1976) and chapter four in Dunning (1993).

[2] Pushing forward Ricardo's idea of comparative advantage, factor endowments predict the patterns of production and trade in the Heckscher-Ohlin model, so that countries export products that utilize their most abundant factors of production, and import products that utilize the countries' scarce factors. In contrast to Ricardo, the model does not require differences in productivity across countries. Despite its elegant formulation, the model does not seem to have much empirical validity in actually explaining trade flows.

assets, or portfolio investment when investors did not. Because financial resources would presumably search for their most efficient use, differences in real interest rates should explain capital flows among countries. These capital flows materialize in MNE activities in other countries as well as geographically diversified portfolios.

This trade approach to the analysis of the MNE based on capital transfers and FDI had important problems that started to be identified in the sixties.[3] MNEs are more than mere financial instruments to transfer capital and, in fact, they actually borrow heavily from local markets. Furthermore, the match between FDI and the growth of MNEs is not very strong empirically.[4] Probably more important, this early approach remains silent about the reasons why a firm may decide to control foreign activities as opposed to using other market-based alternatives.

These important criticisms led several authors in the sixties and seventies to the analysis of the MNE as a monopolistic rent seeker, inspired in the traditional ideas about barriers to competition from Bain (1956) in industrial organization.[5] Hymer (1976) triggered this approach, that tried to understand why foreign firms could compete versus domestic players, which presumably should enjoy the advantages of having local knowledge of customers and resources. To compensate for these inherent disadvantages of foreignness, MNEs arguably own some type of advantage that would need to be transferable to the new countries where competition actually takes place. These potential competitive advantages include brand name, technology, managerial skills, better access to financial resources, and operational economies of scale and vertical integration.[6] Barriers to competition are essential to understanding the advantages of the MNE in its own domestic country as well as the barriers to trade that may prevent it from using exports to exploit such advantages, and also the barriers to imitation from the

---

[3] See Stephen Hymer's (1976) thesis as a seminal contribution to the theory of the MNE written in 1960.

[4] See Hennart (2001) about the limits of trade theories of the MNE. He discusses the three major approaches to the theory of the multinational, i.e., trade, industrial organization, and TCE/internalization, and focuses particularly on this last approach.

[5] In addition to the seminal work of Hymer (1976), this approach based on industrial organization economics was further developed by Kindleberger (1969), Aliber (1970), Caves (1974), and Knickerbocker (1973).

[6] See Kindleberger (1969).

local players in the new markets. Thus, from this perspective the competitive advantages behind MNEs are mainly due to structural market
failures associated with limits to competition.

This theory of the MNE based on industrial organization highlighted
the importance of what later would be called "ownership advantages"
by Dunning (1981). However, it does not make clear why and under
what circumstances the MNE is the best organizational form to transfer
these advantages to the markets abroad. The MNE can be regarded as
one type of mode of entry into new markets, but any potential competitive advantage may be exploited through other governance structures,
such as exports and joint ventures. Based on a Coasian comparative
analysis of using the market versus the hierarchy for managing international transactions, transaction costs economics (TCE)/internalization
theory seeks to explain why interdependencies across countries are
better handled through the MNE instead of through other market-
based alternatives. The MNE is essentially an organizational form
that allows the most efficient exploitation of these possible ownership
advantages under certain circumstances. Teece (1986: 37) argued that
FDI "stems from the possession by a firm of certain unique assets and
that developing and protecting the rent stream associated with these
assets often requires the extension of some kind of hierarchical control
structure over productive assets which are distributed internationally."
For instance, this would be the case for firms whose competitive advantage is based on their superior technological know-how in conditions
of weak appropriability. Frequent transfers of technology and tacit
knowledge to foreign subsidiaries can be more efficiently carried out
internally by an MNE. This organizational form facilitates the dis-
closure, agreement, and enforcement between parties in international
exchanges in contrast to contracting alternatives, such as exports and
licenses.

This Coasian approach to the analysis of the MNE known as internalization theory in international business was developed independently by researchers in Europe outside the influence of TCE, particularly Buckley and Casson (1976) and Rugman (1982), and in
parallel, by researchers in American schools inspired in TCE, like
Teece (1982b) and Hennart (1982). Though there are some differences across authors, they basically agree that the MNE internalizes cross-border exchanges to solve imperfections in international
markets. Vertically-integrated MNEs can be explained by traditional

TCE arguments of opportunism and asset specificity along the value chain, while horizontal MNEs arguably emerge from market failures of difficult-to-trade assets, like managerial knowledge and goodwill. This TCE/internalization approach has received substantial empirical support, though less clearly for horizontally integrated MNEs.[7]

The internalization theory of the MNE emphasizes the efficiency enhancing features of MNEs over the oligopolistic focus of earlier research inspired in Hymer and industrial organization. However, they need not be interpreted in full opposition. Dunning (1981, 1993) has developed an eclectic model of international production that combines these two approaches as well as the locational advantages that international production may confer.[8] According to this model, the MNE emerges from a combination of three factors. First, the firm must have some unique asset (usually some sort of intangible asset like know-how) that potentially gives it a competitive advantage over competitors in foreign markets (i.e., ownership advantage). Second, the assets must be more economically used or further developed by setting them in certain locations outside the domestic market (i.e., location advantages). Third, the best way to obtain the full value from these unique

---

[7] A meta-analysis of the empirical literature done by Zhao *et al.* (2004) shows clear support for the TCE approach to the MNE. The main variables in TCE, such as asset specificity, uncertainty, and free-riding potential, are associated with the choice of entry mode, though there are important moderating factors like cultural distance and international experience. However, the effect of asset specificity in horizontal MNEs has received mixed results. A recent review of the literature by Brouthers and Hennart (2007) concludes that asset specificity is often not significantly related to entry mode for horizontal MNEs, and claims that information asymmetry between buyer and seller of knowledge has greater explanatory power than asset specificity for this type of MNE.

[8] Locational advantages were stressed by Vernon's (1966) model of international investment and trade in the product life. Vernon's model draws from the ideas of Ricardian comparative advantage and further developments in the analysis of the spatial distribution of factor endowments in order to understand the movement of production across countries. Institutional differences between the home and the host country can also contribute to the choice of the MNE to enter through FDI or contract-based alternatives. See Kogut (1991) and Yiu and Makino (2002) for a learning and institutional perspective on the MNE and the choice of entry mode. From an IO perspective, Porter (1990) explains why the structural characteristics that surround firms in a given location of cluster, particularly greater degrees of competition and the availability of sophisticated customers and related industries, may produce a positive environment that facilitates the emergence of strong players globally.

assets must be internally as a result of market imperfections (i.e., internalization advantage). This eclectic model (or OLI) has received clear empirical support.[9]

Despite the clarity and usefulness of this comprehensive approach to the theory of the MNE, we could debate whether these three advantages are all necessary conditions for the MNE to exist. To some extent, internalization theory already includes the prior existence of an ownership advantage that needs to be internalized, so that only internalization and locational advantages would seem necessary.[10] Even locational advantages do not seem strictly necessary for the MNE as an organizational solution to manage interdependencies across agents situated in different countries, independently of the greater or smaller differences that may exist between these countries.[11] Within a TCE framework, Teece (1986: 28) agrees with the three conditions identified by Dunning in his eclectic model, though he stresses transaction analysis and downplays the other two as mere prerequisites, which "standing alone they do not have a decisive impact on the selection on the firm's boundaries."

However, the relevance of the TCE/internalization approach to the MNE has been questioned by some authors inspired in institutional theory and evolutionary economics. Kogut and Zander (1993) argued that firms are social communities that specialize in the creation and the internal transfer of knowledge. For MNEs we should focus on why their specific organizations with their own accumulated skills in contrast to other firms may be the best option to transfer their knowledge across borders. This knowledge perspective to the MNE can be reinterpreted from a TCE approach (Hennart, 1982; Teece, 1986), but these authors claim that its main argument based on international market failure is overdetermined and there is no need to rely on the notions of opportunism and more generally contract analysis to study the emergence of the MNE. Without recourse to TCE, Kogut and Zander (1993) show that MNEs use wholly owned subsidiaries when the knowledge that they transfer is more complex and less codifiable

---

[9] See Agarwal and Ramaswamy (1992) for one of the early tests of the eclectic model (ownership-location-internalization). Further support is discussed in the review by Brouthers and Hennart (2007) of boundaries of the firm for MNEs.

[10] See Rugman (1982).

[11] See Hennart (2001), who develops a TCE-based theory of the MNE as an internalizer of markets disregarding locational and ownership advantages.

and teachable. Thus, the debate between TCE and the resource-based view (RBV)-knowledge perspective of the firm has been transferred to the international business area and the theory of the MNE, including the issue of contractibility versus transferability. Value analysis of an MNE strategy can also be useful in this international context to reconcile these different perspectives on the nature of the MNE and its emergence.

A value approach to the MNE

The main debates in the theory of the MNE are, not surprisingly, very similar to the different benefits and costs that we discussed in the previous chapter on product diversification. The possible benefits of managing international interdependencies through an MNE are essentially related to the advantages for value creation that hierarchies may have over other modes of entry with regard to (1) resource management, (2) dealing with competitors, and (3) customer relationships. The existing controversies mostly refer to their relative importance.

First, internalization theory stresses the increase in efficiency that results from better management of interdependencies. As Teece (1982b) argues, the joint presence of economies of scope and transaction costs would facilitate the emergence of an MNE to manage international exchanges. However, for the same reasons that we explored in chapter two, any of these two factors alone could also drive the MNE *ceteris paribus*. Economizing in transaction costs may be sufficient to make the MNE the most efficient governance structure, but, if transactions costs are similar inside and outside the hierarchy, differences in operating costs (e.g., driven by economies of scope or superior skills) would also determine which alternative is most efficient, that is, the MNE or the market.

In addition, as Kogut and Zander (1993) showed, integration inside the organization has certain advantages for the creation and transferability of knowledge. Though Teece (1986) explained these knowledge-based advantages in terms of appropriability and contract features, an evolutionary view of the MNE would not regard these contractual issues as relevant to the nature of the MNE. In other words, to the extent that an MNE is the best way to deal with knowledge transfer across borders, contracting issues that arise from opportunism become secondary. Independently of transaction costs, the actual transferability of knowledge inside the organization is likely to be easier under some circumstances because of the intrinsic characteristics of knowledge, for instance, in the transfer of complex tacit knowledge.[12]

Nevertheless, these approaches are not truly inconsistent with each other. The debate within the theory of the MNE replicates similar debates about economies of scope, transaction costs, and resources as determinants of the scope of the firm. These different perspectives actually point to the advantages of the MNE for value creation through better resource management across borders, driven by operational efficiencies, administrative (transaction) costs, and knowledge management. None of them provides a better or more complete answer to the nature of the MNE.

Second, international organization (IO)-based approaches to the MNE, like those of Hymer, Caves, and Kindleberger, highlight the oligopolistic motives behind the MNE and its effects of market power. The MNE may be the best way to deal with potential competitors abroad when it serves to overcome barriers to trade and set up barriers to competition to protect the MNE's competitive advantages. For instance, considering FDI as an oligopolistic reaction to competitors' investments, Knickerbocker (1973) showed that MNEs in more concentrated industries tend to match their moves abroad, so that they enter new markets at around the same time. Thus, there is also a rationale for the MNE as a collection of resources that provides or protects ownership advantages from the effect of competition, in addition to its efficiency-enhancing features. The choice between full ownership versus contractual alternatives is affected by its potential consequences

---

[12] Teece (1986) considers these limits to knowledge transfer as a contracting issue, thus including knowledge transferability limitations as one type of disadvantage for a contracting alternative to the MNE. However, this is not truly a limitation that necessarily results from opportunism or even information asymmetry, though it could be on some occasions. As Kogut argued, it may be considered an issue of permeability of knowledge across firm boundaries. Inside firms, knowledge is transferred more efficiently and effectively because resources inside the organization have similar ways to communicate, understand, and even behave. Transferability is not the same as contractibility, though it is considered a prior step to contract design by some TCE scholars. Transferability is partially determined by motivation and opportunism, but also by the cognitive features of people and organizations outside the traditional scope of TCE. See also the contributions of evolutionary economists like Nelson and Winter (1982) to our understanding of how routines and knowledge are created, used, transformed, and discarded by organizations.

on the competitive dynamics among the players both domestically and globally. In this sense the MNE is an instrument with which to create and also to appropriate value versus competitors.

Finally, being an MNE may also have benefits for managing the relationship with customers, independently of firm efficiency and market power. These benefits have not received much attention in the literature as an additional potential reason for the MNE to emerge, and they have typically been subsumed within operational benefits. For instance, having an international presence is widely considered as a critical advantage for MNEs because the firm is exposed to different customers with different needs, which may facilitate new learning and a transfer of skills across locations.[13] MNEs can learn faster when they have exposure to a broader set of markets. Beyond these positive benefits of global learning, customers may value the international presence of larger MNEs when they interact with the same firm in different countries. This is the case of firms like advertising agencies, corporate banking, and consulting that go abroad to follow their MNE customers and even for individual customers who travel frequently and demand similar services in different countries (e.g., hotel chains). In these examples the MNE creates value by reducing the nonmonetary costs of customers, especially those of finding information about local firms providing the services that they need and managing the relationship with them and associated risks.

In summary, the literature on international business has already identified the main advantages and limitations of MNEs versus other modes of entry in foreign markets. Just as we did for diversification, we can analyze the MNE as a collection of value-creating resources and look at how they jointly deal with customers, competitors, and internal and external resources across borders. The MNE emerges to create and capture more value than other ways to arrange interdependencies among resources located in different countries.

This comprehensive approach is quite different from Dunning's OLI model, which also condenses earlier views on the theory of the MNE. A critical feature of Dunning's eclectic model is the need for the joint presence of three necessary conditions, i.e., having ownership, location, and internalization advantages. It is ultimately the existence of

---

[13] The benefits for global learning of the MNE have been stressed by Bartlett and Ghoshal (1989).

internalization advantages that drives the emergence of the MNE, given the prior existence of locational and ownership advantages. The OLI model can be regarded as an elaborate explanation of essentially a TCE/internalization approach that requires two additional assumptions. Contrary to the necessary presence of these three conditions, different determinants of the MNE may exist as independent main effects on the choice of entry mode from a value approach. Though there could be some interaction effects that reinforce each other, the different ways in which MNEs create value are essentially additive rather than multiplicative, as Dunning claims.[14] *Ceteris paribus*, either operational efficiency, knowledge transferability, market power, or customer-driven benefits, are sufficient on their own for the MNE to create value as a collection of geographically dispersed units.

The MNE can be understood basically through a cost/benefit analysis that has been very well explained by Hennart, though he restricted its use to a TCE perspective. In his words (Hennart, 2001: 143–4), "The transaction cost theory of the MNE argues that they arise to organize interdependencies between agents located in different countries. This will occur (1) when organizing these interdependencies within the firm is more efficient than organizing them through the market and (2) when the benefits of organizing interdependencies with the firm are higher than their costs."

In summary, any benefits and costs of using the organization to manage interdependencies across activities in several countries need to be considered. There is no reason to believe that the only benefit of the MNE over other organizational forms to manage interdependencies is that they enjoy less administrative costs (transaction or governance costs). Contractibility issues driven by opportunism and bounded rationality do matter because they affect overall cost efficiency and necessary investments in specialized assets. However, there are also differences, for instance, in the actual transferability of knowledge inside and outside the organization as well as important effects over competitive dynamics and customer relationships. Thus, MNEs can benefit from different sources of value created by putting geographically dispersed resources under the same corporate umbrella.

---

[14] See Agarwal and Ramaswami (1992) for empirical support of different determinants of the MNE from an OLI framework as well as some specific interactions among some of them.

These benefits would need to be compared with the costs of managing these interdependencies through an organization, including the costs at business unit (or geographical subsidiary) and corporate (or MNE) levels.

International presence

Firms decide to go abroad and to increase their international presence for a variety of reasons. It is surprising that the internationalization decisions of firms and the geographical paths that they follow have been studied in relative isolation from the theory of the MNE. Scholars have analyzed different specific motivations for the international expansion of MNEs, such as seeking new markets, resources, greater efficiency, technology, lower risk, and strategic assets, and generally countering the competition.[15]

Finding new customers is probably the most frequent rationale for internationalization. As Penrose (1959) explained, firms have an incentive to expand as long as expansion can provide a way of using their resources more profitably than they are being used. Any critical resource that gives a firm its competitive advantage in its home market, such as specialized knowledge, is a potential candidate for its exploitation in new markets to attract new customers. As long as the competitive advantage is transferable abroad, entering new geographical markets can generate value for new customers, so that the firm may appropriate part of the newly created value.

MNEs often follow an internationalization path that is determined by the transferability of its advantages abroad, driven by variables like geographical, institutional, and cultural distance. Exports are usually the first step to exploit a firm's value-creating resources abroad. Firms gradually increase their involvement in international business as they increase foreign market knowledge and commitment to international presence. Thus, firms go from having occasional export activities and agents abroad to setting up sales subsidiaries and eventually production facilities.[16]

[15] See, for instance, Robock and Simmonds (1989) and Dunning (1993).

[16] See Johanson and Vahlne (1977) for a description of the incremental approach to internationalization (known as "the Uppsala approach"). From an entirely different perspective, Vernon's (1966) international product cycle also explains the evolution of MNEs, starting with home production and exports to

Regardless of the geographical path followed in the internationalization process, some complementary assets in the local markets are
likely to be necessary to fully exploit the value of the resources and
competitive advantages transferred to the new locations. This physical
presence in the new markets may require FDI specifically if the interdependencies among home and foreign locations can be managed more
effectively inside an MNE, as we discussed earlier.

However, firms also expand abroad to reinforce their competitive
advantages and not only to exploit their initial advantages by attracting
customers in new markets. International presence gives the MNE the
opportunity to increase its value creation potential through improved
resource management worldwide and enhanced capability to fight with
competitors at home and abroad. To the extent that they enjoy greater
ownership advantages, more successful companies at home are more
likely to internationalize; in turn, greater internationalization gives
firms some advantages that purely domestic companies cannot enjoy,
such as greater scale, global learning, and market power. This recipro-
cal causality should create a positive correlation between international
presence and profitability, though the empirical evidence is not always
supportive.[17]

From a value perspective geographical subsidiaries should be able
to be more competitive as part of the MNE than as separate organizations. The relationship is potentially bidirectional so that the MNE
can contribute value to each local organization as well as vice versa.
Each subsidiary is comprised by a set of internal resources that compete in its local market for customers and external resources against
other local and multinational players. The MNE can make the subsidiary's strategy more competitive in its own market by transferring
some of its ownership advantages, like brand name, managerial skills,

---

international production and even imports into the original home country. The
process of internationalization in sequential stages has also been studied with
regard to other variables like MNE organizational structure and innovation.
However, empirical research has provided mixed results. For instance, Benito
and Gripsrud (1992) did not find support for the claim that firms first
internationalize to culturally close countries; they argued that
internationalization results from discrete rational choices based on a
traditional economic rationale rather than a social learning process.

[17] See Lu and Beamish (2004) for an analysis of the relationship between
geographical diversification and performance based on the different benefits
and costs that take place as internationalization increases.

and technology, which can be further developed anywhere and diffused throughout the organization. Thus, it is essential for the MNE to effectively manage and transfer those organizational resources that can give competitive advantage to its local subsidiaries, just as much as leveraging its international presence to benefit the overall MNE. To achieve this dual goal, at least some elements of the strategy of the MNE in each market would need to be globalized to some degree.

Global strategy

Mere international presence does not create value without some integration of the MNE activities worldwide. Certain elements of the strategy in each local market would need to be globally managed for the MNE to create value above and beyond what each local subsidiary could do on its own. Otherwise there would be no reason for the MNE to exist, while the subsidiaries would have to bear some additional bureaucratic costs. The key question is how much to globalize.

Prahalad and Doz (1987) provide the traditional answer to this question based on two different types of pressure that the MNE needs to balance: global integration versus local responsiveness. The benefits of global integration are relatively greater in industries characterized by multinational customers and competitors, higher investment requirements and technological intensity, and significant pressure for cost reductions and access to inputs. In contrast, the benefits of local responsiveness are likely to be greater when there are substantial differences across countries in customer needs, distribution channels, and structural characteristics as well as substantial intervention from host governments. Some industries may be affected by both types of pressure, but the relative strength of each one should determine how much to globalize each element of the strategy in an analysis that should go down to the level of functional areas and tasks.

This analysis has been expanded by Bartlett and Ghoshal (1989), who claim that MNEs often have to face both pressures and add a third challenge: the benefits generated by global learning. The extent to which the MNE tries to deal with these challenges essentially determines its strategy. Thus, four types of MNE strategy may result, multinational (i.e., local responsiveness), global (i.e., high worldwide integration), international (somewhere between multinational and global), and transnational.[18] Presumably, transnational corporations should be able to manage the three challenges at the same time: global integration, local adaptation, and worldwide learning. Each strategy would have its own implications for the specific role of each local subsidiary and the way that knowledge is managed and transferred across the network of interdependent local organizations within the MNE. Empirical research has shown that the integration benefits of scale are not significant nowadays, but greater technological intensity and less advertising intensity facilitate global integration.[19]

Porter (1986) uses a similar approach to analyze global strategy, though he focuses more directly on value-chain analysis. Essentially, any industry can be characterized along a continuum from multidomestic to global. While in multidomestic industries MNEs manage their subsidiaries like a portfolio with essentially stand-alone operations in each country (usually with a one-time transfer of know-how to first set it up), in global industries there is greater integration of activities worldwide to take full advantage of the linkages among countries. This dichotomy is also consistent with the contrast between the benefits of global integration versus local responsiveness, but it places the emphasis on the configuration and coordination of value-creating activities worldwide. First regarding activity configuration, MNEs decide in how many places should each activity along the value chain be performed and in which specific locations. Second, firms decide how to coordinate these geographically dispersed activities.

These ideas can be included within the value-creating model of strategy introduced earlier. As any organization, each local subsidiary has to deal with its own customers, competitors, and internal and external resources in each country. Some elements of the local organization's strategy can benefit from being managed globally instead of in each subsidiary independently. Global integration and learning refer to possible benefits in the efficient management of resources globally, including lower costs and better knowledge management.[20] Local

[18] See Leong and Tan (1993) for empirical support of this typology, though transnationals do not seem to be truly abundant.
[19] See Kobrin (1991).
[20] Ghoshal (1987) reviewed the three benefits that the existence of countries and, thus, the possibility to set a global strategy may have on achieving efficiency, managing risks, and facilitating learning and adaptation. An MNE may improve how it manages its resources globally to achieve these three goals by

responsiveness relates to the customer benefits associated with locally differentiated versus globally standardized products and, more generally, the MNE's interface with the customer in each market. Finally, there can also be competitive benefits in globally integrating how the firm responds to competitors' actions and managing barriers to competition worldwide.

All of these potential benefits and costs of globalization have been widely studied.[21] Globalization does not happen automatically with international presence and greater integration is not always positive, though there is a clear trend towards greater globalization since Levitt (1983) began drawing attention to it. With their decisions to configure and coordinate their activities worldwide, MNEs can create or destroy value by making their subsidiaries more or less competitive.[22] The complex cross-border integration across subsidiaries in many MNEs has displaced traditional dyadic relationships between the central office and foreign subsidiaries in favor of an organizational network of interdependent units with different roles for each subsidiary and geographically dispersed centers of excellence.[23]

From global presence to global competitive advantage

Gupta and Govindarajan (2001) explain how firms can convert a global presence into a global competitive advantage. Having worldwide presence does not produce competitive advantage on its own. However, multinationals can exploit several specific opportunities to create value in the configuration and coordination of their value-chain activities worldwide. There are five sources of global competitive advantage that need to be adequately managed:

---

taking advantage of its international presence. In particular, international presence gives the MNE the potential to benefit from the differences across countries as well as the economies of scale and scope that international presence generates.

[21] See Yip (1989).

[22] Becerra and Santalo (2003) show that, though the performance of MNEs is primarily determined by local factors and their industries, about ten percent of the performance of MNEs in different regions of the world can be attributed to the MNE as a whole.

[23] See, for instance, Frost *et al.* (2002) for an analysis of centers of excellence.

1. Adapting to local market differences, which is necessary to obtain the benefits of local adaptation to heterogeneous markets.
2. Exploiting economies of global scale, such as spreading fixed costs over larger volume and pooling global purchasing power over suppliers.
3. Exploiting economies of global scope across multiple regions, like providing coordinated services to global customers.
4. Tapping optimal locations for activities and resources, so that each value-chain activity can be performed or managed from the best possible location to enhance performance and reduce costs and risks.
5. Maximizing knowledge transfer across locations, which facilitates innovation and cost efficiency throughout the organization.

Gupta and Govindarajan argue that "capturing these five sources of value requires the firm to optimize on a global basis the organization and management of each value-chain activity." It may be optimal to globalize some activities, like production, while decentralizing others, like advertising. The MNE should assess the optimality of its value chain worldwide and its global architecture, i.e., the number of centers where each activity should be performed and their best locations. Once this optimal architecture is decided, the firm should try to build the requisite competencies at those locations. Finally, the MNE would need to place the appropriate organizational arrangements that allow seamless coordination and the motivation for managers to cooperate across locations, including incentives, planning, teams, and formal and informal rules and procedures.

Optimal globalization that results in a global competitive advantage will require appropriate decisions about the MNE's activity architecture, locational competencies, and global coordination. Each value-chain activity will require its own analysis of the extent to which the five sources of global competitive advantage are specifically relevant for such an activity. When the firm takes advantage of all these possibilities to create value on a global scale, each subsidiary will benefit from being part of the larger network of local organizations that constitute the MNE.

Value analysis in internationalization

There are two critical challenges for international strategy: how can the MNE contribute to the success of its local subsidiaries worldwide, and is the MNE facilitating the potential contribution from the subsidiaries to the MNE's competitive advantage globally? These two questions refer to the transferability and the reinforcement of competitive advantages across locations inside the MNE. The collection of subsidiaries under one corporate umbrella should be able to create more value than they could separately. Let us briefly analyze the case of two retailers with substantial international presence and very different performance in their overseas operations: Wal-Mart and Ikea.

The internationalization of retailers Wal-Mart and Ikea

Wal-Mart is the largest discount store in the world with outstanding performance in its home country. This formidable competitor has the most efficient cost structure in the US in a market segment primarily driven by price. Its cost advantages are built on its large size that gives the firm enormous bargaining power over its suppliers. Wal-Mart is also known for its technological superiority in its logistics and integration with suppliers, which results in lower inventory and operations costs alongside low labor costs. The company also has certain location advantages because a significant proportion of its stores are located in relatively small areas, where they enjoy limited competition and monopoly profits.

Despite the strong advantages of Wal-Mart in its discount stores in the US, the firm has had limited international success abroad. Only its operations in Canada and Mexico have achieved a level of performance not too far from its domestic operations, but the firm even had to exit several of the countries that it entered, like Germany, due to its inability to compete efficiently in some international markets. Their cost advantages do not seem to be transferable abroad, except to nearby countries. Unfortunately for Wal-Mart, their stores outside the US and neighboring countries cannot take advantage from its large size because an important part of its inputs are locally produced and only local demand exerts bargaining power over suppliers. In addition, the complex technology and logistics system cannot be replicated in countries with very different infrastructures. Furthermore, some of the new markets already had very powerful general retailers with costs even lower than Wal-Mart can possibly have, like Aldi and Lidl in Germany. When a Wal-Mart store opens up in a new country, there is not much that its parent company can do to improve its operations and reduce its costs, beyond management skills that may or may not be useful in the new markets. In addition, its international growth does not make the overall MNE stronger. Thus, the success of a Wal-Mart store in Mexico, for instance, does not really make Wal-Mart more competitive in Brazil or China, because the nature of this industry is mostly local with regard to customers, competitors, external inputs, and internal resources.

Ikea is a very different story. The Swedish MNE relies on a fully globalized business strategy. Design and production (including out-sourcing) is globally managed, which gives the firm huge economies of scale. Products are then sent to individual stores, which decide which products should be included in their own catalog from all the available designs. All stores have a similar layout and internal operations as well as identical market positioning that attracts the same type of customer across locations. After walking through the large store customers take their boxed furniture from the lower floor warehouse and take it home to assemble it.

Ikea's strategy is built on very efficient operations both inside the store and in its large-scale batch production. The boxed furniture allows savings in transportation and inventory costs. Customer assem-bly is an important increase in nonmonetary costs, but is compensated for by its immediate carry-out as well as lower prices from savings in firm assembly, transportation, and store space.[24] The business model is especially attractive for price-sensitive customers who want to furnish an entire room or house.

These advantages are clearly transferable to any store in a new country. Its low cost furniture is imported into the store, thus taking full advantage of its large scale and centralized production. The entire business model from production to outbound logistics is managed to minimize transportation and inventory costs. When a new store opens up, it receives not only the skills to manage an exact replica of other stores, but the entire business system, including store layout, low cost inputs, store management, and similar market positioning,

---

[24] Home delivery and assembly options also exist for an extra charge.

global brand name, and advertising. Furthermore, any new Ikea store increases the MNE's global scale and, if used adequately, can help develop new ideas to be used and products to be sold in other locations. Thus, its strategy is based in fully transferable advantages to each local store, which can also contribute to strengthen its global strength. While each Wal-Mart store has to start almost from scratch in each new country, Ikea stores receive an entire tried and tested business model that is fully transferable to each location.

9 | *Strategy and social value*

Markets and social value

Markets are a very powerful mechanism to achieve greater overall allocative efficiency, that is, the most efficient allocation of productive resources to those uses that create most value for society. The benefits and limitations of the market economy to promote social welfare have been analyzed by political economists for over two centuries. The positive effects of markets on social value were already identified in the famous passage about the invisible hand from Adam Smith's *Wealth of Nations*:

Every individual endeavors to employ his capital so that its produce may be of greatest value. He generally neither intends to promote the public interest, nor knows how much he is promoting it. He intends only his own security, only his own gain. And he is in this led by an invisible hand to promote an end which was no part of his intention. By pursuing his own interest he frequently promotes that of society more effectually than when he really intends to promote it. (Smith, 1776)

Welfare economics studies the allocative efficiency of an economy and its income distribution. Following Pareto, an economy can be regarded as efficient when it is impossible to alter the allocation of resources so that a change could make at least one individual better off without hurting another individual. It can be shown that a perfectly competitive market system (i.e., a Walrasian general equilibrium model) results in a Pareto-efficient allocation of resources in an economy.[1]

---

[1] This is known as the first theorem of welfare economics. See Arrow and Debreu (1954) for formal proof of the Pareto efficiency of a Walrasian general equilibrium.

This idea gives strong support for free markets and *laissez-faire* policies. Firms operating in free markets should achieve technical efficiency and maximum social value even if they do not intend to do so. In terms of value, firms end up enhancing customer value even though they actually pursue the maximization of value appropriation. Good strategic decisions in freely competitive markets do not only lead to greater performance for the firm, but they should also promote the overall good for society. Thus, strategic management enhances social welfare and it is not just an issue of value capture in a zero-sum game between competitors and customers.

However, there are two important problems that qualify these conclusions. First, there are several restrictive conditions for free markets to achieve an optimal solution. Because its assumptions are usually not present in the real world, the applicability and realism of the formal proof in favor of an efficient market-driven general equilibrium can be questioned. Second, free markets do not solve any problems of inequality that may exist in the distribution of wealth. Thus, firms do not always promote social value through their strategies in our market economy. There is sometimes a conflict between social value and the goal of firms to appropriate value, which we will analyze in this chapter.

Market imperfections

Free markets would result in an allocation of resources that is Pareto efficient if all markets in the economy were perfectly competitive. However, they rarely, if ever, are so. There are many assumptions for firms operating in free markets to maximize social value. Economic agents across all markets (e.g., consumer products, input factors, labor, and capital) would have to be atomistic (price-takers) and provide homogeneous goods without barriers to competition (free entry and exit) and with freely mobile resources and technologies. Other requirements include perfect information, no externalities or transaction costs, and some more technical assumptions. Their frequent absences are important market imperfections that require some government intervention and market regulation to try to achieve the best possible social welfare. Otherwise, the strategies followed by independent units competing in the market for their own interests may not lead to greater overall economic wealth for society. Let us briefly discuss them.

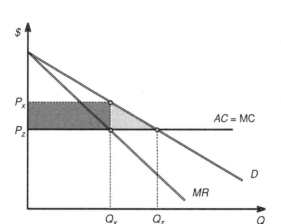

Figure 9.1 Monopoly and deadweight loss

Monopoly

The best-known market imperfection is monopoly. When firms are not atomistic and they can influence prices (i.e., they face a downward sloping demand curve D), their profit maximizing strategy is to set up prices above the perfectly competitive level at the point where marginal revenue (MR) equals marginal cost (MC). Figure 9.1 shows a simple case in which costs are assumed to remain constant, so that MC is equal to average cost (AC). To maximize its profits, the monopoly firm will produce Q_x at price P_x, which goes through the point at which MR = MC. The firm obtains an extra profit above the normal profit required to conduct business, shown by the dark shaded rectangle. This value appropriated by the firm is smaller than the value that would be created if the firm had chosen to produce Q_z at price P_z, which results in no extra profits and a consumer surplus equal to the overall shaded trapezoid. By constraining output Q_x, the monopolist can increase prices and capture extra profits from customers, but the light-shaded triangle is lost for overall society (i.e., the deadweight loss). Some exchanges do not take place, even though the average cost of production is still smaller than the price that some consumers would be willing to pay.

When firms have some monopoly power, value appropriation conflicts with value creation in the short run, because the maximum profit for the firm does not occur alongside the largest combined value for firms and consumers. Furthermore, the dynamic effects of monopoly in the long run can be even more detrimental for society. Monopolists have an easy life that is not subject to the competitive pressure to reduce costs and to enhance its products and services through innovation. Thus, monopoly does not lead to maximum social value and arguably requires some type of government intervention to mitigate its negative effects on social welfare, usually through price regulation that maximizes production with an adequate level of firm profits.

Unfortunately, this is a very complex problem, including its related aspects of oligopolistic collusion and anticompetitive behavior, which does not have a clear practical solution yet. This problem is particularly important in industries with large economies of scale in which there may be a natural monopoly. In those cases, there is a strong argument in favor of closely regulated monopolies, maybe government owned, to take advantage of the ever-decreasing average costs of production. But even then, regulation may create more problems than it solves. Recently deregulated industries like telecommunications and airlines have seen a clear increase in innovation and competitiveness that has resulted in significantly lower prices and new types of firms and services, despite the possible losses in economies of scale of having several firms with large fixed costs.

The possible solutions to the social welfare problems created by monopolies fall inside economics and outside the scope of this book on strategy. However, we need to acknowledge that some degree of monopoly power often exists and the greater it is, the greater the divergence between value appropriation by firms and overall value creation for society, at least in the short run. Firms usually want to appropriate as much value as possible for their own resources and stockholders, which sometimes leads them to design strategies to increase their monopoly power and build barriers to competition. But market dominance, and thus monopoly, may also be the result of a better strategy (i.e., a superior collection of value-creating resources) and the reward for greater efficiency or superior innovation. Thus, monopolies are not necessarily evils to be eradicated in all circumstances, though they often have negative consequences on social welfare on the short and the long run, if left uncontrolled.

Apparently, it is not so much the short-term negative effects associated with the deadweight loss that seem most damaging to social welfare and may be solved with price regulation, but the long-term consequences of lack of competition among firms to create value. It is this latter negative effect on innovation and social welfare that is actively fought by most governments. The short-term extra profits associated with monopoly power are a powerful incentive for firms to create value in new ways, just like patent protection promotes research and development. In contrast, a healthy amount of competition needs to be guaranteed by antitrust agencies to motivate firms to search for new ways to enhance value for customers and to limit the negative effects of monopoly in the long run.

Overall, the welfare losses attributed to monopoly power seem to be modest. Scherer and Ross (1990) conclude that the deadweight welfare loss attributable to monopolistic resource allocation in the US lies somewhere between 0.5 and 2 percent of gross national product (GNP), though other X-inefficiencies induced by monopolies would need to be considered as well, like excessive costs and rent-seeking. Fortunately, monopoly power does not seem to be sustainable in the long run and most governments are determined to maintain a minimum level of competition. Therefore, nowadays a successful firm strategy can hardly rely primarily on value appropriation through monopoly power at the expense of value creation for customers, at least in the long run. Firms need to reconcile the two elements of new value creation for customers and its appropriation by firms, though they may be negatively correlated in the short run in the presence of substantial monopoly power.

Taking a more dynamic perspective, customer value creation and firm profits are likely to evolve together to increase social value, similar to the process of creative destruction described by Schumpeter. To the extent that monopoly power may not be sustainable in the long run, there would be no conflict between customer value and firm value appropriation, and firms should try to maximize both concurrently through time. In this sense, value creation and appropriation point in the same direction towards greater social welfare, though some extra profits may be captured in the short term when firms focus on value appropriation and the occasional exploitation of monopoly power at the expense of social value. However, the existence of some monopoly power does not seem to be an important threat to social welfare as long as governments do not allow sustained barriers to competition and let firms feel the pressure, real or potential, from competition in the market.[2] In conclusion, we may reasonably expect that the design of successful strategies by firms trying to maximize value capture will also contribute to greater social value in the long run, despite the existence of some monopoly power.

Externalities

In addition to the limits to competition associated with monopoly, social value also includes the effect of firm strategies on the economic agents that are not industry stakeholders, but are nevertheless part of society. As we discussed in chapter four, market exchanges may produce positive or negative externalities on third parties who are not resource providers, customers, or competitors in those markets. For instance, a firm may pollute the environment with its factory, but the total nonmonetary cost of a polluted environment and possibly the monetary costs of cleaning it up are suffered by the entire society and not only by the firm and its actual customers.

Externalities are an important problem for markets as a way to allocate and coordinate resources to generate social value. Some strategic decisions by firms may not lead to greater social welfare if all benefits and costs are not properly considered. In other words, when private value diverges from social value, decisions made by private institutions may end up destroying social welfare or not creating as much as it would be possible. In the example of the polluting factory, the economic value created by a factory may be smaller than the damage that is done to the people that live near the factory. The firm would possibly consider only the costs and benefits that have an impact on the value that it creates for its customers and the profits that it can capture, but not the pollution effect. Profitable firm strategies may not increase social value if there are negative externalities that are not accounted for in the firm's (private) performance.

The analysis of externalities essentially requires the proper estimation of all value for the parties directly involved through market exchanges as well as indirectly outside the market system. Only the analysis of economic value can ultimately determine whether the specific action that generates externalities should or should not be

---

[2] See Baumol *et al.* (1982) for an analysis of contestable markets in which the mere potential entry of new competitors may force a monopolist to expand production and lower prices to the perfectly competitive level.

undertaken in order to benefit society as a whole. In our example, both the individuals that suffer the polluting factory and the individuals that benefit from the factory's production have benefits and costs. None has inherently superior rights and the option that generates the largest social value is economically desirable.[3] To maximize social welfare, the party with the ultimate decision to build the factory, presumably the firm or the judge that may settle the issue, would need to internalize any possible externalities of such a decision, so that all social benefits and costs are taken into consideration.

Coase showed that the optimal solution to the problem of externalities consists in having clear and well-defined property rights that can be negotiated through well-functioning markets, i.e., without transaction costs. Continuing with our example, if the right to pollute a certain area belongs to all the people that live in the given location, the firm may buy such a right and fully compensate those people. In that case, the firm would only build the factory if the environmental damage that it creates (i.e., the negative externality) is smaller than the economic value that it can generate. Interestingly, if the right to pollute belongs to the firm, even in that case the factory may not be built if the neighbors were willing to pay more for the factory to be closed down than the value the factory would generate otherwise.[4] To resolve the social problems created by externalities, governments should just define and assign property rights and let markets work to achieve the most efficient allocation of property rights that leads to maximum social value. Essentially, externalities disappear automatically when there is a market for them as long as transaction costs do not impede mutually beneficial agreements between the parties in conflict. Markets for externalities can solve the problems that the existence of externalities create for social value.

Unfortunately, property rights are often very difficult to assign and transaction costs can be very high if there are many parties or people

---

[3] This utilitarian perspective to the maximization of utility and social welfare is widely accepted in mainstream economics since the classical work of John Stuart Mill. However, it could be questioned for social projects outside the traditional activities of profit-seeking businesses. For a debate about cost-benefit analysis and social welfare, see Adler and Posner (2001).

[4] This is known as Coase theorem, which basically says that, in the absence of transaction costs, externalities may be resolved through bargaining between the parties and the socially efficient outcome may be achieved regardless of the initial assignment of property rights.

that should be involved in reaching an agreement. As a result, externalities are likely to make the strategic decisions of firms to maximize profits to diverge from the maximization of social value. To the extent that transaction costs are greater and well-functioning markets are absent, externalities become an important problem and successful firm strategies may not lead to greater social value.

Other market imperfections

In addition to monopoly and externalities, there are other reasons why firms operating in free markets may not lead to the maximization of social value, like the existence of public goods and information asymmetries. These market imperfections may also provide the rationale for some type of market regulation by governments.[5]

Closely related to the problem of externalities, *public goods* are those whose consumption by one person does not reduce its availability to others. Individuals cannot be excluded from enjoying public goods that do not get depleted by their use, for instance, national defense. Any person may free ride on the payments done by others to create or protect such public goods. If they were asked, people could possibly understate their willingness to pay, despite the utility they may receive from them. To solve this problem, governments often provide public goods and force everyone to contribute to their costs. Conceptually, maximum social value would be presumably achieved by setting the sum of the marginal utilities of all individuals equal to the public goods' marginal costs. Beyond this point, providing a greater quantity of public goods would result in greater costs than the additional utility that it creates for overall society. Free markets on their own would not lead to the adequate provision of public goods.

Information asymmetry between the firm and its customers about the offered products and services may also lead to market failures. When people have different private information, markets may not perform efficiently, even when there are advantageous exchanges that would create value for both parties. Akerlof (1970) provides a famous example of the market for used cars and how it may collapse when the buyers cannot possibly evaluate the quality of the cars and, thus,

---

[5] See Viscusi *et al.* (2000) for a discussion of the nature of market imperfections and the economics of regulation.

may get a lemon. The sellers of the cars with greater quality may be driven out of the market by the average prices that buyers would be willing to pay, which would be below their true value only known by the sellers. This is an example of adverse selection or hidden characteristics, but there are also informational problems of moral hazard that are particularly important in insurance markets. As Stiglitz and other economists have shown, even small departures from the standard Arrow-Debreau model of small information search costs would dramatically change the nature of the market equilibrium.[6] To solve some of these problems of information asymmetry, economic agents may provide signals of quality and governments may use regulation to force the mandatory provision of information, beyond the law and the liability system.

In sum, there are different reasons why firms operating in free markets may not always lead to the maximum social value. All of them relate directly or indirectly to the limits of markets to facilitate exchanges that would be mutually beneficial to both parties. Broadly defined, there must be some transaction costs that prevent such exchanges from taking place and, consequently, result in market failures. If transaction costs were zero, any potential change that benefits an economic agent more than it damages others could be written and enforced, so that the maximum social welfare would be achievable. There would be markets for everything, which would automatically lead to maximum social value. Even in the case of monopoly, firms could in theory write a contract with each individual customer and a different price (i.e., first-order price discrimination), so that no deadweight-loss would occur.

However, transaction costs do exist and there are market failures driven by imperfections like natural monopolies, externalities, public goods, and information asymmetries. When these market imperfections are greater, there would be greater divergence between the primary goal of firms to maximize value appropriation and the effect of firm strategies on overall social value. In those cases, some type of government intervention may be required to align the private interests of economic agents with those of overall society. Regulation may force economic agents to internalize any possible externalities.

---

[6] For a review of the main ideas in the economics of information, see Stiglitz (2000).

Unfortunately, government involvement to solve market failures may result in greater destruction of social value, because regulation is far from perfect. Well-intentioned regulation may actually destroy value driven by political forces that serve objectives other than economic efficiency.[7] This is a critical challenge for public policy and administration, but not for our purposes in business strategy. Strategic management is concerned with understanding and improving firm performance and, as we have seen above, successful strategies generally lead to greater social value, except in the presence of substantial market imperfections.

Wealth distribution

Firms are the active mechanism for resource combinations to create value for society, though the strategic decisions of firms operating in free markets do not always lead to the maximization of overall social value. Despite the existence of some market imperfections, successful firm strategies create much value for customers, stockholders, resource owners, and overall society. However, firms and the market-driven economy in general are not effective in reducing inequalities and solving other social issues apart from economic value creation.

For most economists, wealth redistribution and the cost of other social welfare programs should be funded by individuals and firms via taxes. Society cannot rely on voluntary donations to solve the problems of equity in the world. Arguably, these programs should be managed by specialized public and nongovernment organizations (NGOs) with social goals aside efficiency and the maximization of economic value. Without the direct intervention of government to redistribute wealth through taxation, free markets would not be sufficiently effective to increase equality and achieve a variety of social goals. In fact, firms target primarily those customers based on their willingness to pay for their services, so that the needs of people with greater wealth receive far more attention than those of poorer and more needy people.[8] Firms would only contribute very slowly to greater equality, for instance, through their impact on the resource side by searching for lower costs and relocating productive resources to emerging countries.

---

[7] See Wolf (1979) about "nonmarket failure."
[8] However, firm strategies can also be targeted to those situated at the bottom of the pyramid. See Prahalad (2006).

Marxist theories have gone much further in the criticisms of the negative effect of free market systems on social inequality. They claim that firms exploit workers and free markets even increase inequality both inside domestic markets and across countries on a global scale. Today very few well-trained economists, if any at all, would argue in favor of central planning systems to run an economy. As we discussed in chapter three, the superiority of free markets is well established both from a theoretical point of view as well as empirically. The Chinese economic explosion driven by private firms in a moderately free economic context (though not yet politically free) is a very clear example in contrast to the terrible economic conditions and widespread poverty in Cuba. There is no doubt that firms operating in free markets with an adequate level of regulation to deal with market imperfections are the best known way to increase society's overall wealth. However, other mechanisms need to exist to improve social welfare challenges, like wealth distribution or social discrimination. Markets will not solve these problems with the effectiveness and the urgency that they require.

There is substantial debate regarding the role of firms in society beyond its responsibilities for economic value creation and appropriation. Most often firm strategies do not intend to actively improve social welfare issues such as quality and poverty. These questions are often not considered part of the economic responsibilities of businesses regarding value creation, though firms could also be held responsible for their lack of contribution to solving these problems. We will now turn to the question of where the corporate social responsibility of firms ends and its implications for their performance.

Corporate social responsibility

The free market system has important limitations with regard to its potential to maximize social wealth and, even more so, its distribution among the members of society. We can thus raise the critical question for managers regarding corporate social responsibility: how far should firms go in their social responsibilities beyond their well-known functions in the creation of customer value and its partial appropriation for its own resources and stockholders? In other words, should firms engage in voluntary actions designed to improve social or environmental conditions in addition to allocating resources and making profits?

The traditional orthodox view is represented by Milton Friedman, though it goes back to Adam Smith's defense of self-interest in driving our economy.[9] Friedman (1970) claimed that there is one and only one social responsibility of business: to manage resources and activities to increase its profits as agents of its shareholders and owners of the firm. In his own words:

In a free-enterprise, private-property system, a corporate executive is an employee of the owners of the business. He has direct responsibility to his employers. That responsibility is to conduct the business in accordance with their desires, which generally will be to make as much money as possible while conforming to the basic rules of the society, both those embodied in law and those embodied in ethical custom. (Friedman, 1970)

Any voluntary action by managers to promote social good at the expense of stockholders (similarly for workers and customers via lower salaries and higher prices respectively) can be regarded as an unfair and ineffective tax for this subset of individuals. Managers may give themselves the right to tax other people's wealth and determine how much to use for the social purposes that they choose subjectively. Friedman argues that corporate managers do not have this right and, in fact, they are not civil servants that have been elected to carry out this type of duty, including setting tax rates and deciding how to use the proceeds among all possible social problems.

At first sight, Friedman's view may seem very conservative and not very conducive to social change and improvement. However, this is not really so. By trying to maximize profits, managers will create much value for overall society, including customers, employees, and owners. This wealth can later be redistributed by governments through taxation that funds social programs. Rather than giving managers a self-appointed role in the solution of social problems, this responsibility is assigned to specialized people and agencies, which are controlled through the appropriate political institutions. For Friedman, social programs should not be dictated and executed voluntarily by managers at the expense of a reduced number of contributors, whether they be stockholders, customers, or workers of the firm. Instead, social

---

[9] In one of his most famous quotes about self-interest in business transactions, Adam Smith (1776) said: "It is not from the benevolence of the butcher, the brewer, or the baker, that we expect our dinner, but from their regard to their own self-interest."

programs should be managed and controlled by governments, which impose mandatory taxes to firms and individuals based on their income and decide which social projects deserve priority. The responsibility of firms is limited to financing these programs through taxes. In other words, corporate social responsibility (CSR) is forced upon firms via taxation and the proceeds are used by specialized agencies, not by managers acting on voluntary altruistic intentions.

The issue at hand is whether there is an additional social responsibility of managers beyond this indirect responsibility through taxes. Contrary to Friedman, the defenders of CSR claim that firms have other social responsibilities beyond their economic and legal duties.[10] Certainly, firms are not responsible for solving all social problems, such as poverty or discrimination, but they may be held accountable for social problems in the areas in which they are directly or indirectly involved, such as safety and air pollution for car manufacturers or exploitation and discrimination within their organizations.[11] Aguilera *et al.* (2007) argue based on institutional theory that firms need to obtain legitimacy and not focus exclusively on economic performance. Firm are socially responsible not only to shareholders, but also to other stakeholders that are directly or indirectly affected by the firms' business activities, such as customers, employees, suppliers, and our community at large.[12] All social groups that have some type of stake in a business's actions are likely to exert some pressure for the firm to be responsive to their interests. Thus, firms have relational motives to

---

[10] See Wood (1991) for an integrated approach to the early thinking in strategic management about CSR. She analyzes the social responsibilities categories identified by Carroll (1979), i.e., economic, legal, ethical, and discretionary responsibilities, at three levels of analysis: institutional, organizational, and individual. Aguilera *et al.* (2007) provide a different model based on three motives for engaging in CSR: instrumental, relational, and moral. They stress the interactions between the different levels of CSR analysis, from individual, through the organizational, to the national and transnational levels, and how CSR ultimately affects social change.

[11] See Preston and Post (1975) for the principle of public responsibility that gives boundaries to the social responsibility of firms.

[12] See Freeman (1984) for a stakeholder management perspective on strategy. This view, also in line with the Business Roundtable (see Baron, 2006), considers managers as agents of different stakeholders, so that they are responsible to several groups or constituencies and not only to shareholders, thus contrary to Friedman.

engage in CSR to deal with all of these groups in order to gain and keep their legitimacy in society.

The CSR activities performed by firms may have some impact on their competitiveness in the market and ultimately their financial performance. On the one hand, these activities have some cost that is born by the firm, primarily by the stockholders as the group entitled to keep the firm's residual income. On the other hand, CSR may strengthen the competitive advantage of the firm, for instance, when it increases its reputation or serves as a source of differentiation. A cost-benefit analysis would indicate whether the former effect is greater or smaller than the later one and, thus, there is an overall positive or negative impact of CSR on firm performance.[13] Either impact may be expected in theory, including no relationship between CSR and firm performance. Actually, the empirical evidence is mixed with studies pointing in all directions, though more evidence seems to be converging towards a positive correlation that probably results from bidirectional causality.[14] To the extent that CSR may indeed increase firm performance, everyone including Friedman would agree that firms should engage in CSR for purely instrumental reasons, that is, to maximize their financial viability in the long run. From this strategic CSR view, the economic and legitimacy arguments become parallel and the controversy disappears with regard to whether or not CSR activities should be performed by firms. Instrumental CSR makes everyone better off, including overall society as well as stockholders.[15]

This approach to strategic CSR is fully consistent with the notion of nonmarket strategy and its adequate management. Baron (2006) argues that market and nonmarket strategies should be somehow linked to value-creation for society. However, these two types of

[13] See McWilliams and Siegel (2001) for a cost-benefit analysis of CSR and the factors that influence supply and demand for CSR activities.

[14] See Orlitzky *et al.* (2003) for a meta-analysis of the literature on CSR and performance that supports this conclusion. However, McWilliams and Siegel (2000) claim that empirical studies that find a positive association (e.g., Waddock and Graves, 1997) are mis-specified and, once the appropriate controls are introduced in the model, there is no significant relationship between CSR and firm performance.

[15] Porter and Kramer (2006) analyze the combined economic and social benefits of corporate philanthropy when it is grounded on the firm's competitive context, i.e., when philanthropy is focused on the environmental condition that most enhances the firm's productivity.

strategy are very different in how they are analyzed and managed. He claims that the nonmarket environment can be analyzed in terms of issues, interests, institutions, and information. Issues are the basic unit of analysis and the focus of nonmarket strategy. Associated with each issue are the institutional arenas in which the issue will be addressed, the interests at stake, and the information available to the interested parties. After considering these elements of the nonmarket environment, the firm will have to define its positioning with regard to nonmarket issues in three spaces: public sentiment, political space, and legal space. To the extent that market and nonmarket strategies are effectively integrated in the strategic management of CSR, the firm will be able to participate in the public processes that ultimately affect the business opportunities for the firm and its competitiveness. Under these circumstances, nonmarket strategy should be able to create value for both the firm and overall society.

Apart from the clear arguments in support of strategic CSR and nonmarket strategy, it is more difficult to justify voluntary social expenditures by firms when they impose a cost on their owners. It can be argued that at least some stockholders may value CSR in its own right and be willing to accept somewhat lower financial returns.[16] However, just like investors can diversify for risk minimization purposes on their own better than firms can do for them, they can also decide about their altruistic social concerns according to their own preferences instead of assigning this responsibility to the managers of the firm. Thus, there is a clear rationale for CSR for instrumental or strategic reasons including the need to maintain legitimacy, but the arguments in favor of managers taking a social responsibility beyond these reasons indirectly associated with economic value creation is much more questionable. We need to analyze from both an economic and an ethical point of view whether firms should engage in social activities that actually reduce shareholder's wealth.

When does CSR pay off?

Burke and Logsdon (1996) argue that some CSR activities are done purely for social reasons without implications for the firm's competitive advantage, but many of them can be categorized as strategic

---

[16] See MacKey *et al.* (2007).

CSR that may yield substantial benefits to the firm. Strategic CSR activities contribute to the creation of value by the firm and jointly serve the business interests of the firm as well as societal interests. There are five conditions for CSR to be strategic:

- *Centrality*: programs and policies must be closely related to the organization's mission as opposed to being broad-based corporate philanthropy.
- *Specificity*: the firm should be able to capture some of the benefits created by CSR activities rather than simply creating public goods, whose value cannot be appropriated by the firm.
- *Proactivity*: firms that recognize critical trends and environmental changes early will be better positioned to take advantage of opportunities or to counter threats.
- *Voluntarism*: to create value for a firm, its CSR activities must exceed the minimum standards of externally imposed compliance requirements.
- *Visibility*: CSR activities should be highly visible so that the firm may gain recognition from internal and external stakeholders.

This model essentially adapts the traditional strategic analysis of economic value creation to CSR activities. In particular, it highlights the importance for firms to proactively scan the environment and change it through voluntary programs that give social recognition to the firm. As part of a firm's overall business and social strategy, strategic CSR creates value for the firm and also for society.

Value creation and CSR

Firms actually fund social programs and sometimes argue that they ought to do so regardless of their financial implications. Furthermore, financial markets do not seem to punish these socially responsible firms, though it is not clear that they are rewarded for it either. The social responsibility of firms is to a large extent an ethical issue that we will analyze in the next section, but we will also study it now from a purely economic perspective as a guideline for strategic decision making about activities and resources.

In the first place, it seems clear that a firm should only assign to itself a certain social activity to the extent that it is the most appropriate organization to carry it out effectively.[17] This can only happen when the social activities and the firm's core business are very closely linked within their scope of public responsibility. Otherwise, other organizations, including NGOs, would probably be more skilled and efficient in managing activities for social goals. Just like for diversification decisions, not any social activity can be performed equally well by every firm. CSR can be questioned even from a social perspective if those activities can be carried out better by other organizations rather than by the specific firm that takes the social responsibility for itself. Thus, boundary decisions around CSR activities should be analyzed with regard to the social value that the specific firm can create for society, including its overall benefits and costs.

The critical question is how far should the firm go in those social activities where it can create social value, but also reduce its profitability. These activities actually constitute a transfer of wealth from stockholders to the rest of society. There are good arguments for and against profit maximization as a guideline for this type of (nonstrategic) CSR decisions. On the one hand, we could claim along Friedman that the role of firms in society is primarily to create economic value and any other social responsibility can be better managed through other means, particularly government regulation and taxes. Any deviation from this essential task of business will be ultimately bad for society because there will be less overall wealth to distribute through whichever social programs the government can dictate. Only strategic CSR that improves profitability should be undertaken. On the other hand, managers are not exclusively responsible to the stockholders and they receive pressure from other stakeholders to be sensitive to their needs. This social sensitivity may lead the firm to sometimes trade off profits for other social goals. This is the controversy to resolve.

Firms carry out a variety of productive activities for profit seeking purposes, but they also may engage in CSR activities for social reasons as well. Obviously, business activities constitute the core of the firm. Organizations create economic value for customers and distribute part of it among the collection of resources that constitutes the firm, including the residual to which the stockholders are entitled as providers of

---

[17] See Porter and Kramer (1999), who argue that: "A foundation creates value when it achieves an equivalent social benefit with fewer dollars or creates greater social benefit for comparable costs."

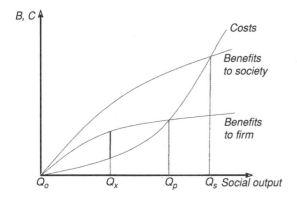

Figure 9.2 Cost–benefit analysis of CSR activities to the firm and overall society

internal capital. Business decisions are presumably taken to maximize economic value, though there are some imperfections in the market system that sometimes cause a divergence between overall social value creation and its appropriation by firms. Leaving these market imperfections aside, it is clear that profit maximization results in the largest economic value for society driven by the invisible hand of markets. Our capitalistic society and the sustained increase in overall wealth that it produces are based on this economic responsibility of firms operating in free markets. Profit making is a good approach to create economic value for both the firm and society.

In contrast, CSR activities are not necessarily performed for the sake of making profits and they should probably not be done only for this reason. Certainly, CSR may indeed have a positive effect on the business side, which we have called instrumental or strategic CSR. Even Friedman would agree that strategic CSR increases shareholders' wealth and overall social welfare in such a case. However, I will argue that these activities, i.e., the voluntary social output of firms, may not be set by managers at the point where they maximize profits and this makes sense even from an economic perspective.

We can draw on Husted and Salazar (2006) to clarify this point. Figure 9.2 shows a graph of the benefits of the firm's social output for overall society and those benefits that may be specifically captured by the firm through greater willingness to pay from its customers, due for instance to positive reputation. The figure also includes the costs of the CSR activities to the firm. In point Q_x the marginal costs of doing any additional CSR equals its marginal benefits to the firm, so that the solid segment in the line would correspond to the largest profits for the firm, i.e., where both functions have the same tangent. At this point the firm does only instrumental strategic CSR.

The firm could produce greater social output if it were to expand CSR until total revenue from CSR equaled total costs in Q_p without incurring any losses from their CSR activities. At this point shareholders would have the same overall profits than if the firm did not engage in any CSR at all in Q_o, but society would benefit from the greatest possible amount of voluntary social output by the firm without transferring wealth from stockholders to the rest of society. Even greater social output in point Q_s is the best situation for overall society, so that all CSR activities that provide more social benefits than their costs are provided. However, the firm would incur substantial losses in Q_s because its own benefits are much smaller than its costs, which would affect its competitiveness on the business activities of the firm. Husted and Salazar (2006) make a strong case in support of strategic CSR that maximizes firm profits. They claim that the key to the production of social output is the capability of the social investor to make strategic investments in CSR that result in additional benefits or lower costs for the firm. In contrast to purely altruistic investments of firms, they suggest that firms should link the business and social activities together to jointly create more value for both the firm and overall society. The largest social value would be created when firms engage in strategic CSR, so that they can move up the benefits function to the firm and move down the cost function of CSR as much as possible. After linking strategically CSR and business activities, they ultimately suggest that strategic CSR should be kept at the level at which the firm maximizes its overall profits in Q_x. To the contrary, I will argue based on a combination of both economic and ethical arguments that CSR can be and it is often expanded until Q_p, where the firm would be about to start incurring losses from its social output, i.e., the point at which social output is maximized and stockholders suffer no penalty over the situation without any CSR in Q_o.

Without any doubt, no CSR at all can be discarded from the two points of view, stockholders' and society's. Both points Q_x and Q_p are preferable to Q_o. They would result in a Pareto improvement in social welfare and stockholders would not suffer any penalty. Similarly, point Q_s can also be rejected because it results in a substantial loss to stockholders and the business activities of the firm. Even though any point between Q_p and Q_s is good for society (i.e., the benefits provided by these social activities are greater than their overall costs), firms acting in their own interests would not have any incentive to generate so much social output that actually reduces stockholder's compensation from business activities. A profit guideline will not drive firms to the level of social output that is optimal for society because the benefits that they generate for society are externalities to the firm (i.e., there are two different benefits functions: to the firm and to overall society). Free markets are not the appropriate system to allocate resources to social activities and only through public policy (e.g., tax incentives or regulation) can government motivate the firm to increase its social output above Q_p.

A critical question is whether firms maximize their profits from only strategic CSR activities in Q_x or further expand their social output to Q_p, as it would be socially preferable. For the firm, this situation is apparently equivalent to the quantity setting decision of business production in a monopoly. Just like firms restrict their business production to increase profits, they could also restrict their social output to maximize profits from their CSR activities. In both cases, government can intervene with regulation and taxes, though we know from abundant experience in regulated industries that this solution can create greater problems than it solves. For business activities, the pressure from competition and the fight for profits motivate firms to expand their production and to innovate, so that the market system induces the continuous creation of economic value. Unfortunately, free markets and profit seeking are not similarly effective in solving noneconomic social problems. In contrast to business activities, competition in CSR among firms will not drive them to expand social output from Q_x to Q_p and further. Because of its noneconomic nature, social output generates very large externalities that are not accounted for by markets and, furthermore, it does not share the competitive features of product markets in perfect competition.

In other words, the invisible hand would not lead automatically to the best solution in Q_s and social output would probably even fall short of Q_p. Though free markets are clearly the best system for the creation of economic value, the profit motive as a guideline for CSR activities would result in too little social output and probably not targeted in the best possible direction. Profits are just not a sound standard for decision making not associated with economic value creation and they should not guide firm decisions about what and how much social output should be provided. The key point is that social output is not analogous to product markets in which competition drives economic production close to its maximum value for overall society at the perfectly competitive level. Thus, we could normatively reject profit maximization as an appropriate guide for CSR activities based on purely economic arguments, and we should search for an alternative way for firms and society to manage their social output. An alternative standard to profit maximization that is acceptable to stockholders and overall society will have to be used for CSR activities to be voluntarily increased to Q_p by firms. Any level of social output above Q_p will require some type of government intervention.

A dual standard for business and CSR activities

To solve this issue, a dual standard can be suggested for business versus social activities. Business activities are carried out for profit maximization, which leads to maximum economic value for society as well. In contrast, I will argue that CSR activities are usually undertaken to maximize social output, subject to the constraint of no losses for the firm and its stockholders (point Q_p). Based on this dual standard, firms produce as much social output as possible, so long as their costs do not clearly outweigh the potential benefits that they may generate, e.g., in legitimacy and reputation for the firm.

This dual standard for business and CSR activities and the different treatment that they receive inside firms provide a middle ground where the supporters of Friedman's orthodox views can meet with the defenders of voluntary CSR by firms beyond profit seeking. Whereas value appropriation drives business decisions, the improvement of social welfare is likely to determine the voluntary investment in CSR, but subject to the reasonable constraint that they should have a neutral impact on firm performance. CSR is fully supported by the benefits that it may produce to the firm, so that no cost is finally suffered by stockholders for the firm's involvement in CSR and they do not provide extra profit either. Essentially, social output is maximized and financed with the potential returns obtained from the firm's strategic CSR activities, if they exist, and then fully returned to society.

This dual standard can be proposed in the best interests of society. Maximizing CSR subject to a no-loss constraint probably describes reasonably well how at least some firms seem to approach their CSR responsibilities. However, the dual standard to CSR can be criticized on both positive and normative grounds. First, based on the traditional assumptions of economic behavior, self-interest could make the suggestion to expand social output from Q_x to Q_p unrealistic, just like a naïve recommendation for monopolists to voluntarily increase production in the best interests of society. In other words, firms may not actually behave like this standard suggests because they do not have economic incentives to do so. Second and in the opposite direction, some people may believe based on ethical considerations that firms should go even further than Q_p in their level of CSR despite suffering some costs. That is, we can make the normative statement that this standard assigns insufficient ethical duties to firms. The analysis of whether this rule is good for society and reasonably realistic takes us into the realm of ethics and human behavior.

Ethics and social strategy

Ethics is an important part of philosophical inquiry that has implications for all aspects of human life, including business management.[18] It is evident that firms indeed have ethical responsibilities and even Friedman acknowledges ethical boundaries on firm behavior. Because organizations are created, owned, and managed by individuals, it is evident that the actions of organizations will have consequences that can be scrutinized for their ethical implications. Firms do not exist in an ethical vacuum outside human influence and responsibility. In the end, managers and owners are ethically responsible for the actions of their firms.

However, the idea that firms have ethical responsibilities does not imply that managers can impose on shareholders the cost of any social programs at their discretion based on ethical reasons. It does not seem intuitively fair that an agent hired specifically to increase the wealth of

---

[18] For a review of ethics in philosophy, see MacIntyre (1998). A critical distinction can be made between theories of the good (classical and utilitarian perspectives on ethics) and theories of the right, including Kant (2008), and Rawls (1999). Traditional economic thinking can clearly be placed within the utilitarian tradition represented by John Stuart Mill (2001).

the principal should use the firm's assets to improve the world at the cost of shareholders and against their will. As Kant pointed out, moral duties are self-imposed and we constitute our own moral authority.[19] Ethical duties tie one's behavior to a code of conduct, but people (managers) could hardly propose a code that truly affects other people (shareholders) and not their own sacrifice exclusively. Consequently, it cannot be argued that it is ethical for managers to undertake any social action at the expense of stockholders with which they may not agree. Forcing these costs on shareholders cannot be defended on moral grounds, though society as a whole can impose on itself corporate and individual taxes to redistribute wealth for equity (i.e., ethical) reasons through its government.

Though managers have moral duties when deciding their firm strategy, they should only be held responsible for those that all shareholders and overall society would agree that they are ethically obliged to. If the law or the ethical tradition does not require the firm to carry out those programs, any costly social initiative decided voluntarily by managers goes beyond the attributions that they are entitled to, as noted by Friedman. Thus, generally acceptable ethical duties should determine the level of social output provided by firms. The main problem is that it is not clear what these generally acceptable ethical principles are. However, this is a problem with ethics itself, not with the economic analysis of Friedman. The problem is that it is hard for us to agree on which are our moral duties as individuals and, thus, the ethical responsibilities of firms within society. More generally and

---

[19] Kant believes that ethical duties can only be universal and everyone is subject to a *categorical imperative* without exceptions and regardless of the consequences of those ethical duties. Unfortunately, the analysis of the potential to consistently universalize an ethical rule has important limitations as a guide for ethics. For instance, the same action can be defined using very different rules, some of which may be consistently universalized. Furthermore, even if we disregard the technical guideline about the potential to consistently universalize a rule without incurring in a contradiction (which is ultimately a prerequisite for a rule, but it does not reject universal rules that may be unethical anyway), the categorical imperative ultimately leads to a universal situation whose desirability and, ultimately, goodness needs to be assessed (MacIntyre, 1998). Contrary to his own intentions, Kant's categorical imperative implicitly includes an analysis of consequences to this approach to ethics presumably based on absolute conceptualizations of right and wrong versus the good or bad consequences of actions stressed by the utilitarian approach to ethics, which is mainstream in economics.

independently of economics and strategic management, we just do not have a good answer to a very important question about ethics: how much should I sacrifice myself for the greater good of overall society? In our case, is it ethical to give up some profitability to improve social conditions?

This question shares some similarities with the prisoner's dilemma game.[20] This well-known game describes a situation in which individuals trying to achieve their best outcome independently end up obtaining a lower pay-off than they could obtain if they had cooperated and trusted in each other's nonselfish choice in the game. If the game is played a finite number of times, the equilibrium solution has both players choosing an option that is not in their joint best interests. For cooperation and the best joint solution to emerge, the game needs to be infinite without a too high discount rate or be played on a sufficiently large number of occasions with the players believing that there is some chance that the rival may behave cooperatively.[21] From a game theory perspective it is difficult to understand the emergence of cooperation in the short run, though detrimental selfish behavior may be prevented under certain circumstances. However, altruistic behavior does occur, despite its apparent contradiction with self-interested behavior particularly in the short run.[22]

It is evident that a world with infinitely selfish individuals would be both a terrible place in which to live and economically backward. It is not good for all of us as a whole to rely on the unbounded pursuit of selfish goals disregarding the dynamic interplay with other people, as the pay-off structure in the prisoner's dilemma shows. Some actions, such as stealing for individuals and collusion among firms, are legally prohibited to restrain excessive selfishness against the interests of overall society. As an internal complement to the external enforcement of social interests, ethical prescriptions based on the assessment of goodness for overall society also lead to actions that maximize overall social value against the immediate benefits to selfish individuals. In addition to the law and the institutions that force cooperation among

---

[20] For an introduction to game theory, see for instance Kreps (1990). For a detailed discussion of cooperation and the prisoner's dilemma game in particular see Axelrod (1984).

[21] See Radner (1980), and Kreps and Wilson (1982).

[22] See, for instance, Becker (1976) or Frank (1988), who analyze altruism and passions from an economic approach.

individuals, internal moral duties temper excessive selfishness that resolve situations like the prisoner's dilemma. Somewhat paradoxically, it is good for us to choose strategies that are apparently bad for us.

The decision for the managers of the firm about the appropriate level of social output in Figure 9.2 is ultimately an ethical issue regarding the level of selfishness that society could expect and require from the firm. Q_x represents maximum selfishness and Q_s maximum altruism. We can analyze from an ethics perspective the amount of social output of the firm that can be widely accepted by overall society, including firm stockholders, which should presumably lead to the maximum good for overall society. The intermediate point Q_p represents a moderately selfish solution that is consistent with the general social interest and an ethical rule potentially acceptable for stockholders.

On the one hand, it may be claimed that firms should restrict their involvement in CSR to Q_x so that they maximize overall profits, including those generated by the strategic use of CSR. This argument would place profit maximization as an unrestricted goal over any other possible consideration guiding the firm's behavior, so that any legal action that increases profits should be undertaken by managers if and only if it leads to profit maximization. However, it does not seem intuitively right to believe that individuals and firms should try to make as much money as possible in all the things they do, even within the constraints of the law.

Certainly, firms do not have an economic incentive to move from Q_x to Q_p, but they should do so for the same reasons for which we allow profits in our society. We allow profit maximization to guide our economy because they lead to the greatest possible creation of wealth for society, so that this motivation is clearly ethical from an utilitarian perspective. Note that there are other economic systems in which profits are regarded as unethical and they are not allowed, like in a Marxist economy and in the medieval Catholic system that considered charging interest as a sin. What makes profits ethical today is our strong belief that by pursuing profits we are indeed contributing to the economic development of society. Profits not associated with such goal are prohibited by the legal system (e.g., profitable practices that restrict competition or mafia extortion to "protect" people from suffering damages).

By increasing their social output to Q_p, firms are not contributing to maximizing economic value, but they are increasing social welfare as much as they can without negatively affecting their core business activities. From a purely ethical perspective, profits as a guide for social activities can be regarded as excessively selfish and detrimental to overall society. Philanthropy for financial reasons is not well targeted to its better uses and it may not be philanthropy at all. Instead, nonbusiness criteria should drive nonbusiness activities because they ultimately lead to greater social good. Arguably, everyone including stockholders could see the benefits of and agree with an ethical rule that limits the search for profits only to the traditional business activities of firms, but not to CSR activities presumably intended to improve social welfare.

On the other hand, it does not seem reasonable to expect that this ethical obligation for firms to improve social conditions for their own sake is unbounded. Ethics cannot justify a voluntary increase in social output to Q_x. There is a limit to the altruism that we can expect from managers and firms in their discretionary social output. The natural limit for social output is the cost that it has for the owners of the firm. Only fair and equitable sacrifice that increases overall social welfare can be required from individuals. While stockholders may agree that the firm should provide as much social output as possible alongside its profit-seeking business activities, they may also require that these CSR activities should not have an onerous burden on them. If certain social programs are clearly good for society, then they should be mandated by government and their cost fully and equitably shared among all of society's members, rather than being financed by a limited group of shareholders.

Taking into consideration both sides of the argument, point Q_p in Figure 9.2 emerges as a reasonable level of social output that we can both expect and demand from firms. This point is neither absolutely egoistic nor altruistic, but it represents a moderate level of selfishness that allows the greatest social value to be generated by the firm without forcing losses on stockholders. As a guideline for CSR activities, Q_p maximizes the overall social output voluntarily provided by firms without having a negative impact on the return from their business activities. Any point below or above Q_p can be rejected for ethical reasons; lower social output does not lead to the greatest possible good for society, while greater social output imposes an unfair burden on a reduced number of individuals (i.e., the firm's owners).

Despite the economic and ethical arguments in favor of Q_p as the optimal level of voluntary social output for firms, this is ultimately a discretionary decision that it does not intend to maximize profits, but it has positive effects for society. Only a moral obligation can ultimately lead managers to provide any social output greater than Q_x voluntarily. The ethical standard proposed in this chapter has the clear benefit of leading to a better world for everyone without requiring an excessively altruistic transfer of wealth from the firm's stockholders to the rest of society. This is a guideline that could be generally agreed including stockholders and, thus, it can be used to identify the social output to which the firm can be ethically obliged in its strategy.

Value analysis in corporate social responsibility

Let us analyze one of the emblematic cases of CSR and its connection to business strategy. The Body Shop is a very clear example of how a firm can contribute to improve society in addition to the economic value that it creates through its business strategy. The approach to CSR in this firm has changed substantially in the last few years, but its key traditional features can allow us to study the main issues behind CSR management.

CSR in The Body Shop

The Body Shop (TBS) was created by the charismatic entrepreneur Anita Roddick in Great Britain in the seventies, when the concern for the environment had begun to grow in Western Europe. TBS was clearly positioned against traditional cosmetics firms and built its own distribution channel and a strong green differentiation with prices below the traditional branded players like L'Oreal, but above the low cost players. The firm grew very rapidly through franchises based on several practices that attracted socially conscious female consumers to its wide range of cosmetics products. For instance, the firm did not test its products on animals, did not use advertising, recycled all of its packaging, used only generic brand names with the products' exotic ingredients, and employed mostly women for its franchised stores. Its famous chief executive officer (CEO) often criticized its competitors very harshly and presumably disregarded stockholders' interests, though she actually received several marketing awards and led the highly successful firm for about two decades. The firm entered into highly political campaigns ranging from saving the whales to reducing worldwide poverty. When the firm's performance was not as expected in the late nineties, a new CEO replaced Roddick in 1998 and, a year before she died in 2007, she sold her participation in The Body Shop and the entire firm to the French cosmetics giant, L'Oreal.

The success of this company is based on a solid business strategy based on unique positioning and a franchised distribution channel, which allowed the firm to surpass the huge barriers to competition in this profitable industry, particularly in distribution and advertising. In addition to its business strategy, the firm is frequently used as a great example of strategic CSR and the benefits that it can bring to the firm, mainly through reputation and internal motivation of its employees.

The green differentiation and its unique model in the cosmetics industry can be studied using the traditional models for the analysis of business strategy, but we are particularly interested in its CSR activities and voluntary practices. Very clearly, its positioning in social issues complement and help reinforce its business model. In particular, we should analyze its social output with respect to its quantity (has TBS gone too far or not in its CSR activities?) and its direction (did TBS get into social areas where it should not be involved?). These are ultimately questions about social value and the appropriate boundaries of the firm in its social strategy.

Regarding the activities with purely social goals, the firm has been openly involved in social programs presumably for the benefits to overall society. It is hard to see whether TBS merely uses environmental protection to obtain larger profits or its CSR is indeed out of a sense of social duty aside stockholders' interests. However, this debate can obscure the analysis rather than help us understand the use of CSR in TBS. Evidently, it is quite reasonable for firms to try to obtain profits. TBS does so through its business strategy that includes a unique positioning on environmental and social issues, especially during its early years. The firm connects both business and social positioning particularly well in order to try to increase its profits. Both profits and social concerns are compatible and TBS makes money alongside being socially conscious. It has a sound business strategy and a socially conscious CSR sitting on top of it. This is what strategic CSR is all about and there is no dilemma between both goals, as shown by point Q_x in Figure 9.2.

The key question is whether TBS goes beyond Q_x in its social output and whether it does some activities to achieve social goals aside from stockholders' interests. In other words, has TBS moved closer to Q_p or even beyond it? We would need to know Roddick's and her management team's intentions and whether they engaged in any social programs for reasons other than the maximization of profits. Their real motives are hidden to us, but it does not seem that all the social programs that they funded over the years were done to maximize profits, even if they increased the firm's reputation. Roddick's public statements clearly point in this direction, though it may just be a communication strategy. Despite the possible instrumental motives behind its CSR, many of these social activities were strictly voluntary and, at least apparently, the firm probably did not need to go as far as it usually went just to build and sustain its green reputation. Some of its programs can be regarded as purely social, voluntarily aimed at improving social conditions and the environment in general.

On the other hand, the social programs of CSR were always a source of potential conflict with stockholders after the firm went public and the amount dedicated to social activities was limited to just a few million dollars per year. The firm is clearly not run as a foundation, though it has built a strong pro-environment reputation in parallel to its CSR activities. It is the firm's business performance that attracts investors, some of them probably aimed at pure social goals, despite the social projects in which the firm is involved. Overall, it seems that TBS may have produced more social output than Q_x, but it has limited its CSR to a level that is acceptable to stockholders, probably somewhere around Q_p. A greater amount of social output is not likely to be allowed by stockholders.

With regard to the direction of its CSR, TBS has implemented a variety of green practices as a cosmetics firm, the costs (and reputation benefits) of which are transferred to its socially sensitive customer base via higher prices. These socially responsible practices are closely related to the firm's business activities and they are clearly good for customers and stockholders, thus creating economic and social value in the direction that society demands.

However, some of the social programs that are more distant from the firm's business activities have been much more controversial. For instance, when TBS gets involved actively in depressed regions, it is not clear that it can contribute to economic development there better than local government or professional NGOs can. Furthermore, politically charged campaigns can damage the firm's reputation rather than enhance it. In the last decade, TBS has been much more careful in its social programs and it even asked its charismatic founder to refrain from claiming that her own personal values about hot social or political issues represent the entire firm.

We can see in the case of TBS how firms can be socially responsible as well as economically successful. This example can be interpreted through the CSR value model suggested earlier, though this is evidently not the only possible interpretation. At least apparently, stockholders allow some CSR activities for purely social goals, but they place limits on them arguably at the level when they start affecting negatively business performance and their own compensation. From a value perspective, only those social activities that potentially create some benefits to the firm above their costs are likely to be allowed by stockholders, even though these activities may not always be actually undertaken to maximize profits. In contrast, general social programs in which TBS cannot especially contribute to their achievement and which generate no possible benefit to the firm could hardly be acceptable by stockholders for both economical and ethical reasons. Thus, the boundaries of the firm around social activities can also be understood in terms of value analysis, i.e., the maximum contribution of the firm to social value that is consistent with profit maximization from the business strategy of the firm.

10 | *Value analysis in strategy*

Economic value and the theory of the firm

Throughout this book we have explored the firm as a collection of heterogeneous resources whose role in society, its organizational boundaries, and its actual performance is inherently associated with the creation of economic value for customers and its capture by the firm's resources and owners. This perspective builds primarily from the resource-based view (RBV) and comparative cost-benefit analysis to understand how value creation and appropriation drive the main strategic decisions of the firm. Certainly, there are other economic and sociological approaches that can serve to study why firms exist and their role in society, but the analysis of economic value is particularly useful to investigate some of the fundamental issues in strategic management. We can now summarize what a value perspective can contribute to the key questions about the theory of the firm that we identified in chapter one.

What is a firm?

We have drawn from the conceptualization of the firm as a collection of tangible and intangible resources suggested by Edith Penrose and further expanded in the RBV. This concept of the firm can be refined to make it as useful as possible for strategy research and practice. Because we are specifically interested in strategic analysis, I suggested in chapter three that the administrative framework that constitutes a firm should be defined in terms of the reach of the strategy around the collection of resources that compete together versus other firms in the market. Thus, from a strategy perspective the firm is essentially a competitive unit with one strategy to attract customers and capture economic value versus other firms.

A firm strategy defines how the collection of resources that we call "the firm" competes as an aggregated unit in the markets for customers and resources. To the extent that different resources are part of a joint strategy, we can say that they are part of the same firm as far as strategic management is concerned. This strategic definition of the boundaries of the firm may or may not be equivalent to other conceptualizations, such as similar ownership, formal accounting reporting, strength of social ties, and nature of contractual links. Strategy is evidently the core concept in strategic management and, thus, it makes sense for our analytical purposes to study the firm as a collection of resources that behave in the market as one competitive unit with its own strategy, as opposed to the definition of the firm based on ownership that is prevalent in the contracting view of the firm.

It may be difficult at times to identify with precision the limits of the strategy and which resources are actually inside or outside the firm. This problem also occurs in other conceptualizations of the firm, for instance, for hybrid forms of governance between the market and the hierarchy in transaction costs economics (TCE). However, even though it is difficult to place precise boundaries around the resources that constitute a firm, it is much better to do so based on the reach of the strategy than any alternative guideline about firm boundaries, because we are particularly interested in why and under what circumstances different strategies may fail or succeed.

A firm's resources could potentially be spun off and compete as an independent unit or below another firm's umbrella. The owners of these potentially separable resources voluntarily give up the responsibility for strategic decision making to the aggregated combination of resources that we call the firm. Thus, the firm emerges as a collective unit with one strategy to manage its relationship with customers and external resources in competition with other players in the market. Being part of one strategy is what gives a collection of resources its strategic boundaries as one competitive unit in the market. The resources inside the firm jointly share at least some part of their interaction or interface with other players in the market, i.e., customers, competitors, and external resources. Figure 6.1 in chapter six shows the three main elements of a firm strategy, that is, the management of value-creating resources, the firm's market positioning, and its competitive dynamics versus other players in the market.

Why do firms exist?

The existing approaches to the theory of the firm highlight different aspects of what firms do ranging from their decision-making features to solving contractual problems among their internal resources. Though firms are often very complex organizations with a great variety of purposes and effects on society, we have stressed one critical function of firms: the creation of economic value.

The suggested role of firms as economic value-creating combinations of resources puts the emphasis on why firms exist in the first place rather than on what they do. Firms are not just production plants, but they may engage in manufacturing in order to create economic value for customers. We allow independent firms to exist and to compete in the market because they are effective instruments in creating value for society. This is their key task in our economy, which we have analyzed in chapter four.

Economic theories of the firm have focused primarily on the efficiency side of value creation, probably because the theory of demand is almost entirely isolated from the theory of production in which the theory of the firm has been traditionally placed. However, we know well in strategy that reducing costs is certainly not the only strategy for firms and, most often, it is not even a key goal for high-performing organizations. Firms often disrupt the market and innovate radically, which can be understood better in terms of overall customer value creation rather than mere efficiency seeking.

However, it would not be realistic to say that firms have an unselfish goal to create value for society, which leads their strategic business decisions. The resources that comprise the firm ultimately want to capture as much value as possible for themselves. For this reason, different resources join those firms where they can contribute more to creating value for customers (i.e., greater willingness to pay), so that they may appropriate part of that economic value. As Adam Smith noted over two centuries ago, even though pure self-interest drives the decisions of resource owners, they end up producing economic value for themselves, customers, and overall society, so that resources are allocated by this invisible hand where they create most value for society. Though the presence of market failures like monopoly power and externalities may produce deviations among the resources' private and social value, only by creating value for customers in the long run can firms generate higher compensation for their own resources. This is the main reason for firms to exist and it should not be surprising that value creation guides their main decisions about business, corporate, international, and even social strategy.

What determines firms' boundaries?

One of the critical strategic decisions of firms is their choice of vertical integration and horizontal diversification across industries and business activities. We analyzed in chapter three how firms can change the value they create by moving effectively the boundaries around certain resources, so that they may be more competitive as part of one firm strategy. For instance, TCE has explored how transaction costs often change when firms integrate different activities within a hierarchical structure. We expanded this comparative analysis of corporate boundary decisions to other noncontractual factors that may influence the value that firms create for customers and, consequently, how much they can capture for their own resources.

We have discussed how and why putting two sets of resources under the same corporate umbrella can have important internal and external effects on the value that they create, either through greater benefits for customers or lower overall costs, including transaction costs. Comparative cost-benefit value analysis can guide firms in deciding which activities should be done inside their organization and which should be carried out by other firms. It is ultimately the overall economic value that two sets of resources can create and capture from the rest of the market that determines whether it makes sense to merge them or keep them as independent competitive units, each one with its own business strategy. We applied this type of value analysis to different corporate-level strategic decisions about firm boundaries, including diversification, internationalization, and even corporate social responsibility (CSR) activities.

Contracting issues and, in particular, the incentives to invest in specialized assets are important determinants of the efficiency that a change in corporate boundaries could produce, but there is more to value creation than contractual and even operational efficiency. Firms are not comprised of interchangeable Lego pieces that can be reconfigured to create any organization. TCE acknowledges that there are cospecialized assets the joint operations of which can increase their efficiency considerably. The contracting view focuses on the incentives to invest in specialized assets and its implications for efficiency, but resource heterogeneity and asset specificity have implications even beyond investment incentives and the most efficient assignment of the residual control rights. Firm boundaries are important because the value that resources can create depends on which other resources they are combined with, i.e., the extent to which they are part of a joint strategy along with other resources. For instance, we analyzed in chapter seven how placing specific businesses under the same corporate umbrella can generate benefits for them with regard to the main elements of their strategy: customer relationships, competitive dynamics, the management of internal resources, and the relationship with external resources.

We have traditionally studied issues of relatedness and asset specificity to understand diversification decisions in strategy, but it is ultimately the value specificity of different resource combinations that may lead them to be part of a specific firm or a separate competitive unit with its own independent strategy in the market. Only under some circumstances will resources benefit from being part of a larger firm strategy. In fact, their competitiveness may even be negatively affected when the additional business and corporate costs outweigh the benefits of integrating two units under one corporate umbrella. Firms should expand or retreat to combine just those resources whose value-creation potential is actually increased by sharing at least part of the strategy with the other resources inside the firm. The joint value-creation potential of internal resources ultimately determines the boundaries of the firm.

What causes performance differences across firms?

Value creation determines which resources should be combined within one firm strategy (i.e., its boundaries) and also its final performance as a composite competitive unit. However, the causality traditionally proposed in some RBV arguments needs to be refined and properly understood in terms of resource combinations.

Firms do not have superior performance because they have superior resources, which is an oversimplified conclusion from a resource-based perspective. Firstly, the causality in this sentence is actually reversed. It is the future expected net cash flow that a resource can generate that determines its superiority over other resources. As Fisher (1930) noted many decades ago, "the value of the crop does not depend on the value of the land. On the contrary, the value of the land depends on the expected value of its crops." It is not the greater quality of the resource that results in greater sales, production, or profits; to the contrary, it is the output that a resource produces that may lead us to say that it has greater quality or value. Superior performance is the reason why we could say that a firm may possess a superior resource, rather than vice versa. Explaining superior performance based exclusively on the inherent characteristics of resources is putting the cart before the horse. For example, having smarter and better trained people may be regarded as a strategic resource for a consulting firm, but it is truly the superior solutions that they can provide to customers that truly gives human resources its strategic relevance.

To understand performance and the value or superiority of internal resources we will have to look outside the firm to what it does for its customers and at what overall cost. Those resources that critically allow the firm to attract more customers at an accessible cost can then be considered superior. Thus, the focus of strategic analysis should not be in the resources as such and its inherent features, but in the value that the resource can create in combination with others. For this analysis we will have to look outside the firm and how its strategy around a collection of specific resources deals with customers, competitors, and external resources.

Secondly, even if we can identify superior resources after doing an analysis of the value that they create, their possession within the firm does not guarantee superior performance for the firm. The owner of such a resource will require as much compensation as they can for its contribution to the overall value created by the firm. Thus, we need to take into consideration the question of appropriability of the returns generated by the resources and under what conditions the firm may capture part of the created value.

As analyzed in chapter five, there are three possible reasons why resource contributors to the firm may not fully capture the value that they jointly create through its strategy. Profits exist because (1) it is sometimes impossible to know *a priori* how much value resources can create, (2) different resource combinations can result in different value being created and the resulting synergy is shared between resource owners and the firm through bargaining, and (3) firms can develop new firm-level resources that nobody directly contributed to the firm, and the value that these organizational resources produce is captured by the firm's owners.

In summary, the analysis of economic value can help us understand what firms do in our market-driven economy, their main strategic decisions, and their performance. Firms are essentially collections of resources to deal jointly with customers, competitors, and other resources. By being part of one broader firm strategy, cospecialized resources may be able to create more value for customers and capture a larger part for themselves than they could do through an alternative strategy, e.g., competing on their own or as part of another firm. Only under certain circumstances do some resource combinations produce more value that the resource contributors demand as compensation and, thus, generate some profits for the firm's owners.

Implications for strategy research and practice

Economic value analysis can have important implications for strategic management, including the issues of business, corporate, international, and social strategy that we discussed in chapters six through nine. More specifically, the focus on value creation and appropriation can affect strategy research and practice with respect to (1) the strategic definition of firm boundaries, (2) the critical relevance of the customer's perspective in driving strategic decisions, (3) the sources for differentiation available to managers, and (4) the analysis of industry change and replacement.

The strategic definition of firm boundaries

The field of strategy is concerned with top management decisions about the direction that a firm takes in the market, i.e., its behavior at certain levels of aggregation (business versus corporate) and its presence in different arenas (geographical coverage and even social activities). The firm, the business unit, or the national subsidiary often constitute the unit of analysis at which the strategy is defined. Top managers have the responsibility to design and execute the strategy that links certain assets and resources within a given but changeable administrative framework. Unfortunately, we have not explored in sufficient depth in strategic management why the competitiveness of a set of resources changes when they are part of a strategy at a broader level of aggregation. We have not even studied when and why two resources can be considered part of a strategy. In other words, we do not have a strategic definition of the boundaries of the competitive unit the strategy of which we want to analyze. Instead, we have just borrowed an organizational or legal conceptualization of the firm, unit, or subsidiary, which may not necessarily be appropriate for strategic analysis.

Firm boundaries are defined by top managers and we need to understand better when it makes sense to put certain resources and not others under the control of top managers, so that they may set their strategic direction and behavior in the market as part of one competitive unit. Neither the RBV nor TCE have been able to fully capture the competitive consequences of making these critical decisions about firm boundaries, though they have provided important insights. Value analysis can take these two perspectives somewhat further because it can serve to address some of their limitations.

With regard to the contracting view of the firm, we criticized its over-reliance in opportunism, its excessive focus on efficiency driven by one type of costs, and, in the end, its limited usefulness for managerial decision making. Though its contributions to our understanding of firm boundaries should not be underestimated, TCE and other contractual perspectives constitute primarily a theory of investment incentives that explains firm ownership. However, it leaves out on purpose some aspects of corporate decisions that are critical for strategic management. TCE and property rights regard asset specificity as an exogenous variable that ultimately determines governance structure and firm ownership. But asset specificity, or more generally value specificity, is a critical endogenous variable in which strategy scholars are particularly interested. The key question for us is: under what condition does it make economic sense for two sets of resources to be combined within one broader competitive strategy? Lowering potential transaction costs and facilitating necessary investment are clearly part of the answer, but they are neither the only ones nor probably the most important reasons for setting firm boundaries. We need to comprehend better what makes two resources cospecialized in the first place and current explanations of firm boundaries based on investment incentives are just not sufficient.

We will have to look outside the firm to understand why its strategy can create more or less value by combining only certain specific resources. A technological answer based only on economies of scope along the presence of transaction costs is an important improvement on the neoclassical theory of the firm based exclusively on technology, but it still places excessive emphasis on efficiency issues for the understanding of competitiveness and profits. Value analysis includes efficiency consequences of moving firm boundaries, but it also considers any possible reason why two resources may be more competitive together within one strategy than competing as separate units, even when there may be no exchanges between them at all and they just share a joint interface in the market. Besides the internal implications for the efficient management of resources, we should also take into consideration the effects of firm boundaries in creating new value for customers (e.g., through differentiation and innovation) and capturing a greater part of the created value versus competitors and external resources (e.g., through market power).

In contrast, economic value analysis pushes forward the RBV into an area where it has made little progress, i.e., the boundaries of the competitive unit that constitute the firm. In contrast to the analysis of resource development and inimitability where the RBV has provided important insights, we have not explored in strategic management when two resources can be regarded as related and the conditions under which core competencies should be combined within a firm strategy, though these concepts are presumably closely associated with firm boundaries from an RBV. We need a better understanding of what firms do as combiners of resources above and beyond what these resources could do on their own or within other firms.

The strategic boundaries of the firm are established around a collection of internal resources and the firm's strategy defines the internal management of resources as well as their interface with external resources, customers, and competitors. When different resources are combined within a firm strategy, we are effectively changing how they are interdependently linked, which affects their internal efficiency and their dynamic capabilities to innovate as well as their relationship with customers, external resources, and competitors. These are important internal and external changes in how firms behave that we analyzed in chapter three and later on. Some of these organizational changes have been studied in depth by organization theorists, and their importance led Simon (1991) to assert that we should label our modern industrialized societies more appropriately as "organizational economies" rather than "market economies." However, we still need to study further from a strategy perspective how the changes in organizational boundaries influence the competitiveness of these resources and the value that these resources can jointly create and capture for themselves.

Focus on the customer's perspective

Value analysis places customers and their perspective at the center of a firm's strategy. It is ultimately the value created for customers that is distributed among the resources that comprise the firm, its owners, and its customers, who may be willing to pay a higher price for the firm's products and services (i.e., customers' surplus). Only creating more value for customers or increasing the firm's efficiency in delivering customer value can there be growth and profits for the firm and its resources. Thus, efficient value creation for customers should be the main goal for the firm in the long term, even though the firm truly wants to capture returns for itself and its internal resources. I have argued that this superordinate goal guides the firm's strategic decisions regarding market positioning, resource management, and competitive dynamics.

The critical role of the customer's perspective in guiding the firm's business strategy was already acknowledged by Peter Drucker (1954), who claimed that "there is only one valid definition of business purpose: *to create a customer*" (Drucker, 1954, 37, italics in original text). He further added:

It is the customer who determines what a business is. For it is the customer, and he alone, who through being willing to pay for a good or for a service, converts economic resources into wealth, things into goods. What the business thinks it produces is not of first importance – especially not to the future of the business and to its success. What the customer thinks he is buying, what he considers "value," is decisive – it determines what a business is, what it produces, and whether it will prosper. (Drucker, 1954, 37)

Drucker was an insightful thinker and a seminal contributor to the marketing field, but not really influential in the development of the strategy field. Many strategy researchers, like Barney (2001) and Makadok and Coff (2002), believe that the analysis of customer value falls outside the domain of strategy and the RBV in particular. They argue that strategic management, like all fields, has to rely on exogenously determined constructs. This would be the case for the notion of customer value, which we can draw from the theory of customer utility in marketing and microeconomics. These authors suggest that strategy research should focus primarily on explaining above normal economic performance and the top manager's strategic decisions to capture value. These are the areas where presumably strategy researchers can have a legitimate claim of expertise, but not in what customers consider valuable and are willing to pay for.

To the contrary, other strategy scholars believe that we should study value creation for customers in addition to its appropriation by the firm (Ghoshal *et al.*, 2000; Priem and Butler, 2001; DeSarbo *et al.*, 2001; Lepak *et al.*, 2007). I have argued that, unless we have a better understanding of how firms create value for customers, we would not be able to provide useful recommendations to management about firm boundaries and which strategies lead to greater performance. The value (Barney, 1997) or relevance (Grant, 2005) of resources are so critical for our understanding of firm performance that we just cannot leave outside our field the analysis of how, why, and how much value firms create for their customers through their different strategies in the market.

Some central concepts within the strategy field are implicitly related to value analysis and they would benefit from their explicit connection to the customer's perspective. For instance, Porter's generic strategies of differentiation and cost leadership are actually built on the two main sources of value creation. However, a value perspective questions the idea that being "stuck in the middle" is inherently an ill-advised choice for market positioning. It is the customers' perspective that defines value and they consider both benefits and costs when making their purchasing decisions, including their own monetary and non-monetary costs. As we discussed in chapters four and six, firms may concentrate mostly on just a few of these criteria that drive customers' choices in order to differentiate their products from competition, but customer value is ultimately determined by all of them at the same time, so that there are trade-offs to be made. If fact, many highly successful companies, such as Dell and Toyota, have been able to maintain for many years a successful mixed strategy that is ultimately focused on overall value creation for the customer and not on only one of its components, unique benefits or lower costs.

Most likely, strategy scholars will not feel obliged or interested in studying what precise product features drive customer preferences and behavior, which clearly fit better within the marketing field. However, we should not forget that the success of a strategy ultimately depends on the value that it can create for customers and the total costs that it involves. The potential for creating customer value can and should be studied at the firm-level of analysis that characterizes the strategic decisions that top managers take. Just like strategy draws from and contributes to the finance literature in the analysis of diversification and acquisitions, for instance, there are some topics in marketing that are also important for strategic management, if they are adapted to the cross-functional nature of the field and its focus on the entire organization, its direction, and its performance. The analysis of how and why strategic resources generate customer value is one of these topics.

Sources of differentiation

The contrast between enhancing customer benefits (i.e., differentiation) versus competing in costs (i.e., cost leadership) has occupied a central place in our field for several decades. There is some research on strategies to increase a firm's efficiency, particularly restructuring, downsizing, and divestments, though the importance of operational efficiency is generally underplayed in strategy, maybe excessively. However, it is unfortunate that there has been very little research about the options for firms to differentiate and how customer value systematically differs across contexts. Despite differentiation being such a critical concept in strategy, we still do not know much about it at the firm level of analysis.

To build differentiation that truly attracts customers, it is first necessary to understand the sources for customer value. Many if not all highly successful strategies are based on redefining the rules of the game in order to create value for customers in radically new ways. For instance, Kim and Mauborgne (1997) analyze how Kinepolis has revolutionized the customer's experience of going to a movie theater, and there are many other examples, such as Ikea and Apple's iPod, which changed how customers buy furniture and listen to portable music respectively. Only through the analysis of what customers truly value and the associated costs in making it happen can new sources of innovation and differentiation be found.

Firms may build a unique positioning in the market changing this combination of benefits and costs, including the possibilities for vertical and horizontal differentiation and the corresponding costs for customers, both monetary and nonmonetary. We have noted that it is very difficult to build sustainable differentiation examining only the intrinsic and directly observable characteristics of the product. As patents are not very effective in most industries and can often be circumvented, product features can usually be copied through relatively simple resource combinations with near perfect replicability. In contrast, nonmonetary customer costs are much harder for firms to observe and manage, such as those dealing with product information, accessibility, and actual usage.

New sources of differentiation can be obtained by firms that focus on these nonmonetary customer costs, which have not received as much attention as the direct intrinsic benefits of products and services. For instance, firms that selectively provide useful information about other similar or complementary products can create much value for the customer, who may not know about them, but would likely be interested in buying them. From books to financial products, firms often provide extra information about related products of potential interest for customers, which creates value above the product they initially want to buy. Similarly, strategies like Domino's Pizza and Home Depot are clearly built on easier and more convenient access to relatively standardized products, while companies like Apple stress ease of use and reduced need for learning. Other firms like Travelocity and similar mediators reduce all of these nonmonetary costs to customers in order to facilitate the most convenient information about, access to, and easy booking of other firms' travel-related services.

Rather than competing in what the products and services that they are selling actually do, these firms focus on the nonmonetary costs that consuming the product imposes on customers and, thus, create value by actively managing them. Firms manage the features of their products and services, but it is ultimately the benefits and costs that they provide to customers that determine value. Thus, managers may find new sources of differentiation by reducing the nonmonetary costs of customers when consuming a product, as opposed to improving the intrinsic features of the products and services.

Industry change and replacement

The tools for industry analysis and positioning like Porter's five-forces model, are well-established and they are particularly useful in stable environments. However, we do not yet have a useful model for the dynamic analysis of how an industry creates value for customers and when its business model is more likely to change or be fully replaced by a new one.

It is relatively easy to analyze familiar and reasonably stable industries, including the alternatives for resource management, market positioning, and competitive dynamics. In contrast, it is much more challenging to analyze how industry players may be affected by the emergence of new substitutes and complementors, especially when their resources are very different but target similar customers and needs. Sometimes technological development results in the replacement of one type of product by another without really changing the way that value is created for the customer, such as the substitution of compact disks (CDs) for vinyl records in the music industry. In other occasions, the entire industry is shaken and the business model radically changed, like the ongoing substitution of music CDs by internet-download models.

The role of specific players within an industry may go through important changes that affect their relative contribution to value creation and, thus, their bargaining power and profitability. New industries emerge and others disappear driven by the value that they create for customers. For instance, firms and artists are experimenting new ways to deliver the music that customers want in the most effective way. The value that listening to music creates for customers will be distributed very differently among resource contributors (particularly musicians), firms (music companies and intermediaries), and customers, who are now paying far less than they used to.

To understand why industry restructuring and the emergence of entirely new players occur, we would have to analyze the value that different players contribute within a business model. Sometimes the marginal contribution to customer value is particularly difficult to estimate. Only relative costs may be clearly observable, but not the customer's willingness to pay for a given activity, the effect of which on the product or service is not clearly identifiable by the customer, like record labels for the buyer of music. While music companies used to sell a physical product to customers, the digitalization of music and its easy exchange among customers (still illegal) has destroyed the ability of record companies to capture the value they create for customers by facilitating their access to recorded music. New conceptual frameworks are needed to help managers analyze industry changes and the relative benefits and costs for customers of these changes in existing or potential business models, including but going beyond greater efficiency.

Towards a value theory of the firm in strategic management

This book started by reviewing the unique nature of strategic management as an applied multidisciplinary field that has been heavily influenced by the economics-based theories of the firm, such as international organization (IO) economics, TCE, and the RBV. I have argued that, despite substantial advancement in different areas, we still need a comprehensive theory of the firm specifically designed to address the fundamental questions of interest for strategic management, like the boundaries of firm strategy and its performance implications. This theory should be broad enough to absorb the rich set of ideas that currently exist about strategy from different perspectives as well as push forward into new areas that have not been studied yet.

The analysis of value creation and appropriation through firm strategy has the potential to evolve into such a theory. Borrowing from the RBV, we have defined the firm as a combination of resources that comprise a competitive unit in the markets for customers and resources against other competitors. We have stressed the strategic definition of its boundaries based on the collective interface of the firm's internal resources versus customers, competitors, and external resources. Moving these boundaries around different sets of resources can have important effects on the value that the firm may create for society and how much it can appropriate for its internal resources and its owners. Thus, the comparative analysis of governance structure for transactions can be incorporated into the efficiency aspect of value analysis and further expanded to any additional benefit or cost of moving firm boundaries around different resource combinations. Contracting and resource analysis can be integrated this way under the umbrella of value analysis into a broader coherent approach.

Beyond the boundaries of the firm strategy, value analysis also helps us understand the performance of firms by focusing on what firms can do for customers by managing resources in competition with other players in the market. This approach brings back the customer to the center of strategic management. The strategy field has probably been excessively concerned with capturing value through building barriers to competition and increasing the firm's bargaining power versus resource providers and customers. The appropriation of value is certainly a critical aspect of strategy, but it is the ability to create value for customers that determines the performance of firms in the long term. Firms create value for customers by combining certain specific resources and, later on, the potential replicability of these resource combinations by competitors determines the sustainability of profits. Without creating value for customers, the firm cannot capture any part of such value to compensate its resources and its owners.

Despite value creation being the critical role for firms in our society, strategy scholars may have overlooked its importance in driving strategic decisions. For an applied field like strategic management, it is quite surprising to hear most CEOs talk continuously about meeting the needs of their customers, but we can see only scarce analysis in our field of what firms do to create customer value. This book is only one step in this direction and suggests that firms can create value by enhancing customer benefits through horizontal and vertical differentiation and product innovation as well as reducing monetary and nonmonetary customer costs. These latter costs in particular have received less attention, though they are likely to become more important as a way to create value for customers. Strategy scholars still have a full agenda to explore firm strategy from a value perspective in much greater detail.

Areas for future research

We have argued that the strategy of one firm defines how it deals as one collective unit with three critical stakeholders in the market: customers, resources, and competitors. The interaction among the three corners of the model presented in Figures 3.1 and 6.1 results in the three main elements of a firm's strategy: resource management process, market positioning, and competitive dynamics. Most current research on strategy content can be placed within one of them. The analysis of value creation and appropriation in these elements of firm strategy raises several questions that deserve to be studied by future research.

With regard to resource management, it is clear that firms follow different economic logics in what they do and they should be studied by strategy researchers and well understood by managers. Based on Stabell and Fjeldstad (1998), we have discussed three major types of activity configurations, i.e., value chains, professional service firms, and value networks. Most theoretical development has taken place in the analysis of manufacturing firms, but there has been limited progress in how firms actually create value for customers through other underlying technologies since the work in organization theory of Thompson (1967). In particular, network-based firms are becoming more important in our economy and we have just started to study their unique characteristics and strategic challenges, including the fight between standards and the management of relationships between complementors in layered network services. New underlying technologies will certainly emerge with unique features in how they create value for customers and their own strategic implications. In-depth empirical analysis of industries with similar economic logic will be required as opposed to large cross-sectional studies of very different firms that are still most frequent. We should also explore how and when firms should combine different competitive logics within the same strategy, including their implications for corporate strategy and organizational structure.

There is also an important void between the strategic analysis at a very high level of abstraction of skills and learning on the one side, and the more operational aspects of firm strategy like divestments, post-merger integration, reengineering, and value-chain deconstruction, for instance, on the other. Firms make important strategic decisions about the resources that they gather and how they are managed that are closely connected to the market positioning of the firm and the customers that they want to attract. The link resources-activities-customers still needs further development, even for manufacturing firms and value-chain analysis. Better tools should be developed to help managers in the analysis of strategic resources and activities and their impact on the customer's willingness to pay, thus exploiting the potential of the RBV in guiding managerial decision making and value creation.

Research on market positioning can also be pushed forward through value analysis beyond generic strategies. As noted earlier, there has been only scarce conceptual development and empirical research about differentiation, despite being such a critical concept in strategic management. We still do not know what makes a company and its products different from the perspective of the customer, i.e., what they value in different contexts and how their evaluation affects strategic decisions of firms. Research on vertical and horizontal differentiation in marketing and economics can be useful to understand better the strategic implications of differentiation, including its effects on resource development and barriers to competition.

Also regarding market positioning, it is surprising that pricing strategy has not been studied in our field in much depth. Pricing decisions are often considered tactical rather than strategic and only firm costs are usually analyzed as a strategic option. However, some pricing decisions are hard to reverse and they may have an important effect on a firm's performance, particularly in the early stages of firm evolution or when a new product is launched. Pricing needs more empirical analysis because the ability to raise prices over costs ultimately determines profits. Relative prices and overall sales are important aspects of a firm's performance that have not been directly studied yet. Existing research often uses ratios like ROA as a performance measure, but it does not distinguish between the sales that firms are able to attract and their relative costs in doing so as separate sources of value. We should also study the extent to which firms are able to raise prices as a result of market power or an indicator of superior customer value.

With regard to competitive dynamics, this area of research has been particularly fertile in the strategy field in the last two decades, including research on actions and reactions, first-mover advantages, and resource inimitability. Much of this research focuses on value capture against competitors, but some topics regarding value creation have also been studied, such as inter-firm cooperation and the dual role of competition and cooperation between different players in the market. It is the value-creating side of managing resources differently from competitors that deserve greater attention. In particular, we need structured and reasonably comprehensive models to compare how resource profiles differ among competitors and how they are expanded and protected through competitive actions.

As noted earlier, value analysis can be especially relevant to study industry change and replacement in our highly competitive and changing economy. The Schumpeterian process of creative destruction continuously reconfigures industry structure and the role of the different players in the market. Firms adjust their strategy to be more competitive and generate more value for customers, so that the resources that they comprise can capture greater value. Thus, they dynamically redefine their business and adjust their external boundaries to incorporate only certain resources within their backward integration decisions, as well as specific competitors and customers in their choice of horizontal and forward integration respectively. The potential for new value creation for customers, often identifying an entirely new type of industrial or end consumers, is likely to play a key role in these models of industry change and replacement that still need to be developed.

These are just some issues that deserve to be studied regarding strategic decisions about resource management, market positioning, and competitive dynamics. The analysis of how firms create and appropriate value through their strategies can be helpful in our understanding of how all of these decisions are linked interdependently and, thus, facilitate a more coherent development of the field of strategic management.

Limitations of value analysis

Economic value analysis is sufficiently broad to incorporate most of the fundamental ideas in the field of strategy about the theory of the firm, but it has some limitations that should also be discussed.

It is clear that value analysis cannot be applied to all strategic decisions. It is most applicable to issues of strategy content, particularly to the fundamental questions about the role of firms, their boundaries, and their performance. Therefore, value analysis is only pertinent to understand the firm's market behavior, its strategic alternatives to deal with customers, resources, and competitors, and their performance consequences. However, there are many topics about strategy process that have a weak indirect link with value creation and appropriation. There are process-related issues about how top managers conceive of and carry out the (content) strategy of their firms for which value analysis is not particularly useful, such as managerial cognition and decision-making processes. All strategic decisions ought to have an impact in the firm's behavior in the market for them to have performance consequences, but process issues are sometimes only remotely connected to creating customer value and the behavior of the firm in the market. In these cases, the direct analysis of the customers' willingness to pay, their nonmonetary costs, and firm efficiency is not likely to provide much insight. Instead, other variables become more salient, such as organizational flexibility, individual cognition, and decision-making speed, while their implications on customer value remain implicit.

All theories have boundaries and it is not really a problem that value analysis should be restricted to issues of strategy content. However, it is possible to question whether the strategy field really needs a comprehensive theory of the firm and, furthermore, whether value analysis truly adds new insight to our understanding of the strategic choices of firms and their market performance.

On the most positive side, a value theory of the firm could help reconcile different theoretical approaches into one internally consistent body of literature, thus solving some unnecessary controversies like knowledge versus contracting perspectives on the boundaries of the firm and industry structure versus internal resource explanations of firm performance. This integration would be positive to the extent that it may serve to map existing ideas and push forward the development of the field. A synthesis around the concept of economic value allows researchers to identify partially overlapping topics and how they are connected, so that it could facilitate making incremental contributions to a more structured body of knowledge, its teaching, and its practice. In this sense, we have discussed three main areas of strategy research dealing with resource management, market positioning, and competitive dynamics, which jointly explain value creation and appropriation by the firm as a collection of resources. Beyond this integration and the clarification it provides, value analysis can also help push forward research on topics like industry competitive logics, pricing strategy, and industry replacement, as examples of areas for future research suggested above.

To the contrary, some researchers will prefer a different structure for the field, such as the strategic management process described in many undergraduate textbooks that goes from external analysis to strategy formulation, implementation, and control. Still other scholars may not favor any structure at all that could limit research into fruitful directions, even if they are disconnected and may generate debates and even contradictions. Though the analysis of value creation and appropriation can answer the main questions that a theory of the firm should address, only its further development may turn the current notion of value from a rhetorical concept into a workable and useful guideline for strategic decisions.

The challenges that researchers will have to face in order to develop a value theory of the firm in strategy are quite substantial. Many aspects of competitive dynamics and resource management have been studied by strategy scholars for at least two decades, but the analysis of market positioning and customer value remains understudied, virtually reduced to the applied analysis of value chains suggested by Porter. Understanding customer benefits and overall costs is likely to be a critical challenge for strategy researchers in the near future, including how to deal with measurement problems. This objective may take strategy to new territory that was considered the exclusive domain of marketing experts, but its implications for the entire organization, its direction, and its performance also make it of necessary interest to strategy researchers as well.

However, despite its importance, strategy cannot always be reduced to comparative cost-benefit analysis, even if it is conducted at the level of the entire organization and what it can do for its customers. Certainly, creating customer value and doing it efficiently are the ultimate goals of firms and why they exist. It is the fact that they do so by combining and developing unique resources in a continuous fight with other players in the market that gives strategic management its distinct nature and applied focus on competition and choice. The interaction among the different elements of firm strategy and their final effect on value creation and appropriation constitute the basis for the understanding of what firms do and their performance. It is in this sense that a value theory of firm strategy could be useful to research and practice.

Further reading

1 Introduction

Andrews (1971). *The Concept of Corporate Strategy*. Highly influential early book in strategic management that stresses the fit between internal resources and external opportunities. It develops a well-rounded picture of the strategic responsibilities of leaders and the entire process of strategy analysis, formulation, and implementation, including the values and social responsibilities of firms and top managers.

Rumelt, Schendel, and Teece (1994). *Fundamental Issues in Strategy*. This collection of articles discusses some of the main topics in the field of strategic management from very different perspectives. Rather than providing a balanced overview of state-of-the-art theories in the early nineties, the book describes some of the most influential ideas, including an interesting debate about the relationship between game theory and strategic management.

Hitt, Freeman, and Harrison (2001). *The Blackwell Handbook of Strategic Management*. Quite a comprehensive, edited volume that reviews some of the main topics in the strategic management field. A good insight into state-of-the-art research strategies at the turn of the century.

Early influential books in strategy include: Barnard (1938). *The Functions of the Executive*; Selznick (1957). *Leadership in Administration*; Chandler (1962). *Strategy and Structure*; Ansoff (1965). *Corporate Strategy*; Miles and Snow (1978). *Organizational Strategy, Structure, and Process*; and Schendel and Hofer (1979). *Strategic Management*.

Simon (1957). *Administrative Behavior*; March and Simon (1967). *Organizations*; and Cyert and March (1963). *A Behavioral Theory of the Firm*. These books develop an analysis of the firm from a decision-making approach and they discuss human behavior inside organizations through concepts like bounded rationality, attention, information processing, rewards, conflict, dominant coalitions, and organizational control. Classic books in organization theory.

Morgan (2006). *Images of Organization*. Comprehensive review of different conceptualizations of the firm in organization theory through metaphors, such as organizations as machines, organisms, brains, or political systems.

2 The contracting view of the firm

Mahoney (2005). *Economic Foundations of Strategy*. Useful review of the main economic approaches discussed in this chapter, including the resource-based view (RBV) and dynamic capabilities.

Williamson (1975). *Markets and Hierarchies*; and Williamson (1985). *The Economic Institutions of Capitalism*. Oliver Williamson covers in these two books the main ideas of his approach to transaction costs economics (TCE). The books are an essential contribution to the understanding of firms from a contracting perspective.

Hart (1995). *Firm Contracts, and Financial Structure*. A key book for a formal property rights approach (incomplete contracting) to the theory of the firm, applied particularly to issues of corporate finance.

Putterman and Kroszner (1996). *The Economic Nature of the Firm*. A selection of classical readings in economics about the theory of the firm, from Smith and Knight to Coase, Williamson, Hart, Demsetz, Teece, and others.

Scherer and Ross (1990). *Industrial Market Structure and Economic Performance*. This classical textbook in industrial organization reviews the main ideas and the accumulated empirical research based on the structure-conduct-performance model. Though this book does not cover the theory of the firm, it is still highly recommended for strategy students.

Tirole (1988). *The Theory of Industrial Organization*. A main textbook for the new industrial organization. The emphasis is on theory development through game theoretic analysis, including questions addressed by the theory of the firm.

3 The nature of the firm in strategy

Penrose (1959). *The Theory of the Growth of the Firm*. Seminal analysis of the growth of the firm from an economic perspective that has inspired the resource-based view of the firm. The conceptualization of the firm as a collection of resources and its process of growth is analyzed in detail.

Barney (1997). *Gaining and Sustaining Competitive Advantage*. A graduate-level textbook in strategic management entirely developed from a RBV.

Nelson and Winter (1982). *An Evolutionary Theory of Economic Change*. A highly influential book on the evolutionary analysis to organizations, including the critical role of organizational routines. Essential to understand economics as an evolutionary process.

Foss (2005). *Strategy, Economic Organization, and the Knowledge Economy*. Arguably, the first serious attempt at integrating TCE and the RBV into a strategic theory of the firm. Interesting and insightful.

4 Creating economic value

Schumpeter (1934). *The Theory of Economic Development*. A classical book from the influential Austrian economist, particularly insightful in his analysis of the entrepreneurial process of creative destruction.

Porter (1985). *Competitive Advantage*. In this book Porter further expands his influential ideas about business and corporate strategy. In particular, he proposes the use of value chain analysis to build cost leadership or differentiation.

Copeland, Koller, and Murrin (1990). *Valuation: Measuring and Managing the Value of Companies*. Traditional financial approach to measuring firm value. Useful manual for financial valuation.

Holbrook (1999). *Consumer Value*. Interesting edited volume of different sources of consumer value from a marketing perspective. Much closer to psychology than to economics or strategy.

5 The appropriation of value by firms

Knight (1921). *Risk, Uncertainty and Profit*. Traditional analysis of profits and the firm before transaction costs were introduced to economics by Coase, based primarily on entrepreneurial risk and uncertainty.

Obrinsky (1983). *Profit Theory and Capitalism*. Excellent review of profit theory in economics from the classical authors to Marxist, Knightian, and Keynesian approaches. Particularly focused on macroeconomic implications and why it is so difficult for economic models to explain profits adequately.

Mueller (1986). *Profits in the Long Run*. Influential empirical analysis of sustained firm profits and the possible explanations why they persist in the long run.

Geroski, Gilbert, and Jacquemin (1990). *Barriers to Entry and Strategic Competition*. Review of the formal theoretical literature in economics on mobility barriers, conditions of entry and exit, and dynamic models of pricing and entry.

6 Business strategy

Porter (1980). *Competitive Strategy*. Arguably, the most influential book in strategy. Complete manual to analyze industries and take strategic moves to build a superior position in the market. Heavily based on industrial organizational economics, particularly the structure-conduct-performance and the game-theoretic literature to competitive dynamics.

Grant (2005). *Contemporary Strategy Analysis*. Mainstream graduate-level textbook in strategic analysis that has seen six revised editions, the most recent in 2007.

Grimm, Lee, and Smith (2006). *Strategy as Action*. Insightful analysis of strategy as taking actions and reacting to competitors' actions. This applied book develops a comprehensive and useful approach to understand recent ideas on competitive dynamics in strategic management.

Dixit and Nalebuff (1991). *Thinking Strategically*. The contributions to strategy from a game theory perspective are very clearly explained in this book for a nontechnical audience. Excellent introduction to the most useful aspects of game theory.

Besanko, Dranove, Shanley, and Schaefer (2004). *Economics of Strategy*. Mainstream textbook to strategy from an applied microeconomics perspective.

Beath and Katsoulacos (1991). *The Economic Theory of Product Differentiation*. Detailed and well-integrated discussion of the early theoretical literature in economics about product differentiation.

7 Corporate strategy

Collis and Montgomery (1998). *Corporate Strategy*. Graduate-level textbook on corporate strategy from a resource-based approach, including elements of both strategy content and process.

Goold, Campbell, and Alexander (1994). *Corporate-level Strategy*. This book describes with many useful examples how the corporate office can create (or destroy) value. Highly applied analysis of strategic management of diversified corporations.

Haspeslagh and Jemison (1991). *Managing Acquisitions*. Excellent applied analysis of how firms can create value through acquisitions.

Bamford, Gomes-Casseres, and Robinson (2003). *Mastering Alliance Strategy*. Useful applied analysis of the entire process of alliance management.

8 International strategy

Dunning (1992). *Multinational Enterprises and the Global Economy*. One of the mainstream books in international business with a new updated edition. Particularly good review of the theory of the multinational enterprise (MNE), which is condensed into the ownership-location-internalization eclectic paradigm.

Bartlett and Ghoshal (1989). *Managing Across Borders*. Insightful analysis of the modern MNE. This influential book highlights the nature of the MNE as a network of geographical subsidiaries and the need for worldwide learning.

Gupta, Govindarajan, and Wang (2008). *The Quest for Global Dominance*. A state-of-the-art practical analysis of the challenges for firms to build, manage, and exploit global presence.

Classical books on the theory of the MNE include Buckley and Casson (1976). *The Future of the Multinational Enterprise*; Caves (1982). *Multinational Enterprise and Economic Analysis*; Rugman (1982). *New Theories of the Multinational Enterprise*; and Hennart (1982). *A Theory of Multinational Enterprise*.

9 Strategy and social value

Friedman (1970). "The Social Responsibility of Business is to Increase its Profits." In this well-known article from *New York Times Magazine*, Friedman explains the traditional orthodox approach in economics to the firm's social responsibility. Essential reading.

Freeman (1984). *Strategic Management*. Seminal and highly influential book on stakeholder theory.

Baron (2006). *Business and its Environment*. Mainstream textbook on business and society from an economic perspective.

Adler and Posner (2001). *Cost-benefit Analysis*. This edited volume includes some excellent articles about the strengths and weaknesses of cost-benefit analysis in welfare economics from a variety of perspectives.

References

Adler, M. D., and Posner, E. A. (2001). *Cost-benefit Analysis: Legal, Economic, and Philosophical Perspectives*. Chicago: University of Chicago Press.

Agarwal, S., and Ramaswami, S. N. (1992). "Choice of Foreign Market Entry Mode: Impact of Ownership, Location and Internalization Factors." *Journal of International Business Studies, 23*(1), 1–27.

Aguilera, R. V., Rupp, D. E., Williams, C. A., and Ganapathi, J. (2007). "Putting the S Back in Corporate Social Responsibility: a Multilevel Theory of Social Change in Organizations." *The Academy of Management Review, 32*(3), 836–863.

Akerlof, G. (1970). "The Market for Lemons: Qualitative Uncertainty and the Market Mechanism." *Quarterly Journal of Economics, 84*(3), 488–500.

Alchian, A., and Demsetz, H. (1972). "Production, Information and Economic Organization." *American Economic Review, 62*(5), 777–795.

Alchian, A. A. (1965). "The Basis of Some Recent Advances in the Theory of Management of the Firm." *The Journal of Industrial Economics, 14*(1), 30–41.

Aliber, R. Z. (1970). "A Theory of Foreign Direct Investment." *The International Corporation*, 17–34.

Alvarez, S. A., and Busenitz, L. W. (2001). "The Entrepreneurship of Resource-Based Theory." *Journal of Management, 27*(6), 755.

Amabile, T. M. (1983). *The Social Psychology of Creativity*. New York: Springer-Verlag.

Amihud, Y., and Lev, B. (1981). "Risk Reduction as a Managerial Motive for Conglomerate Mergers." *The Bell Journal of Economics, 12*(2), 605–617.

Amit, R., and Schoemaker, P. J. H. (1993). "Strategic Assets and Organizational Rent." *Strategic Management Journal, 14*(1), 33–46.

Anderson, C. R., and Zeithaml, C. P. (1984). "Stage of the Product Life Cycle, Business Strategy, and Business Performance." *The Academy of Management Journal, 27*(1), 5–24.

Anderson, J. C., and Narus, J. A. (1998). "Understand What Customers Value." *Harvard Business Review*, 53–65.

Andrews, K. R. (1987 [1971]). *The Concept of Corporate Strategy*. Homewood, Ill.: Dow Jones-Irwin.

Ansoff, H. I. (1965). *Corporate Strategy*. New York: McGraw-Hill.

Arrow, K. J. (1974). *The Limits of Organization*. New York: W. W. Norton.

Arrow, K. J., and Debreu, G. (1954). "Existence of an Equilibrium for a Competitive Economy." *Econometrica*, 22(3), 265–290.

Axelrod, R. (1984). *The Evolution of Corporation*. New York: Basic Books.

Baiman, S. (1982). "Agency Research in Managerial Accounting: A Survey." *Journal of Accounting Literature*, 1(1), 154–210.

Bain, J. S. (1956). *Barriers to New Competition*. Boston: Harvard University Press.

Bamford, J. D., Gomes-Casseres, B., and Robinson, M. S. (2003). *Mastering Alliance Strategy*. San Francisco, Calif.: Jossey-Bass.

Barnard, C. I. (1938). *The Functions of the Executive*. Cambridge, Mass.: Harvard University Press.

Barney, J. B. (1986). "Strategic Factor Markets." *Management Science*, 32(10), 1231–1241.

(1990). "The Debate between Traditional Management Theory and Organizational Economics: Substantive Differences or Intergroup Conflict?" *The Academy of Management Review*, 15(3), 382–393.

(1991). "Firm Resources and Sustained Competitive Advantage." *Journal of Management*, 17(1), 99.

(1997). *Gaining and Sustaining Competitive Advantage*. Harlow: Addison-Wesley.

(2001). "Is the Resource-Based View a Useful Perspective for Strategic Management Research? Yes." *The Academy of Management Review*, 26(1), 41–56.

Barney, J. B., and Arikan, A. M. (2001). "The Resource-Based View: Origins and Implications." In M. A. Hitt, R. E. Freeman and J. S. Harrison (Eds.), *Handbook of Strategic Management* (124–188): Oxford: Blackwell.

Baron, D. P. (2006). *Business and Its Environment*. Upper Saddle River, N.J.: Pearson Education.

Baron, R. A., and Shane, S. A. (2008). *Entrepreneurship: A Process Perspective*. Mason, Ohio: South-Western.

Bartlett, C. A., and Ghoshal, S. (1989). *Managing Across Borders*. Cambridge, Mass.: Harvard Business School Press.

Baumol, W. J., Panzar, J. C., and Willig, R. D. (1982). *Contestable Markets and the Theory of Industry Structure*. London: Harcourt Brace Jovanovich.

Beath, J., and Katsoulacos, Y. S. (1991). *The Economic Theory of Product Differentiation*. Cambridge: Cambridge University Press.

Becerra, M., and Santalo, J. (2003). "An Empirical Analysis of the Corporate Effect: The Impact of the Multinational Corporation on the Performance of its Units Worldwide." *Management International Review*, 43, 7–23.

Becker, G. S. (1976). "Altruism, Egoism, and Genetic Fitness: Economics and Sociobiology." *Journal of Economic Literature*, 14(3), 817–826.

Benito, G. R. G., and Gripsrud, G. (1992). "The Expansion of Foreign Direct Investments: Discrete Rational Location Choices or a Cultural Learning Process?" *Journal of International Business Studies*, 23(3).

Berger, P. G., and Ofek, E. (1995). "Diversification's Effect on Firm Value." *Journal of Financial Economics*, 37(1), 39–65.

Berle, A., and Means, G. C. (1933). *The Modern Corporation and Private Property*. New York: Macmillan.

Besanko, D., Dranove, D., Shanley, M., and Schaefer, S. (2004). *Economics of Strategy*. Hoboken, N.J.: Wiley.

Bettis, R. A., and Hall, W. K. (1982). "Diversification Strategy, Accounting Determined Risk, and Accounting Determined Return." *The Academy of Management Journal*, 25(2), 254–264.

Bower, J. L, Bartlett, C. A., Christensen, C. R., Pearson, A. E., and Andrews, K. R. (1991). *Business Policy*. (Seventh edition). Homewood, Ill.: Richard Irwin.

Bowman, C., and Ambrosini, V. (2000). "Value Creation versus Value Capture: Towards a Coherent Definition of Value in Strategy." *British Journal of Management*, 11(1), 1–15.

Bowman, E. H., and Helfat, C. E. (2001). "Does Corporate Strategy Matter?" *Strategic Management Journal*, 22(1), 1–23.

Brandenburger, A., and Nalebuff, B. J. (1996). *Co-Opetition*. New York; London: Currency Doubleday.

Brandenburger, A., and Stuart, H. (1996). "Value-Based Business Strategy." *Journal of Economics and Management Strategy*, 5, 5–24.

Brouthers, K. D., and Hennart, J. F. (2007). "Boundaries of the Firm: Insights from International Entry Mode Research." *Journal of Management*, 33(3), 395.

Brown, S. L., and Eisenhardt, K. M. (1995). "Product Development: Past Research, Present Findings, and Future Directions." *The Academy of Management Review*, 20(2), 343–378.

Buckley, P. J., and Casson, M. (1976). *The Future of the Multinational Enterprise*. London: Macmillan.

Burke, L., and Logsdon, J. M. (1996). "How Corporate Social Responsibility Pays Off." *Long Range Planning*, 29(4), 495–502.

Burns, T. B., and Stalker, G. M. (1961). *The Management of Innovation.* London: Tavistock Publications.

Busenitz, L. W., and Barney, J. B. (1997). "Differences between Entrepreneurs and Managers in Large Organizations: Biases and Heuristics in Strategic Decision-Making." *Journal of Business Venturing, 12*(1), 9–30.

Calori, R., and Ardisson, J. M. (1988). "Differentiation Strategies in 'Stalemate Industries'." *Strategic Management Journal, 9*(3), 255–269.

Camerer, C. F. (1991). "Does Strategy Research Need Game Theory?" *Strategic Management Journal, 12,* 137–152.

Campa, J. M., and Kedia, S. (2002). "Explaining the Diversification Discount." *The Journal of Finance, 57*(4), 1731–1762.

Campbell, A., Goold, M., and Alexander, M. (1995). "Corporate Strategy: The Quest for Parenting Advantage." *Harvard Business Review, 73*(2), 123.

Campbell-Hunt, C. (2000). "What have we Learned about Generic Competitive Strategy? A Meta-Analysis." *Strategic Management Journal, 21*(2), 127–154.

Carroll, A. B. (1979). "A Three-dimensional Conceptual Model of Corporate Performance." *The Academy of Management Review, 4*(4), 497–505.

Carroll, G. R. (1993). "A Sociological View on Why Firms Differ." *Strategic Management Journal, 14*(4), 237–249.

Caves, R. E. (1974). *International Trade, International Investment, and Imperfect Markets.* Princeton, N.J.: Princeton University Press.

(1982). *Multinational Enterprise and Economic Analysis.* Cambridge: Cambridge University Press.

Caves, R. E., and Porter, M. E. (1977). "From Entry Barriers to Mobility Barriers: Conjectural Decisions and Contrived Deterrence to New Competition." *The Quarterly Journal of Economics, 91*(2), 241–262.

Caves, R. E., and Williamson, P. J. (1985). "What Is Product Differentiation, Really?" *The Journal of Industrial Economics, 34*(2), 113–132.

Chamberlin, E. (1933). *The Theory of Monopolistic Competition.* Cambridge: Harvard University Press.

Chandler, A. D. (1962). *Strategy and Structure: Chapters in the History of the Industrial Enterprise.* Cambridge: MIT Press.

Chatterjee, S. (1986). "Types of Synergy and Economic Value: the Impact of Acquisitions on Merging and Rival Firms." *Strategic Management Journal, 7*(2), 119–139.

Chatterjee, S., and Wernerfelt, B. (1991). "The Link between Resources and Type of Diversification: Theory and Evidence." *Strategic Management Journal*, 12(1), 33–48.

Chen, M. J., and Miller, D. (1994). "Competitive Attack, Retaliation and Performance: an Expectancy–Valence Framework." *Strategic Management Journal*, 15(2), 85–102.

Cheung, S. N. S. (1998). "Presidential Address." *Economic Inquiry*, 36, 514–521.

Child, J. (1972). "Organizational Structure, Environment and Performance: The Role of Strategic Choice." *Sociology*, 6(1), 1.

Chiles, T. H., and McMackin, J. F. (1996). "Integrating Variable Risk Preferences, Trust, and Transaction Cost Economics." *The Academy of Management Review*, 21(1), 73–99.

Christensen, C. R., Andrews, K. R., Bower, J. L., and Learned, E. P. (1978). *Business Policy: Text and Cases*. Homewood, Ill.: R. D. Irwin.

Coase, R. H. (1937). "The Nature of the Firm." *Economica*, 4(New series) 386–405.

(1960). "The Problem of Social Cost." *Journal of Law and Economics*, 3(1).

(1988). "The Nature of the Firm: Origin, Meaning, Influence." *Journal of Law, Economics, and Organization*, 4(1), 3–47.

Coff, R. W. (1999). "When Competitive Advantage Doesn't Lead to Performance: the Resource-Based View and Stakeholder Bargaining Power." *Organization Science*, 10(2), 119–133.

Cohen, W. M., and Levinthal, D. A. (1990). "Absorptive Capacity: A New Perspective on Learning and Innovation." *Administrative Science Quarterly*, 35(1).

Collis, D. J. (1994). "Research Note: How Valuable are Organizational Capabilities?" *Strategic Management Journal*, 15, 143–152.

Collis, D. J., and Montgomery, C. A. (1998). *Corporate Strategy: A Resource-Based Approach*. Boston, Mass.: Irwin.

Conner, K., and Prahalad, C. K. (1996). "A Resource Based View of the Firm: Knowledge Versus Opportunism." *Organization Science*, 7(5), 407–501.

Conner, K. (1991). "A Historical Comparison of Resource-Based Theory and Five Schools of Thought within Industrial Organization Economics: Do we Have a New Theory of the Firm?" *Journal of Management*, 17(1), 121.

Copeland, T. E., Koller, T., and Murrin, J. (1990). *Valuation: Measuring and Managing the Value of Companies*. New York: Wiley.

Cottrell, T., and Nault, B. R. (2004). "Product Variety and Firm Survival in the Microcomputer Software Industry." *Strategic Management Journal*, 25(10), 1005–1025.

Cubbin, J., and Geroski, P. (1987). "The Convergence of Profits in the Long Run: Inter-firm and Inter-industry Comparisons." *The Journal of Industrial Economics*, 35(4), 427–442.

Cyert, R. M., and March, J. G. (1992 [1963]). *Behavioral Theory of the Firm* (Second edition). Oxford: Blackwell.

d'Aspremont, C., Gabszewicz, J. J., and Thisse, J. F. (1979). "On Hotelling's Stability in Competition." *Econometrica*, 47(5), 1145–1150.

Damanpour, F. (1991). "Organizational Innovation: a Meta-Analysis of Effects of Determinants and Moderators." *The Academy of Management Journal*, 34(3), 555–590.

Das, T. K., and Teng, B. S. (2000). "A Resource-Based Theory of Strategic Alliances." *Journal of Management*, 26(1), 31.

Datta, D. K., Pinches, G. E., and Narayanan, V. K. (1992). "Factors Influencing Wealth Creation from Mergers and Acquisitions: a Meta-Analysis." *Strategic Management Journal*, 13(1), 67–84.

Day, G. S., Shocker, A. D., and Srivastava, R. K. (1979). "Customer-oriented Approaches to Identifying Product–Markets." *Journal of Marketing*, 43(4), 8–19.

de Vasconcellos, J. A. S., and Hambrick, D. C. (1989). "Key Success Factors: Test of a General Theory in the Mature Industrial–Product Sector." *Strategic Management Journal*, 10(4), 367–382.

Deephouse, D. L. (1999). "To be Different, or to be the Same? It's a Question (and Theory) of Strategic Balance." *Strategic Management Journal*, 20(2), 147–166.

Demsetz, H. (1967). "Toward a Theory of Property Rights." *The American Economic Review*, 57(2), 347–359.

(1982). "Barriers to Entry." *American Economic Review*, 72(1), 47–57.

(1988). "The Theory of the Firm Revisited." *Journal of Law, Economics and Organization 4*, 141–161.

DeSarbo, W. S., Jedidi, K., and Sinha, I. (2001). "Customer Value Analysis in a Heterogeneous Market." *Strategic Management Journal*, 22(9), 845–857.

Dess, G. G., and Davis, P. S. (1984). "Porter's (1980) Generic Strategies as Determinants of Strategic Group Membership and Organizational Performance." *The Academy of Management Journal*, 27(3), 467–488.

Dickson, P. R., and Ginter, J. L. (1987). "Market Segmentation, Product Differentiation, and Marketing Strategy." *Journal of Marketing*, 51(2), 1–10.

Dierickx, I., and Cool, K. (1989). "Asset Stock Accumulation and Sustainability of Competitive Advantage." *Management Science*, 35(12), 1504–1513.

DiMaggio, P., and Powell, W. (1983). "The Iron Cage Revisited: Institutional Isomorphism and Collective Rationality in Organizational Cost Explanation." *Journal of Economic Behavior and Organization*, 4, 305–336.

Dixit, A. K., and Nalebuff, B. J. (1991). *Thinking Strategically*. New York: Norton.

Dixit, A. K., and Stiglitz, J. E. (1977). "Monopolistic Competition and Optimum Product Diversity." *The American Economic Review*, 67(3), 297–308.

Dobb, M. (1973). *Theories of Value and Distribution since Adam Smith: Ideology and Economic Theory*. Cambridge: Cambridge University Press.

Donaldson, L. (1990). "The Ethereal Hand: Organizational Economics and Management Theory." *The Academy of Management Review*, 15(3), 369–381.

Drucker, P. F. (1954). *Practice of Management*. New York: Harper.

(1985). *Innovation and Entrepreneurship*. London: Heinemann.

Dunning, J. H. (1981). *The Eclectic Theory of the MNC*. London: Allen and Unwin.

(1993). *Multinational Enterprises and the Global Economy*. Wokingham: Addison-Wesley.

Eisenhardt, K. M. (1989). "Agency Theory: an Assessment and Review." *The Academy of Management Review*, 14(1), 57–74.

Eisenhardt, K. M., and Zbaracki, M. J. (1992). "Strategic Decision Making." *Strategic Management Journal*, 13(8), 17–37.

Fama, E. F. (1980). "Agency Problems and the Theory of the Firm." *Journal of Political Economy*, 88, 288–307.

Ferrier, W. J., Smith, K. G., and Grimm, C. M. (1999). "The Role of Competitive Action in Market Share Erosion and Industry Dethronement: a Study of Industry Leaders and Challengers." *The Academy of Management Journal*, 42(4), 372–388.

Fisher, F. M. (1989). "Games Economists Play: a Noncooperative View." *The RAND Journal of Economics*, 20(1), 113–124.

Fisher, I. (1930). *The Theory of Interest*. New York: Macmillan.

Foss, N. J. (2005). *Strategy, Economic Organization, and the Knowledge Economy*. Oxford: Oxford University Press.

Frank, R. H. (1988). *Passion within Reason*. New York: Norton.

Freeman, R. E. (1984). *Strategic Management: a Stakeholder Approach*. Boston: Pitman.

Friedman, M. (1970). "The Social Responsibility of a Business Is to Increase Its Profits." *The New York Times Magazine*, 13 September.

Frondizi, R. (1971). *What is Value? An Introduction to Axiology*. La Salee. Ill.: Open Court.

Frost, T. S., Birkinshaw, J. M., and Ensign, P. C. (2002). "Centers of Excellence in Multinational Corporations." *Strategic Management Journal*, 23(11), 997–1018.

Fulmer, W., and Goodwin, J. (1988). "Differentiation: Begin with the Customer." *Business Horizons*, 31(5), 159–166.

Galbraith, J. R. (1977). *Organization Design*. Reading, Mass.: Addison-Wesley.

Gale, B. T., and Wood, R. C. (1994). *Managing Customer Value*. New York: Free Press.

Gander, J. P. (1991). "Managerial Intensity, Firm Size and Growth." *Managerial and Decision Economics*, 12(3), 261–266.

Geroski, P. A., Gilbert, R. J., and Jacquemin, A. (1990). *Barriers to Entry and Strategic Competition*. London: Routledge.

Ghoshal, S. (1987). "Global Strategy: an Organization Framework." *Strategic Management Journal*, 8, 425–440.

Ghoshal, S., Bartlett, C., and Moran, P. (2000). "Value Creation." *Executive Excellence*, 17(11), 10–36.

Ghoshal, S., and Moran, P. (1996). "Bad for Practice: a Critique of the Transaction Cost Approach." *The Academy of Management Review*, 21, 13–47.

Gimeno, J., and Woo, C. Y. (1999). "Multimarket Contact, Economies of Scope, and Firm Performance." *The Academy of Management Journal*, 42(3), 239–259.

Goold, M., and Campbell, A. (1998). "Desperately Seeking Synergy." *Harvard Business Review*, 76(5), 131–143.

Goold, M., Campbell, A., and Alexander, M. (1994). *Corporate-level Strategy: Creating Value in the Multibusiness Company*. New York: John Wiley.

Goold, M., and Luchs, K. (1993). "Why Diversify? Four Decades of Management Thinking." *Academy of Management Executive*, 7(3).

Granovetter, M. (1985). "Economic Action and Social Structure: a Theory of Embeddedness." *American Journal of Sociology*, 91(3), 481–510.

Grant, R. M. (1996). "Toward a Knowledge-based Theory of the Firm." *Strategic Management Journal*, 17(10), 109–122.

Grant, R. M. (2005). *Contemporary Strategy Analysis*. Oxford: Blackwell.

Grant, R. M., Jammine, A. P., and Thomas, H. (1988). "Diversity, Diversification, and Profitability among British Manufacturing Companies, 1972–84." *The Academy of Management Journal*, 31(4), 771–801.

Grimm, C. M., Lee, H., and Smith, K. G. (2006). *Strategy as Action*. New York; Oxford: Oxford University Press.

Grossman, S., and Hart, O. (1986). "The Costs and Benefits of Ownership. A Theory of Vertical and Lateral Integration." *Journal of Political Economy*, *94*, 691–719.

Gulati, R. (1995). "Does Familiarity Breed Trust? The Implications of Repeated Ties for Contractual Choice in Alliances." *The Academy of Management Journal*, *38*(1), 85–112.

Gulati, R., and Singh, H. (1998). "The Architecture of Cooperation: Managing Coordination Costs and Appropriation Concerns in Strategic Alliances." *Administrative Science Quarterly*, *43*(4), 781–784.

Gupta, A. K., and Govindarajan, V. (2001). "Converting Global Presence into Global Competitive Advantage." *Academy of Management Executive*, *15*, 45–58.

Gupta, A. K., Govindarajan, V., and Wang, H. (2008). *The Quest for Global Dominance*. New York: John Wiley.

Hambrick, D. C., and Fredrickson, J. W. (2005). "Are you Sure you Have a Strategy?" *The Academy of Management Executive*, *19*(4), 51–62.

Hamel, G. (1991). "Competition for Competence and Inter-partner Learning within International Strategic Alliances." *Strategic Management Journal*, *12*(4), 83–103.

Harrigan, K. R. (1980). *Strategies for Declining Businesses*. Lexington: Lexington Books.

Harris, M., and Raviv, A. (1979). "Optimal Incentive Contracts with Imperfect Information." *Journal of Economic Theory*, *20*(2), 231–259.

Hart, O. D. (1985). "Monopolistic Competition in the Spirit of Chamberlin: a General Model." *The Review of Economic Studies*, *52*(4), 529–546.

(1995). *Firms, Contracts, and Financial Structure*. Oxford: Clarendon Press.

Haspeslagh, P. C., and Jemison, D. B. (1991). *Managing Acquisitions: Creating Value through Corporate Renewal*. London: Free Press.

Hayek, F. A. (1945). "The Use of Knowledge in Society." *The American Economic Review*, *35*, 519–530.

Hennart, J. F. (1982). *A Theory of Multinational Enterprise*. Ann Arbor: University of Michigan Press.

(1988). "A Transaction Costs Theory of Equity Joint Ventures." *Strategic Management Journal*, *9*(4), 361–374.

(2001). "Theories of the Multinational Entreprise." In A. M. Rugman and T. Brewer (Eds.), *Handbook of International Business*. London: Oxford University Press.

Hennart, J. F., and Reddy, S. (1997). "The Choice between Mergers/ Acquisitions and Joint Ventures: the Case of Japanese Investors in the United States." *Strategic Management Journal, 18*(1), 1–12.

Hill, C. W. L., and Hansen, G. S. (1991). "A Longitudinal Study of the Cause and Consequences of Changes in Diversification in the US Pharmaceutical Industry 1977–86." *Strategic Management Journal, 12*(3), 187–199.

Hitt, M. A., Freeman, R. E., and Harrison, J. S. (2001). *The Blackwell Handbook of Strategic Management*. Oxford: Blackwell.

Hitt, M. A., Harrison, J. S., and Ireland, R. D. (2001). *Mergers and Acquisitions: a Guide to Creating Value for Stakeholders*. Oxford: Oxford University Press.

Holbrook, M. B. (1999). *Consumer Value: A Framework for Analysis and Research*. London: Routledge.

Holmstrom, B. (1979). "Moral Hazard and Observability." *The Bell Journal of Economics, 10*(1), 74–91.

Holmstrom, B., and Roberts, J. (1998). "The Boundaries of the Firm Revisited." *The Journal of Economic Perspectives, 12*(4), 73–94.

Hoskisson, R. E., Hitt, M. A., Wan, W. P., and Yiu, D. (1999). "Theory and Research in Strategic Management: Swings of a Pendulum." *Journal of Management, 25*(3), 417.

Hotelling, H. (1929). "Stability in Economic Competition." *Economic Journal, 39*(153), 41–57.

Huber, G. P. (1991). "Organizational Learning: the Contributing Processes and the Literatures." *Organization Science, 2*(1), 88–115.

Husted, B. W., and Salazar, J. (2006). "Taking Friedman Seriously: Maximizing Profits and Social Performance." *Journal of Management Studies, 43*(1), 75–91.

Hymer, S. (1976). *The International Operations of National Firms*. Cambridge, Mass.; London: MIT Press.

Inkpen, A. C. (2001). "Strategic Alliances." *The Blackwell Handbook of Strategic Management*, 409–432.

Inkpen, A. C., and Dinur, A. (1998). "Knowledge Management Processes and International Joint Ventures." *Organization Science, 9*(4), 454–468.

Jacobsen, R. (1988). "The Persistence of Abnormal Returns." *Strategic Management Journal, 9*(5), 415–430.

Jarrell, G. A., Brickley, J. A., and Netter, J. M. (1988). "The Market for Corporate Control: the Empirical Evidence since 1980." *The Journal of Economic Perspectives, 2*(1), 49–68.

Jensen, M. C. (1988). "Takeovers: Their Causes and Consequences." *The Journal of Economic Perspectives, 2*(1), 21–48.

Jensen, M. C., and Meckling, W. (1976). "Theory of the Firm: Managerial Behavior, Agency Costs, and Capital Structure." *Journal of Financial Economics*, 3(4), 305–360.

Jensen, M. C., and Ruback, R. S. (1983). "The Market for Corporate Control: the Scientific Evidence." *Journal of Financial Economics*, 11(1–4), 5–50.

Johanson, J., and Vahlne, J. E. (1977). "The Internationalization Process of the Firm: a Model of Knowledge Development and Increasing Foreign Market Commitments." *Journal of International Business Studies*, 8(1), 23–32.

John, C. H. S., and Harrison, J. S. (1999). "Manufacturing-based Relatedness, Synergy, and Coordination." *Strategic Management Journal*, 20(2), 129–145.

Jones, G. R., and Hill, C. W. L. (1988). "Transaction Cost Analysis of Strategy–Structure Choice." *Strategic Management Journal*, 9(2), 159–172.

Joskow, P. L. (1987). "Contract Duration and Relationship-specific Investments: Empirical Evidence from Coal Markets." *The American Economic Review*, 77(1), 168–185.

Kant, I. (2008). *On the Metaphysics of Morals and Ethics*. Radford, Va.: Wilder Publications.

Katz, M. L., and Shapiro, C. (1985). "Network Externalities, Competition, and Compatibility." *The American Economic Review*, 75(3), 424–440.

Kekre, S., and Srinivasan, K. (1990). "Broader Product Line: a Necessity to Achieve Success?" *Management Science*, 36(10), 1216–1231.

Keller, K. L. (1993). "Conceptualizing, Measuring, and Managing Customer-based Brand Equity." *Journal of Marketing*, 57(1), 1–22.

(2007). *Strategic Brand Management: Building, Measuring, and Managing Brand Equity*. Upper Saddle River, N.J.: Prentice Hall.

Khanna, T., Gulati, R., and Nohria, N. (1998). "The Dynamics of Learning Alliances: Competition, Cooperation, and Relative Scope." *Strategic Management Journal*, 19(3), 193–210.

Kim, D. J., and Kogut, B. (1996). "Technological Platforms and Diversification." *Organization Science*, 7(3), 283–301.

Kim, W. C., and Mauborgne, R. (1997). "Value Innovation: the Strategic Logic of High Growth." *Harvard Business Review* (Jan–Feb), 103–112.

Kindleberger, C. P. (1969). *American Business Abroad. Six Lectures on Direct Investment*: New Haven and London: Yale University Press.

Kirzner, I. M. (1979). *Perception, Opportunity and Profit: Studies in the Theory of Entrepreneurship*. Chicago: University of Chicago Press.

(1997). "Entrepreneurial Discovery and the Competitive Market Process: an Austrian Approach." *Journal of Economic Literature*, 35(1), 60–85.

Klein, B., Crawford, R. G., and Alchian, A. A. (1978). "Vertical Integration, Appropriable Rents, and the Competitive Contracting Process." *Journal of Law and Economics*, 21, 297–326.

Knickerbocker, F. T. (1973). *Oligopolistic Reaction and Multinational Enterprise*. Boston, Harvard University.

Knight, F. H. (1921). *Risk, Uncertainty and Profit*. New York: Houghton Mifflin.

Kobrin, S. J. (1991). "An Empirical Analysis of the Determinants of Global Integration." *Strategic Management Journal*, 12, 17–31.

Kogut, B. (1988). "Joint Ventures: Theoretical and Empirical Prospects." *Strategic Management Journal*, 9, 319–332.

Kogut, B. (1991). "Country Capabilities and the Permeability of Borders." *Strategic Management Journal*, 12(1), 33–47.

Kogut, B., and Zander, U. (1993). "Knowledge of the Firm and the Evolutionary Theory of the Multinational Enterprise." *Journal of International Business Studies*, 24(4), 625–645.

(1996). "What Firms Do? Coordination, Identity, and Learning." *Organization Science*, 7(5), 502–518.

(2003). "Knowledge of the Firm and the Evolutionary Theory of the Multinational Corporation." *Journal of International Business Studies*, 34(6), 516–529.

Kotha, S., and Vadlamani, B. L. (1995). "Assessing Generic Strategies: an Empirical Investigation of Two Competing Typologies in Discrete Manufacturing Industries." *Strategic Management Journal*, 16(1), 75–83.

Kotler, P., and Armstrong, G. (1993). *Marketing: an Introduction*. Englewood Cliffs, N.J.: Prentice Hall.

Kotler, P., and Zaltman, G. (1971). "Social Marketing: an Approach to Planned Social Change." *Journal of Marketing*, 35(3), 3–12.

Kreps, D. M. (1990). *Game Theory and Economic Modelling*. Oxford: Clarendon Press.

Kreps, D. M., and Wilson, R. (1982). "Reputation and Imperfect Information." *Journal of Economic Theory*, 27(2), 253–279.

Lancaster, K. (1990). "The Economics of Product Variety: a Survey." *Marketing Science*, 9(3), 189–206.

Lawrence, P. R., and Lorsch, J. W. (1967). *Organization and Environment*. Boston, Mass.: Harvard Business School Press.

Leong, S. M., and Tan, C. T. (1993). "Managing across Borders: an Empirical Test of the Bartlett and Ghoshal [1989] Organizational Typology." *Journal of International Business Studies*, 24(3), 449–464.

Lepak, D. P., Smith, K. G., and Taylor, M. S. (2007). "Value Creation and Value Capture: a Multilevel Perspective." *The Academy of Management Review*, 32(1), 180–194.

Levinthal, D. (1988). "A Survey of Agency Costs of Organizations." *Journal of Economic Behavior and Organization, 9*, 153–185.

Levitt, T. (1983). "The Gobalization of Markets." *Harvard Business Review, 61*(3).

——— (1986). *The Marketing Imagination*. London: Collier Macmillan.

Libecap, G. D. (1989). *Contracting for Property Rights*. Cambridge: Cambridge University Press.

Lieberman, M. B., and Montgomery, D. B. (1988). "First-mover Advantages." *Strategic Management Journal, 9*, 41–58.

Liebeskind, J. P. (1996). "Knowledge, Strategy, and the Theory of the Firm." *Strategic Management Journal, 17*, 93–107.

Lippman, S. A., and Rumelt, R. P. (1982). "Uncertain Imitability: an Analysis of Interfirm Differences in Efficiency under Competition." *The Bell Journal of Economics, 13*(2), 418–438.

Lu, J. W., and Beamish, P. W. (2004). "International Diversification and Firm Performance: the S-curve Hypothesis." *Academy of Management Journal, 47*(4), 598–609.

MacCrimmon, K. R. (1993). "Do Firm Strategies Exist?" *Strategic Management Journal, 14*, 113–130.

Machlup, F. (1967). "Theories of the Firm: Marginalist, Behavioral, Managerial." *The American Economic Review, 57*(1), 1–33.

MacIntyre, A. C. (1998). *A Short History of Ethics*. Notre Dame, Ind.: University of Notre Dame Press.

Mackey, A., Mackey, T. B., and Barney, J. B. (2007). "Corporate Social Responsibility and Firm Performance: Investor Preferences and Corporate Strategies." *The Academy of Management Review, 32*(3), 817–835.

Madhok, A. (2002). "Reassessing the Fundamentals and Beyond: Ronald Coase, the Transaction Cost and Resource-based Theories of the Firm and the Institutional Structure of Production." *Strategic Management Journal, 23*(6), 535–550.

Magenheim, E. B., and Mueller, D. C. (1988). "Are Acquiring-firm Shareholders Better Off after an Acquisition?" in J. C. Coffee, L. Lowenstein, and S. Rose-Ackerman (Eds.) *Knights, Raiders, and Targets the Impact of the Hostile Takeover*. Oxford: Oxford University Press.

Mahoney, J. T. (1992). "The Choice of Organizational Form: Vertical Financial Ownership versus Other Methods of Vertical Integration." *Strategic Management Journal, 13*(8), 559–584.

——— (2005). *Economic Foundations of Strategy*. Thousand Oaks, Calif.: Sage.

Mahoney, J. T., and Pandian, J. R. (1992). "The Resource-based View within the Conversation of Strategic Management." *Strategic Management Journal, 13*(5), 363–380.

Maister, D. H. (1997). *Managing the Professional Service Firm*. New York: Free Press.

Majumdar, S. K., and Ramaswamy, V. (1994). "Explaining Downstream Integration." *Managerial and Decision Economics, 15*(2), 119–129.

Makadok, R., and Barney, J. B. (2001). "Strategic Factor Market Intelligence: an Application of Information Economics to Strategy Formulation and Competitor Intelligence." *Management Science, 47*(12), 1621–1638.

Makadok, R., and Coff, R. (2002). "The Theory of Value and the Value of Theory: Breaking New Ground versus Reinventing the Wheel." *Academy of Management Review, 27*(1), 10–13.

March, J. G., and Simon, H. A. (1967 [1958]). *Organizations*. New York: John Wiley.

Mason, E. S. (1939). "Price and Production Policies of Large-scale Enterprise." *The American Economic Review, 29*(1), 61–74.

Mayo, E. (1945). *The Social Problems of an Industrial Civilisation*. Boston: Harvard University.

McGahan, A. M., and Porter, M. E. (1997). "How Much does Industry Matter, Really?" *Strategic Management Journal, 18*, 15–30.

McGregor, D. (1960). *The Human Side of Enterprise*. New York: McGraw-Hill.

McWilliams, A., and Siegel, D. (2001). "Corporate Social Responsibility: a Theory of the Firm Perspective." *The Academy of Management Review, 26*(1), 117–127.

Miles, R. E., and Snow, C. C. (1978). *Organizational Strategy, Structure, and Process*. New York: McGraw-Hill.

Milgrom, P. R., and Roberts, J. F. (1992). *Economics, Organization and Management*. Englewood Cliffs, N.J.: Prentice Hall.

Mill, J. S. (2001). *Utilitarianism*. Edited by E. Sher. Indianapolis, Ind.: Hackett Publishing.

Miller, D. (1986). "Configurations of Strategy and Structure: Towards a Synthesis." *Strategic Management Journal, 7*(3), 233–249.

(1992). "The Generic Strategy Trap." *Journal of Business Strategy, 13*(1), 37–41.

Mintzberg, H. (1978). "Patterns in Strategy Formation." *Management Science, 24*(9), 934–948.

(1988). "Generic Strategies: Toward a Comprehensive Framework." *Advances in Strategic Management, 5*(New series 1), 67.

Mintzberg, H., Ahlstrand, B. W., and Lampel, J. (1998). *Strategy Safari*. New York: Free Press.

Montgomery, C. A., and Hariharan, S. (1991). "Diversified Expansion by Large Established Firms." *Journal of Economic Behavior and Organization, 15*(1), 71–89.

Morck, R., Shleifer, A., and Vishny, R. (1990). "Do Managerial Motives Drive Bad Acquisitions." *Journal of Finance, 45*(1), 31–48.

Morgan, G. (2006). *Images of Organization*. London: Sage.

Mueller, D. C. (1986). *Profits in the Long Run*. Cambridge: Cambridge University Press.

Murphy, P. E., and Enis, B. M. (1986). "Classifying Products Strategically." *Journal of Marketing, 50*(3), 24–42.

Nadler, D. A., Tushman, M. L., and Nadler, M. B. (1997). *Competing by Design*. Oxford: Oxford University Press.

Narver, J. C., and Slater, S. F. (1990). "The Effect of a Market Orientation on Business Profitability." *Journal of Marketing, 54*(4), 20–35.

Nayyar, P. R. (1993). "On the Measurement of Competitive Strategy: Evidence from a Large Multiproduct US Firm." *The Academy of Management Journal, 36*(6), 1652–1669.

Nelson, R. R., and Winter, S. G. (1982). *An Evolutionary Theory of Economic Change*. Cambridge, Mass.: Belknap Press.

North, D. C. (1990). *Institutions, Institutional Change and Economic Performance*. Cambridge: Cambridge University Press.

Nutt, P. C. (1998). "How Decision Makers Evaluate Alternatives and the Influence of Complexity." *Management Science, 44*(8), 1148–1166.

Obrinsky, M. (1983). *Profit Theory and Capitalism*. Oxford: Robertson.

Orlitzky, M., Schmidt, F. L., and Rynes, S. (2003). "Corporate Social and Financial Performance: a Meta-analysis." *Organization Studies, 24*(3), 403.

Palich, L. E., Cardinal, L. B., and Miller, C. C. (2000). "Curvilinearity in the Diversification–Performance Linkage: an Examination of over Three Decades of Research." *Strategic Management Journal, 21*(2), 155–174.

Park, C. (2003). "Research Notes and Commentaries: Prior Peformance Characteristics of Related and Unrelated Acquirers." *Strategic Management Journal, 24*, 471–480.

Payne, A., and Holt, S. (2001). "Diagnosing Customer Value: Integrating the Value Process and Relationship Marketing." *British Journal of Management, 12*(2), 159–182.

Penrose, E. T. (1959). *The Theory of the Growth of the Firm*. Oxford: Blackwell.

Perloff, J. M., and Salop, S. C. (1985). "Equilibrium with Product Differentiation." *The Review of Economic Studies, 52*(1), 107–120.

Perrow, C. (1986). *Complex Organizations: A Critical Essay* (third edition). New York: Random House.

Peteraf, M. A. (1993). "The Conerstones of Competitive Advantage: a Resource-based View." *Strategic Management Journal*, 14(3), 179–191.

Peters, W., and Waterman, R. (1982). *In Search of Excellence*. New York: Harper and Row.

Pigou, A. C. (1932). *The Economics of Welfare*. New York: Macmillan.

Pisano, G. P. (1990). "The R&D Boundaries of the Firm: an Empirical Analysis." *Administrative Science Quarterly*, 35(1), 153–176.

Porter, M. E. (1980). *Competitive Strategy: Techniques for Analyzing Industries and Competitors*. New York: Free Press.

(1985). *Competitive Advantage: Creating and Sustaining Superior Performance*. New York: Free Press.

(1987). "From Competitive Advantage to Corporate Strategy." *Harvard Business Review*, 65(3), 43–59.

(1990). *The Competitive Advantage of Nations*. New York: Free Press.

(1991). "Towards a Dynamic Theory of Strategy." *Strategic Management Journal*, 12, 95–117.

(1996). "What's Strategy?" *Harvard Business Review*, 74(6), 61–78.

Porter, M. E., and Kramer, M. R. (1999). "Philanthropy's New Agenda: Creating Value." *Harvard Business Review*, 77(6), 121–130.

(2002). "The Competitive Advantage of Corporate Philanthropy." *Harvard Business Review*, 80(12), 56–68.

(2006). "Strategy and Society: the Link between Competitive Advantage and Corporate Social Responsibility." *Harvard Business Review*, 84(12), 78–92.

Powell, T. C. (2001). "Competitive Advantage: Logical and Philosophical Considerations." *Strategic Management Journal*, 22(9), 875–888.

Prahalad, C. K. (2006). *The Fortune at the Bottom of the Pyramid*. Upper Saddle River, N.J.: Wharton School.

Prahalad, C. K., and Bettis, R. A. (1986). "The Dominant Logic: a New Linkage between Diversity and Performance." *Strategic Management Journal*, 7(6), 485–501.

Prahalad, C. K., and Doz, Y. L. (1987). *The Multinational Mission*. New York: Free Press.

Prahalad, C. K., and Hamel, G. (1990). "The Core Competencies of the Corporation." *Harvard Business Review*, 68(3), 79–91.

Prahalad, C. K., and Ramaswamy, V. (2004). "Co-creating Unique Value with Customers." *Strategy and Leadership*, 32(3), 4–9.

Pratt, J. W., and Zeckhauser, R. J. (1985). *Principals and Agents: the Structure of Business*. Boston, Harvard Business School Press.

Preston, L. E., and Post, J. E. (1975). *Private Management and Public Policy*. Englewood Cliffs, N.J.: Prentice Hall.

Priem, R. L., and Butler, J. E. (2001). "Is the Resource-based View a Useful Perspective for Strategic Management Research?" *The Academy of Management Review*, 26(1), 22–40.

Putterman, L. G., and Kroszner, R. (1996). *The Economic Nature of the Firm: A Reader*. Cambridge: Cambridge University Press.

Radner, R. (1980). "Collusive Behavior in Noncooperative Epsilon-equilibria of Oligopolies with Long but Finite Lives." *Journal of Economic Theory*, 22(2), 289–303.

Ramirez, R. (1999). "Value Co-production: Intellectual Origins and Implications for Practice and Research." *Strategic Management Journal*, 20(1), 49–65.

Rappaport, A. (1986). *Creating Shareholder Value*. New York: Free Press.

Rasmusen, E. (2007). *Games and Information*. Oxford: Blackwell.

Ravenscraft, D. J., and Scherer, F. M. (1987). *Mergers, Sell-Offs, and Economic Efficiency*. Washington, D.C.: Brookings Institution Press.

Rawls, J. (1999). *A Theory of Justice*. Cambridge, Mass.: Harvard University Press.

Raymond, V. (1966). "International Investment and International Trade in the Product Cycle." *Quarterly Journal of Economics*, 80(2), 190–207.

Reed, R., and DeFillippi, R. J. (1990). "Causal Ambiguity, Barriers to Imitation, and Sustainable Competitive Advantage." *The Academy of Management Review*, 15(1), 88–102.

Richardson, G. B. (1972). "The Organisation of Industry." *Economic Journal*, 82(327), 883–896.

Rindova, V. P., Williamson, I., Petkova, A. P., and Sever, J. (2005). "Being Good or Being Known: an Empirical Examination of the Dimensions, Antecedents, and Consequences of Organizational Reputation." *The Academy of Management Journal*, 48(6), 1033–1049.

Robinson, J. (1933). *The Economics of Imperfect Competition*. New York: Macmillan.

Robock, S. H., and Simmonds, K. (1989). *International Business and Multinational Enterprises*: Homewood, Ill.: Richard Irwin.

Rosen, S. (1974). "Hedonic Prices and Implicit Markets: Product Differentiation in Pure Competition." *The Journal of Political Economy*, 82(1), 34–55.

Ross, S. A. (1973). "The Economic Theory of Agency." *The American Economic Review*, 63(May), 134–139.

Rugman, A. M. (1982). *New Theories of the Multinational Enterprise*. London: Croom Helm.

Rumelt, R. P. (1974). *Strategy, Structure, and Economic Performance*. Boston, Mass.: Harvard Business School Press.

(1982). "Diversification Strategy and Profitability." *Strategic Management Journal, 3*(4), 359–369.

(1984). "Towards a Strategy Theory of the Firm." *Competitive Strategic Management,* 556–570.

(1986). *Strategy, Structure, and Economic Performance.* Boston, Mass.: Harvard Business School Press.

(1991). "How Much Does Industry Matter?" *Strategic Management Journal, 12*(3), 167–185.

(1997). "The Evaluation of Business Strategy." In H. Mintzberg and J. B. Quinn (Eds.), *The Strategy Process.* Upper Saddle River, N.J.: Prentice Hall.

Rumelt, R. P., Schendel, D., and Teece, D. J. (1994). *Fundamental Issues in Strategy: a Research Agenda.* Boston, Mass.: Harvard Business School Press.

Saloner, G. (1991). "Modeling, Game Theory, and Strategic Management." *Strategic Management Journal, 12,* 119–136.

Salop, S. C. (1979). "Monopolistic Competition with Outside Goods." *The Bell Journal of Economics, 10*(1), 141–156.

Santalo, J., and Becerra, M. (2008). "Competition from Specialized Firms and the Diversification–Performance Linkage." *The Journal of Finance, 63*(2), 851–883.

Schendel, D., and Hofer, C. W. (1979). *Strategic Management: a New View of Business Policy and Planning.* Boston, N.J.: Little Brown.

Scherer, F. M. (1979). "The Welfare Economics of Product Variety: an Application to the Ready-to-eat Cereals Industry." *The Journal of Industrial Economics, 28*(2), 113–134.

(1988). "Corporate Takeovers: the Efficiency Arguments." *The Journal of Economic Perspectives, 2*(1), 69–82.

Scherer, F. M., and Ross, D. M. (1990). *Industrial Market Structure and Economic Performance.* Boston: Houghton Mifflin.

Schumpeter, J. A. (1982). *The Theory of Economic Development.* Edison, N.J.: Transaction Publishers.

Scott, W. R. (1992). *Organizations: Rational, Natural, and Open Systems.* London: Prentice Hall International.

Selznick, P. (1957). *Leadership in Administration: a Sociological Interpretation.* New York: Harper and Row.

Senge, P. M. (1990). *The Fifth Discipline.* New York: Currency Doubleday.

Seth, A., and Thomas, H. (1994). "Theories of the Firm: Implications for Strategy Research." *Journal of Management Studies, 31*(2), 165–191.

Shane, S., and Venkataraman, S. (2000). "The Promise of Enterpreneurship as a Field of Research." *The Academy of Management Review, 25*(1), 217–226.

Shapiro, C. (1989). "The Theory of Business Strategy." *The RAND Journal of Economics*, 20(1), 125–137.

Shapiro, C., and Varian, H. R. (1999). *Information Rules*. Boston, Mass.: Harvard Business School Press.

Shelanski, H. A., and Klein, P. G. (1995). "Empirical Research in Transaction Cost Analysis: a Review and Assessment." *Journal of Law Economics and Organization*, 11, 335–361.

Simon, H. A. (1957). *Administrative Behavior*. New York: Free Press.

    (1982). *Models of Bounded Rationality*. Cambridge, Mass.: MIT Press.

    (1991). "Bounded Rationality and Organizational Learning." *Organization Science*, 2(1), 125–134.

Singh, H., and Montgomery, C. A. (1987). "Corporate Acquisition Strategies and Economic Performance." *Strategic Management Journal*, 8(4), 377–386.

Slater, S. F., and Narver, J. C. (1994). "Market Orientation, Customer Value, and Superior Performance." *Business Horizons*, 37(2), 22–28.

Smith, A. (1776). *An Inquiry into the Nature and Causes of the Wealth of Nations*. London: W. Strahan and T. Cadell.

Smith, K. G., Carroll, S. J., and Ashford, S. J. (1995). "Intra- and Interorganizational Cooperation: Toward a Research Agenda." *The Academy of Management Journal*, 38(1), 7–23.

Smith, K. G., Ferrier, W. J., and Ndofor, H. (2001). "Competitive Dynamics Research: Critique and Future Directions." *Handbook of Strategic Management*, 315–361.

Smith, K. G., Grimm, C. M., and Gannon, M. J. (1992). *Dynamics of Competitive Strategy*. Thousand Oaks, Calif.: Sage Publications.

Sorenson, O. (2000). "Letting the Market Work for You: an Evolutionary Perspective on Product Strategy." *Strategic Management Journal*, 21(5), 577–592.

Spence, M. (1976). "Product Differentiation and Welfare." *The American Economic Review*, 66(2), 407–414.

Spender, J. C. (1989). *Industry Recipes*. Oxford: Blackwell.

Stabell, C. B., and Fjeldstad, O. D. (1998). "Configuring Value for Competitive Advantage: on Chains, Shops, and Networks." *Strategic Management Journal*, 19(5), 413–437.

Stein, J. (2003). "Agency, Information and Corporate Investment." In J. Stein, G. Constantinides, M. Harris, and R. Stulz (Eds.), *Handbook of the Economics of Finance*, Amsterdam: Elsevier Science.

    (1950). "The Development of Utility Theory: Part I and Part II." *Journal of Political Economy*, 58, 307–327.

    (1958). "Ricardo and the 93% Labor Theory of Value." *The American Economic Review*, 48(3), 357–367.

Stigler, G. J. (1961). "The Economics of Information." *Journal of Political Economy, 69*, 213–225.

(1968). "Price and Non-price Competition." *The Journal of Political Economy, 76*(1), 149–154.

Teece, D. J. (1980). "The Economics of Scope and Scale of the Enterprise." *Journal of Economic Behaviour and Organisation, 1*(3), 223–247.

(1982a). "An Economic Theory of Multiproduct Firms." *Journal of Economic Behavior and Organization, 3*, 39–63.

(1982b). *A Transactions Cost Theory of the Multinational Enterprise.* Stanford, Calif.: Graduate School of Business, Stanford University.

(1986). "Transactions Cost Economics and the Multinational Enterprise: an Assessment." *Journal of Economic Behavior and Organization, 7*, 21–45.

(1987). *Technological Change and the Nature of the Firm.* Calif.: University of California, Berkeley Business School.

Teece, D. J., Pisano, G., and Shuen, A. (1997). "Dynamic Capabilities and Strategy Management." *Strategic Management Journal, 18*(7), 509–533.

Thompson, J. D. (1967). *Organizations in Action.* New York: McGraw-Hill.

Tirole, J. (1988). *The Theory of Industrial Organization.* Cambridge, Mass.: MIT Press.

Vasconcellos, J. A. S., and Hambrick, D. C. (1989). "Key Success Factors: Test of a General Theory in the Mature Industrial Product Sector." *Strategic Management Journal, 10*(4), 367–382.

Vernon, R. (1966). "International Investment and International Trade in the Product Cycle." *Quarterly Journal of Economics, 80*(2), 190–207.

Villalonga, B. (2004). "Diversification Discount or Premium? New Evidence from the Business Information Tracking Series." *The Journal of Finance, 59*(2), 479–506.

Viscusi, W. K., Vernon, J. M., and Harrington, J. E. (2000). *Economics of Regulation and Antitrust.* Cambridge, Mass.: MIT Press.

Waddock, S. A., and Graves, S. B. (1997). "The Corporate Social Performance–Financial Performance Link." *Strategic Management Journal, 18*(4), 303–319.

Wernerfelt, B. (1984). "A Resource-based Theory of the Firm." *Strategic Management Journal, 5*(2), 171–180.

Wernerfelt, B., and Montgomery, C. A. (1988). "Tobin's Q and the Importance of Focus in Firm Performance." *The American Economic Review, 78*(1), 246–250.

Williamson, O. E. (1975). *Markets and Hierarchies.* New York: Free Press.

(1985). *The Economic Institutions of Capitalism.* New York: Free Press.

(1991). "Strategizing, Economizing, and Economic Organization." *Strategic Management Journal*, 12, 75–94.

(1993). "Calculativeness, Trust, and Economic Organization." *Journal of Law and Economics*, 36(1), 453–486.

(1999). "Strategy Research: Governance and Competence Perspectives." *Strategic Management Journal*, 20, 1087–1108.

Wolf, C. (1979). "A Theory of Non-market Failure: Framework for Implementation Analysis." *Journal of Law and Economics*, 22(1), 107–139.

Wood, D. J. (1991). "Corporate Social Performance Revisited." *The Academy of Management Review*, 16(4), 691–718.

Yip, G. S. (1989). "Global Strategy." *Sloan Management Review*.

Yiu, D., and Makino, S. (2002). "The Choice between Joint Venture and Wholly-owned Subsidiary: an Institutional Perspective." *Organization Science*, 13(6), 667–683.

Zeithaml, V. A. (1988). "Consumer Perceptions of Price, Quality, and Value: a Means–End Model and Synthesis of Evidence." *Journal of Marketing*, 52(3), 2–22.

Zhao, H., Luo, Y., and Suh, T. (2004). "Transaction Cost Determinants and Ownership-based Entry Mode Choice: a Meta-analytical Review." *Journal of International Business Studies*, 35(6), 524–545.

Index

agency theory, 39
  agency costs, 39
  and risks, 40
  incentives and monitoring in, 40
alliances, 192–195
Andrews, Kenneth, 4, 6
asset specificity, 32, 34, 37
  value specificity, 124

Barney, Jay, 18, 63, 65, 66
barriers to competition, 130
  barriers with asymmetric
    replicability, 132
  barriers with limited substitutability,
    132
  barriers with perfect replicability,
    131
  see also isolating mechanisms
bounded rationality, 14, 32, 34

causal ambiguity, 61
Coase, Ronald, 17, 27–30, 44, 51,
    222
  Coase theorem, 38
competitive dynamics, 160–164
  actions and reactions, 163
  first-mover advantages, 163
corporate social responsibility (CSR),
    226–237
  dual standard for business and CSR,
    236
  relational motivation for CSR, 228
  strategic CSR, 230
cost leadership, 156
  reducing firm costs and value
    creation, 103–104
  versus differentiation, 156
  see also generic strategies
customer value, 255

differentiation strategy, 156
  horizontal differentiation and value
    creation, 97
  sources of differentiation, 257
  vertical differentiation and value
    creation, 96
  see also generic strategies
diversification, 177–186
  diversification discount, 185

entrepreneurship and value creation,
    108
ethics and social strategy, 237–242
evolutionary economics, 59
  routines, 59
externalities, 38, 104, 221
  network effects, 105

firm boundaries, 75, 76, 252
firm growth, 30, 56–59
Friedman, Milton, 227

game theory, 161
  prisonner's dilemma, 239
generic strategies, 94, 141, 156
global competitive advantage, 211
Grant, Robert, 126

Hart, Oliver, 37
heterogeneity across firms, 60, 80,
    124

industry replacement, 259
industry structure, 166
  Porter's five-forces model, 167
innovation, 122
  and value creation, 98, 107
isolating mechanisms, 62
  see also barriers to competition

market for corporate control,
    190
market imperfections, 217–225
mergers and acquisitions, 189–192
monopoly, 218

nexus of contracts, 39
    see also agency theory
nonmonetary customer costs, 100,
    258
    accessibility, 102
    information costs, 101
    usability, 102

opportunism, 32, 34, 42
organizational knowledge, 46,
    59
    and the MNE, 202
    and strategic alliances, 193
    distinctive competence, 6
    dynamic capabilities, 59
    organizational learning, 59

Penrose, Edith, 18, 56
    Penrose effect, 58
Porter, Michael, 94, 167
post-merger performance, 189
profit theory in economics, 114–120
    and bargaining power, 118
    and entrepreneurs, 118
    and monopoly power, 116
    normal profit versus economic
        profits, 115
property rights theory, 35–39
    residual control rights, 37

resource-based view, 18, 56–70
    characteristics of strategic resources,
        63, 126
    profits through resource
        combinations, 127–129
    questions and criticisms, 64–70

Simon, Herbert, 14, 32
segmentation, 153
social welfare, 216
    wealth distribution, 225
strategic management, 3–11
    and economics, 10
    course, 3

early internal-external fit model, 4–5
future research, 261–264
multidisciplinary background, 8
scope of the field, 7
strategy, 71–76
    definitions, 7
    market positioning, 152–160
    nonmarket strategy, 229
    strategic decisions, 142, 143
    typologies, 141
    value-based model of strategy,
        71–76
strategy at different levels, 174
    business-level, 141
    corporate-level, 174
    global, 209–211
synergies, 77, 178

theory of the firm, 11–22
    behavioral theory, 13
    contracting theories, 16, 27–55
    different conceptualizations, 11, 22
    key questions in, 20, 246–252
    neoclassical theory, 11
    resource-based view, 18
    value approach, 21, 71–76, 260
theory of the multinational enterprise,
    198–203
    eclectic model (OLI), 201
    internalization theory, 200
    modes of international entry, 198
    motivation for internationalization,
        207
    ownership advantages, 200
    value approach, 203–207
transaction costs, 27
    contributions to value analysis,
        51
    ex-ante and ex-post, 31
    in vertical integration, 187
    limitations of transaction costs
        economics, 41–51, 54–55
    transaction cost economics, 31–34
trust, 43

uncertainty, 28, 121

value, 67
    and pricing strategy, 99–103
    definition of economic value, 85

internal and external effects on the boundaries of the firm, 76

limitations of economic value analysis, 264

valuable resources, 63–70, 91

value in economics, 86–88

value in the fields of finance and marketing, 88–91

value in the strategy field, 91–92

value configuration and underlying technology, 144

value chain, 145–146

value created by professional firms, 147–148

value network, 148–152

value creation, 92–104

at corporate level, 175

in CSR activities, 231

through enhancing customer benefits, 95–98

through reducing monetary and nonmonetary customer costs, 99–103

through reducing firm costs, 103–104

vertical integration, 186–189

Williamson, Oliver, 31, 34

Printed in the United States
by Baker & Taylor Publisher Services